THE GLOBAL CASINO

Nick Middleton

Fourth Edition

HODDER
EDUCATION
AN HACHETTE UK COMPANY

First published in Great Britain in 2008 by
Hodder Education, an Hachette UK Company,
338 Euston Road, London NW1 3BH

www.hoddereducation.com

© 2008 Nick Middleton

Hachette UK's policy is to use papers that are natural, renewable and
recyclable products and made from wood grown in sustainable forests.
The logging and manufacturing processes are expected to conform to the
environmental regulations of the country of origin.

The advice and information in this book are believed to be true and
accurate at the date of going to press, but neither the authors nor the publisher
can accept any legal responsibility or liability for any errors or omissions.

British Library Cataloguing in Publication Data
A catalogue record for this book is available from the British Library

Library of Congress Cataloging-in-Publication Data
A catalog record for this book is available from the Library of Congress

ISBN 978 0340 957165

5 6 7 8 9 10

Cover photo © Nick Middleton
Typeset in 10pt ACaslon Regular by Pantek Arts Ltd, Maidstone, Kent
Illustrations by Art Construction and Ailsa Allen, Oxford University Centre for the Environment
Printed and bound in Italy

What do you think about this book? Or any other Hodder
Education title? Please send your comments to the feedback
section on www.hoddereducation.com.

Contents

Preface

This book is about environmental issues: concerns that have arisen as a result of the human impact on the environment and the ways in which the natural environment affects human society. The book deals with both the workings of the physical environment and the political, economic and social frameworks in which the issues occur. Using examples from all over the world, I aim to highlight the underlying causes behind environmental problems, the human actions which have made them issues, and the hopes for solutions.

Eighteen chapters on key issues follow the three initial chapters that outline the background contexts of the physical and human environments and introduce the concept of sustainable development. The conclusion complements the book's thematic approach by looking at the issues and efforts towards sustainable development in a regional context. The organization of the book allows it to be read in its entirety or dipped into for any particular topic, since each chapter stands on its own. Each chapter sets the issue in a historical context, outlines why the issue has arisen, highlights areas of controversy and uncertainty, and appraises how problems are being, and can be, resolved, both technically and in political and economic frameworks. Information in every chapter has been expanded and updated to keep pace with the rapid increase in research and understanding of the issues. The chapters are followed by expanded critical guides to further reading on the subjects – including some sources freely available online – guides to relevant sites on the World Wide Web and sets of questions that can be used to spark discussion or as essay questions.

I decided on the title *The Global Casino* because there are many parallels between the issues discussed in this book and the workings of a gambling joint. Money and economics underlie many of the 18 issues covered here, which can be thought of as different games in the global casino, separate yet interrelated. Just like a casino, environmental issues involve winners and losers. The casino's chance element and the players' imperfect knowledge of the outcomes of their actions are relevant in that our understanding of how the Earth works is far from perfect. The casino metaphor also works on a socio-economic level, since some individuals and groups of individuals can afford to take part in the games actively, while others are less able to do so. Some groups are more responsible for certain issues than others, yet those who have little influence are still affected by the consequences. Different individuals and groups of people also choose to play the different games in different ways, reflecting their cultural, economic and political backgrounds and the information available to them.

The stakes are high: some observers believe that the global scale on which many of the issues occur represents humankind gambling with the very future of the planet itself. Everyone who reads this book has some part to play in the 'Global Casino'. I hope that the information presented here will allow those players to participate with a reasonable knowledge of how the games work, the consequences of losing, and the benefits that can be derived from winning.

Acknowledgements

I am indebted to many people who have helped in a variety of ways during the research and writing of four editions of this book. I would particularly like to thank the innumerable undergraduates at the Oxford colleges of St Anne's and Oriel who have been exposed to my efforts at communicating the essence of environmental issues. These many tutorials have provided the foundations for this book. My thanks also go to the technical staff at the School of Geography and the Environment, University of Oxford for their patient and efficient help: Ailsa Allen, Peter Hayward, David Sansom and Neil McIntosh, who between them drew most of the figures, and Martin Barfoot for photographic work. Thanks also to my editors at Arnold for their encouragement and inputs.

The publishers and I are grateful to the following for allowing me to reproduce their photographs: iStockphoto.com/Donald Swartz (Figure 1.6); iStockphoto.com/Andrey Mirzoyants (Figure 1.12); iStockphoto.com/Silvrshootr (Figure 3.8); NASA (Figures 4.4, 4.7, 5.6, 7.9, 9.8, 21.4); UNEP (Figure 5.5); iStockphoto.com/Frank Leung (Figure 6.9); iStockphoto.com/franck camhi (Figure 9.3); iStockphoto.com/Henryk Lippert (Figure 9.7); iStockphoto.com/Ian Bracegirdle (Figure 11.3); iStockphoto.com/Damir Cudic (Figure 13.5); UNEP GRID (Figure 13.6); Katsuhiro Abe, Japan Meteorological Agency (Figure 14.6 © Australian Bureau of Meteorology); Mark Carwardine (Figure 15.6); iStockphoto.com/Ben Jeayes (Figure 16.3); iStockphoto.com/Rob Hill (Figure 17.3); US Department of Energy (Figure 18.5); iStockphoto.com/alohaspirit (Figure 19.1); Rio Tinto plc (Figure 19.5); iStockphoto.com/manxman (Figure 20.5), and iStockphoto.com/Daniel Stein (Figure 22.3). All the other photographs are my own.

Thanks are also due to the following for allowing me to reproduce figures: American Association for the Advancement of Science (Figures 9.6, 15.2, 20.3); American Geographical Society (Figure 13.7); American Scientist (Figure 6.6); Arnold Publishers (Figures 1.1, 1.10, 1.11, 2.5, 13.2 and 21.6); Battle McCarthy architects (Figure 10.13); Blackwell Publishers (Figure 7.2); Cambridge University Press (Figure 2.1, after Kates, R.W., Turner, B.L. II and Clark, W.C., 1990, The great transformation, in Turner, B.L. II, Clark, W.C., Kates, R.W., Richards, J.F., Mathews, J.T. and Meyer, W.B. (eds) *The earth as transformed by human action*: 1–17; Figures 2.4, 2.7, 2.10 from Lonergan, S.C., 1993, Impoverishment, population, and environmental degradation: the case for equity, *Environmental Conservation* 20: 328–34 © Foundation for Environmental Conservation; Figure 14.5 from Lal, R., 1993, Soil erosion and conservation in West Africa, in Pimental D. (ed.) *World soil erosion and conservation*: 7–25; and Figure 14.5 from Davis, M.B., 1976, Erosion rates and land use history in southern Michigan, *Environmental Conservation* 3: 139–48); Convention on Long-range Transboundary Air Pollution Steering Body to the Cooperative

Programme for Monitoring and Evaluation of the Long-range Transmission of Air Pollutants in Europe (EMEP) (Figure 12.3); Elsevier (Figure 19.3 after Khalaf, F.I. 1989 Desertification and aeolian processes in Kuwait. *Journal of Arid Environments* 12: 125-145, © Elsevier 1989); European Environment Agency (Figures 16.11 and 22.4, © EEA, Copenhagen, 1977); Geological Society Publishing House (Figure 17.4); HMSO (Figure 17.1) − Crown Copyright material is reproduced with the permission of the Controller of HMSO; International Tanker Owners Pollution Federation Ltd (Figure 6.11); The Intergovernmental Panel on Climate Change (Figures 11.1, 11.2 and 11.4); International Soil Reference and Information Centre/ASSOD project (Figure 14.9); IOP Publishing Ltd (Figure 8.4 after Wood, L.B., 1982, *The restoration of the tidal Thames*. London, Hilger); John Wiley & Sons (Figure 7.3 from Bird, E.F.C., 1985, *Coastline changes: a global review*; Figure 8.2 after Pasternak *et al.*, 2001 Impact of historic land-use change on sediment delivery to a Chesapeake Bay subestuarine delta. *Earth Surface Processes and Landforms* 26: 409-427. Figure 9.4, after Tolouie, E., West, J.R. and Billam, J., 1993, Sedimentation and desiltation in the Sefid-Rud reservoir, Iran, in McManus, J. and Duck, R.W. (eds) *Geomorphology and sedimentology of lakes and reservoirs*: 125–38; and Figure 9.5 after Chien, N., 1985, Changes in river regime after the construction of upstream reservoirs, *Earth Surface Processes and Landforms* 10: 143–59, all copyright John Wiley & Sons Limited, reproduced with permission); Jared Scheidman Designs (Figure 20.9); McGill-Queen's University Press (Figures 11.6 and 21.2); Mono Lake Committee (Figure 8.7 source: 1850-1912 from Stine, Scott based on occasional observations and San Francisco precipitation, 1912-79 from LADWP and USGS compilations, 1979-present from Los Angeles Aqueduct Daily Reports and observations by the Mono Lake Committee. Compiled by the Mono Lake Committee); Norwegian Polar Institute (Figure 6.12); Oxford University Press (Figure 4.10 from Whitmore, T.C., 1998, *An introduction to tropical rain forests*, 2nd edn; Figure 12.5 after Shahgedanova, M. 2002 Air Pollution. In Shahgedanova, M. (ed) *The Physical Geography of Northern Eurasia*: 476-496, and Figure 14.2, after Cooke, R.U. and Doornkamp, J.C., 1990, *Geomorphology in environmental management*, 2nd edn, all by permission of Oxford University Press); Pan American Health Organisation (figure 10.11, for information about PAHO publications, visit www.paho.org); Permanent Service for Mean Sea Level (PSMSL), Proudman Oceanographic Laboratory (Figure 11.8); National Oceanic and Atmospheric Administration (NOAA) (Figure 21.9); Royal Swedish Academy of Sciences (Figure 12.10 and 19.4); Scott W. Nixon (Figure 7.4); Springer (Figures 15.1 and 16.8); Swedish Society for Anthropology and Geography (Figure 14.3); Swiss Re (Figure 21.3 from sigma 2/07); Taylor & Francis (Figures 7.7, 8.3, 9.1, 21.6 and 21.11); UN Environment Programme (UNEP) (Figures 5.1, 5.7, 6.7, 8.8 (b), 10.5 and 10.8); University of Chicago Press (Figure 4.3 from Kummer, D.M., 1991, *Deforestation in the postwar Philippines*); World Resources Institute (Figure 6.3).

Every effort has been made to trace the copyright holders of reproduced material. If, however, there are inadvertent omissions and/or inappropriate attributions these can be rectified in any future editions.

1 The Physical Environment

TOPICS COVERED

Classifying the natural world, Natural cycles, Timescales, Spatial scales, Time and space scales, The state of our knowledge

KEY WORDS

biome, productivity, biogeochemical cycle, clathrates, feedback, threshold, timelag, resistance, resilience, natural archive, palaeoenvironmental indicator

The term environment is used in many ways. This book is about issues that arise from the physical environment, which is made up of the living (biotic) and non-living (abiotic) things and conditions that characterize the world around us. While this is the central theme, the main reason for the topicality of the issues covered here is the way in which people interact with the physical environment. Hence, it is pertinent also to refer to the social, economic and political environments to describe those human conditions characteristic of certain places at particular times, and to explain why conflict has arisen between human activity and the natural world. This chapter looks at some of the basic features of the physical environment, while Chapter 2 is concerned with the human factors that affect the ways in which the human race interacts with the physical world.

CLASSIFYING THE NATURAL WORLD

Geography, like other academic disciplines, classifies things in its attempt to understand how they work. The physical environment can be classified in numerous ways, but one of the most commonly used classifications is that which breaks it down into four interrelated spheres: the lithosphere, the atmosphere, the biosphere and the hydrosphere. These four basic elements of the natural world can be further subdivided. The lithosphere, for example, is made up of rocks that are typically classified according to their modes of formation (igneous, metamorphic and sedimentary); these rock types are further subdivided according to the processes that formed them and other factors such as their chemical composition. Similarly, the workings of the atmosphere are manifested at the Earth's surface by a typical distribution of climates; the biosphere is made up of many types of flora and fauna, and the hydrosphere can be subdivided according to its chemical constituents (fresh water and saline, for example), or the condition or phase of the water: solid ice, liquid water or gaseous vapour.

These aspects of the natural world overlap and interact in many different ways. The nature of the soil in a particular place, for example, reflects the underlying rock type, the climatic conditions of the area, the plant and animal matter typical of the region, and the quantity and quality of water available. Suites of characteristics are combined in particular areas called ecosystems. These ecosystems can also be classified in many ways. One approach uses the amount of

Ecosystem type	Mean net primary productivity (g C/m²/year)	Total net primary production (billion tonnes C/year)
Tropical rain forest	900	15.3
Tropical seasonal forest	675	5.1
Temperate evergreen forest	585	2.9
Temperate deciduous forest	540	3.8
Boreal forest	360	4.3
Woodland and shrubland	270	2.2
Savanna	315	4.7
Temperate grassland	225	2.0
Tundra and alpine	65	0.5
Desert scrub	32	0.6
Rock, ice and sand	1.5	0.04
Agricultural land	290	4.1
Swamp and marsh	1125	2.2
Lake and stream	225	0.6
Total land	324*	48.3
Open ocean	57	18.9
Upwelling zones	225	0.1
Continental shelf	162	4.3
Algal bed and reef	900	0.5
Estuaries	810	1.1
Total oceans	69*	24.9
Total for biosphere	144*	73.2

*The means for land, oceans and biosphere are weighted according to the areas covered by specific ecosystem types
Source: after Whittaker and Likens (1973)

TABLE 1.1 Annual net primary production of carbon by major world ecosystem types

organic matter or biomass produced per year – the net production – which is simply the solar energy fixed in the biomass minus the energy used in producing it by respiration (see below). The annual net primary production of carbon, a basic component of all living organisms, by major world ecosystem types is shown in Table 1.1. Clear differences are immediately discernible between highly productive ecosystems such as forests, marshes, estuaries and reefs, and less productive places such as deserts, tundras and the open ocean. All of the data are averaged and variability around the mean is perhaps greatest for agricultural ecosystems which, where intensively managed, can reach productivities as high as any natural ecosystem. One of the main reasons for agriculture's low average is the fact that fields are typically bare of vegetation for significant periods between harvest and sowing.

One of the main factors determining productivity is the availability of nutrients, key substances for life on Earth: a lack of nutrients is often put forward to explain the low productivity in the open oceans, for example. Climate is another important factor. Warm, wet climates promote higher productivity than cold, dry ones. Differences in productivity may also go some way towards explaining the general trend of increasing diversity of plant and animal species from the poles to the equatorial regions. Despite many regional exceptions such as mountain tops and deserts, this latitudinal gradient of diversity is a striking characteristic of nature that fossil evidence suggests has been present in all geological epochs. The relationship with productivity is not straightforward, however, and many other hypotheses have been advanced, such as the suggestion that minor disturbances promote diversity by preventing a few species from dominating and excluding others (Connell, 1978).

The relationships between climate and the biosphere are also reflected on the global scale in maps of vegetation and climate, the one reflecting the other. Figure 1.1 shows the world's morphoclimatic regions, which are a combination of both factors. Despite wide internal variations, immense continental areas clearly support distinctive forms of vegetation that are adapted to a broad climatic type. Such great living systems, which also support distinctive animals and to a lesser extent distinctive soils, are called biomes, a concept seldom applied to aquatic zones. Different ecologists produce various lists of biomes and the following eight-fold classification may be considered conservative (Colinvaux, 1993):

1 tundra
2 coniferous forest (also known as boreal forest or taiga)
3 temperate forest

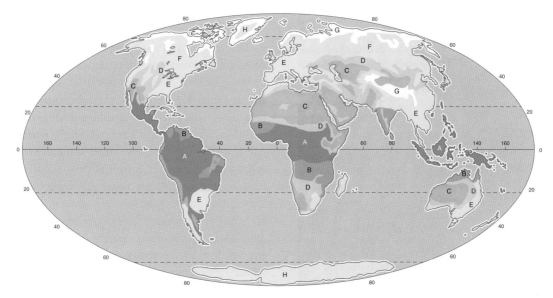

A — Tropical Humid – Rainforest. Rainy climate with no winter. Either constantly moist or with monsoon rains.

E — Warmer Humid – Rainy climate with mild winters. (Includes Mediterranean, Humid Subtropical and Marine West Coast climates).

B — Tropical Humid – Savanna. Rainy climate with either a dry summer or winter season

F — Cooler Humid – Rainy climate with severe winters. (Includes Continental Warm and Cool Summer, and Subarctic climates).

C — Dry – Desert or Arid climate.

G — Polar – Tundra climate.

D — Dry – Steppe or Semi-Arid climate.

H — Polar – Ice Cap. Perpetual frost.

Figure 1.1 Present-day morphoclimatic regions of the world's land surface (Williams *et al.*, 1993).

4 tropical rain forest
5 tropical savanna
6 temperate grassland
7 desert
8 maquis (also known as chaparral).

A striking aspect of the tundra biome is the absence of trees. Vegetation consists largely of grasses and other herbs, mosses, lichens and some small woody plants which are adapted to a short summer growing season. The tundra is also notable for receiving relatively little precipitation and being generally poor in nutrients. The cold climate ensures that the rate of biological processes is generally slow and the shallow soils are deeply frozen (permafrost) for all or much of the year, a condition which underlies about 20 per cent of the Earth's land surface. Many animals hibernate or migrate in the colder season, while others such as lemmings live beneath the snow.

The main tundra region is located in the circumpolar lands north of the Arctic Circle, which are bordered to the south by the evergreen, needle-leaved boreal or taiga forests (Fig. 1.2). Here, winters are very cold, as in the tundra, but summers are longer. Most of the trees are conifers such as pine, fir and spruce. They are tall and have a narrow, pointy shape which means that the snow tends to slide off their branches, while their needles also shed snow more easily than broad leaves. These adaptations reduce the likelihood of heavy snow breaking branches. Boreal forests are subject to periodic fires, and a burn–regeneration cycle is an important characteristic to which populations of deer, bears and

Figure 1.2 Coniferous forest in Finland, the eastern end of a broad region of boreal or taiga forest that stretches to the Russian Far East.

Figure 1.3 An area of primary tropical rain forest, an evergreen biome with great biodiversity, in Panama, Central America.

insects, as well as the vegetation, are adapted. Much of the boreal forest is underlain by acid soils.

The temperate forests, by contrast, are typically deciduous, shedding their leaves each year. They are, however, like the boreal forests in that they are found almost exclusively in the northern hemisphere. This biome is characteristic of northern Europe, eastern China and eastern and midwest USA, with small stands in the southern hemisphere in South America and New Zealand. Tall broadleaf trees dominate, the climate is seasonal, but water is always abundant during the growing season, and this biome is less homogeneous than tundra or boreal forest. Amphibians, such as salamanders and frogs, are present, while they are almost totally absent from the higher-latitude biomes.

The tropical rain forest climate has copious rainfall and warm temperatures in all months of the year. The trees are always green, typically broad-leaved, and most are pollinated by animals (trees in temperate and boreal forests, by contrast, are largely pollinated by wind). Many kinds of vines (llianas) and epiphytes, such as ferns and orchids, are characteristic. Most of the nutrients are stored in the biomass and the soils contain little organic matter. These forests typically display a multilayered canopy (Fig. 1.3), while at ground level vegetation is often sparse because of low levels of light. Above all, tropical rain forests are characterized by a large number of species of both plants and animals.

Savanna belts flank the tropical rain forests to the north and south in the African and South American tropics, a biome known as *cerrado* in Brazil. The trees of tropical savannas are stunted and widely spaced, which allows grass to grow between them. Herds of grazing mammals typify the savanna landscape, along with large carnivores such as lions and other big cats, jackals and hyenas. These mammals, in turn, provide a food source for large scavengers such as vultures. The climate is warm all year, but has a dry season several months long when fires are a common feature. These fires maintain the openness of the savanna ecosystem and are important in mineral cycling.

The greatest expanses of the temperate grassland biome are located in Eurasia (where they are commonly known as steppe – Fig. 1.4), North America (prairie) and South America (pampa), with smaller expanses in South Africa (veldt). There are certain similarities with savannas in terms of fauna and the occurrence of fire, but unlike savannas, trees are absent in temperate grasslands. The vegetation is dominated by herbaceous (i.e. not woody) plants, of which the most abundant are grasses. The climate in this biome is temperate, seasonal and dry. Typical soils tend to be deep and rich in organic matter.

In many parts of the world, where climates become drier, temperate grasslands fade into the desert biome. Hyper-arid desert supports very little plant life and is characterized by bare rock or sand dunes, but some species of flora and fauna are adapted to the high and variable temperatures – the diurnal temperature range is typically high in deserts – and the general lack of moisture. Some water is usually available via precipitation in one of its forms: most commonly rainfall or dew, but fog is important in some coastal deserts (Fig. 1.5). Sporadic, some-times intense, rain promotes rapid growth of annual plants and animals such as locusts, which otherwise lie dormant for several years as seeds or eggs.

A very distinctive form of vegetation is commonly associated with Mediterranean climates in which summers are hot and dry and winters are cool and moist. It is found around much of the Mediterranean Basin (where it is known as maquis), in California (chaparral), southern Australia (mallee), Chile (mat-toral) and South Africa (fynbos). Low evergreen trees (forming woodland) and shrubs (forming scrub) have thick bark and small, hard leaves that make them tolerant to the stresses of climatic extremes and soils that are often low in nutrients. During the arid summer period this biome is fre-quently exposed to fire, which is important to its development and regeneration.

All these natural biomes have been affected to a greater or lesser extent by human action. Much of the maquis, for example, may represent a landscape where forests have been degraded by people, through cutting, grazing and the use of fire. The human use of fire may also be an important factor in maintaining, and possi-bly forming, savannas and temperate grasslands. The temperate forests have been severely altered over long histories with high population densities as people have cleared trees for farming and urban development (Fig. 1.6). Conversely, biomes

Figure 1.4 Temperate grassland in central Mongolia is still predominantly used for grazing. In many other parts of the world such grasslands have been ploughed up for cultivation.

Figure 1.5 This strange-looking plant, the welwitschia, is found only in the Namib Desert. Its adaptations to the dry conditions include long roots to take up any moisture in the gravelly soil and the ability to take in moisture from fog through its leaves. The welwitschia's exact position in the plant kingdom is controversial, but it is grouped with the pine trees.

considered by people to be harsh, such as the tundra and deserts, show less human impact. The anthropogenic influence is but one factor that promotes change in terrestrial as well as oceanic and freshwater ecosystems, because the interactions between the four global spheres have never been static. Better understanding of the dynamism of the natural world can be gained through a complementary way of studying the natural environment. Study of the processes that occur in natural cycles also takes us beyond description, to enable explanation.

Figure 1.6 The US city of New York, part of one of the world's most extensive areas of urban development. Only a few of the original temperate forest trees survive in parks and gardens. Urban areas are now so widespread that they are often treated as a type of physical environment in their own right.

NATURAL CYCLES

A good method for understanding the way the natural world works is through the recognition of cycles of matter in which molecules are formed and reformed by chemical and biological reactions and are manifested as physical changes in the material concerned. The major stores and flows of water in the global hydrological cycle are shown in Figure 1.7. Most of the Earth's water (about 97 per cent) is stored in liquid form in the oceans. Of the 3 per cent fresh water, most is locked as ice in the ice caps and glaciers, and as a liquid in rocks as groundwater. Only a tiny fraction is present at any time in lakes and rivers. Water is continually exchanged between the Earth's surface and the atmosphere – where it can be present in gaseous, liquid or solid form – through evaporation, transpiration from plants and animals, and precipitation. The largest flows are directly between the ocean and the atmosphere. Smaller amounts are exchanged between the land and the atmosphere, with the difference accounted for by flows in rivers and groundwater to the oceans. Fresh water on the land is most directly useful to human society, since water is an essential prerequisite of life, but the oceans and ice caps play a key role in the workings of climate.

Similar cycles, commonly referred to as biogeochemical cycles, can be identified for other forms of matter. Nutrients such as nitrogen, phosphorus and sulphur are similarly distributed among the four major environmental spheres and are continually cycled between them. Carbon is another key element for life on Earth, and the stores and flows of the carbon cycle are shown in Figure 1.8. The major stores of carbon are the oceans and rocks, particularly carbonate sedimentary rocks such as limestones, and the hydrocarbons (coal, oil and natural gas), plus clathrates, or gas hydrates, found mainly in high latitudes and in the oceans along continental margins. Much smaller proportions are present in the atmosphere and biosphere. The length of time carbon spends in particular stores also varies widely. Under natural circumstances, fossil carbon locked in rocks remains in these stores for millions of years. Carbon reaches these stores by the processes of sedimentation and evaporation, and is released from rocks by weathering, vulcanism and sea-floor spreading. In recent times, however, the rate of flow of carbon from some of the lithospheric stores – the hydrocarbons or fossil fuels – has been greatly increased by human action: the burning of fossil fuels,

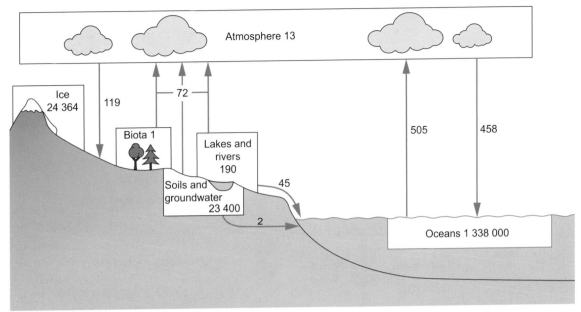

Figure 1.7 Global hydrological cycle showing major stores and flows (data from Shiklomanov, 1993). The values in stores are in thousand km^3, values of flows in thousand km^3 per year.

which liberates carbon by oxidation. Hence, a significant new flow of carbon between the lithosphere and the atmosphere has been introduced by human society and the natural atmospheric carbon store is being increased as a consequence.

Carbon also reaches the atmosphere through the respiration of plants and animals, which in green plants, blue-green algae and phytoplankton is part of the two-way process of photosynthesis. Photosynthesis is the chemical reaction by which these organisms convert carbon from the atmosphere, with water, to produce complex sugar compounds (which are either stored as organic matter or used by the organism) and oxygen. The reaction is written as follows:

$$6CO_2 + 6H_2O \rightarrow C_6H_{12}O_6 + 6O_2$$

This equation shows that six molecules of carbon dioxide and six molecules of water yield one molecule of organic matter and six molecules of oxygen. The reaction requires an input of energy from the sun, some of which is stored in chemical form in the organic matter formed.

The process of respiration is written as the opposite of the equation for photosynthesis. It is the process by which the chemical energy in organic matter is liberated by combining it with oxygen to produce carbon dioxide and water. All living things respire to produce energy for growth and the other processes of life. The chemical reaction for respiration is, in fact, exactly the same as that for combustion. Humans, for example, derive energy for their life needs from organic matter by eating (just as other animals do) and also by burning plant matter in a number of forms, such as fuelwood and fossil fuels.

The flow of converted solar energy through living organisms can be traced up a hierarchy of life forms known as a food chain. Figure 1.9 shows a simple food chain in which solar energy is converted into chemical energy in plants (so-called producers), which are eaten by herbivores (so-called first-order consumers), which,

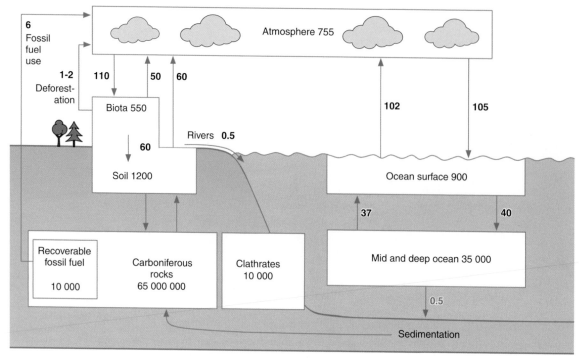

Figure 1.8 Global carbon cycle showing major stores and flows (after Schlesinger, 1991 and Grace, 2004). The values in stores are in units of Pg C, values of flows in Pg C per year. 1Pg C = 10^{15}g C = 1 billion tonnes of carbon as CO_2.

in turn, are eaten by other consumers (primary carnivores), which are themselves eaten by secondary carnivores. An example of such a food chain on land is:

grass → cricket → frog → heron

Each stage in the chain is known as a trophic level. In practice, there are usually many, often interlinked, food chains that together form a food web, but the principles are the same. At each trophic level some energy is lost by respiration, through excretory products and when dead organisms decay, so that available energy declines along the food chain away from the plant. In general terms, animals also tend to be bigger at each sequential trophic level, enabling them to eat their prey safely. This model helps us to explain the basic structures of natural communities: with each trophic level, less energy is available to successively larger individuals and thus the number of individuals decreases. Hence, while plants are very numerous because they receive their energy directly from the sun, they can support only successively fewer larger animals. With the exception of humans, predators at the top of food chains are therefore always rare.

Food chains, the carbon cycle and the hydrological cycle are all examples of 'systems' in which the individual components are all related to each other. Most of the energy that drives these systems comes from the sun, although energy from the Earth also contributes. All the cycles of energy and matter referred to in this section are affected by human action, deliberately manipulating natural cycles to human advantage. One of the human impacts on the carbon cycle has been mentioned, but humans also affect other cycles. The cycle of minerals in the rock cycle is affected by the construction industry, for example. Human activity affects the hydrological cycle by diverting natural flows: the damming of rivers or

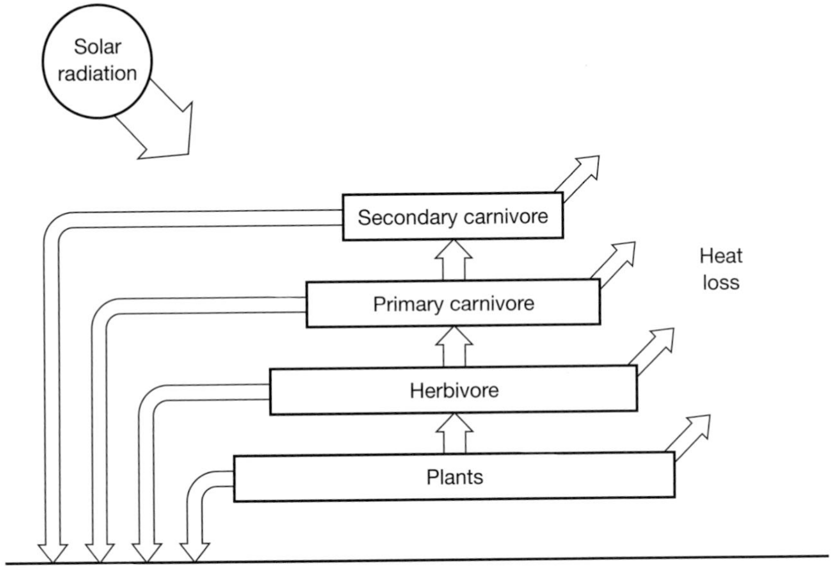

Figure 1.9 Energy flow through a food chain.

extracting groundwater for human use. The nitrogen cycle is affected by concentrating nitrogen in particular places such as by spreading fertilizers on fields. Food chains are widely affected: human populations manipulate plants and animals to produce food.

However, since all parts of these cycles are interrelated, human intervention in one part of a cycle also affects other parts of the same and other cycles. These knock-on effects are the source of many environmental changes that are undesirable from human society's viewpoint. Our manipulation of the nitrogen cycle by using fertilizers also increases the concentration of nitrogen in rivers and lakes when excess fertilizer is washed away from farmers' fields. This can have deleterious effects on aquatic ecosystems. Excess nitrogen can also enter the atmosphere to become a precursor for acid rain. One of the effects of acid rain is to accelerate the rate of weathering of some building stones. A better appreciation of these types of changes can be gained by looking at the various scales of time and space through which they occur.

TIMESCALES

Changes in the natural environment occur on a wide range of timescales. Geologists believe that the Earth is about 4600 million years old, while fossil evidence suggests that modern humans (*Homo sapiens*) appeared between 100 000 and 200 000 years before present (BP), developing from the hominids whose earliest remains, found in Africa, date to around 3.75 million BP (Table 1.2). The very long timescales over which many changes in the natural world take place may seem at first to have little relevance for today's human society other than to have created the world we know. It is difficult for us to appreciate the age of the Earth and the thought that the present distribution of the continents dates from the break-up of the supercontinent Pangaea, which began during the Cretaceous period. Indeed, relative to the forces and changes due to tectonic movements, the

TABLE 1.2 Geological timescale classifying the history of the Earth

Era	Period		Start (million years BP)	Important events
	Quaternary	Holocene	0.01	Early civilizations
		Pleistocene	1.8	First humans
		Pliocene	5	First hominids
		Miocene	22.5	
		Oligocene	38	
		Eocene	54	
Cenozoic	Tertiary	Palaeocene	65	Extinction of dinosaurs
	Cretaceous		136	Main fragmentation of Pangaea
	Jurassic		190	
Mesozoic	Triassic		225	First birds
	Permian		280	Formation of Pangaea
		Pennsylvanian	315	
	Carboniferous	Mississippian	345	
	Devonian		395	
	Silurian		440	First land plants and animals
	Ordovician		500	First vertebrates
Palaeozoic	Cambrian		570	
Precambrian			4600	Formation of Earth

Source: after Goudie (1993a); Colinvaux (1993); Williams et al. (1993).

human impact on the planet is very minor and short-lived. However, such Earth processes do have relevance on the timescale of a human lifetime. Tectonic movements cause volcanic eruptions that can affect human society as natural disasters at the time of the event. Some volcanic eruptions also affect day-to-day human activities on slightly longer timescales, by injecting dust into the atmosphere, which affects climate, for example, and by providing raw materials from which soils are formed. This example also illustrates the fact that the same event may be interpreted as bad from a human viewpoint on one timescale (a volcanic disaster) and good on another timescale (fertile volcanic soils).

It is important to realize that the timescale we adopt for the study of natural systems can affect our understanding as well as our perception of them. Many such systems are thought to be in dynamic equilibrium, meaning that the input and output of matter and energy are balanced, but recognition of dynamic equilibrium in natural systems depends upon the timescale over which the system is studied. To take the Earth as a whole, for example, the idea of dynamic equilibrium has been proposed to explain why the temperature of the Earth has remained relatively constant for the past 4 billion years, despite the fact that the sun's heat has increased by about 25 per cent over that period. The Gaia hypothesis suggests that life on the planet has played a key role in regulating the Earth's conditions to keep it amenable to life (Lovelock, 1989). The theory is not without its critics, but even if we accept it, the dynamic equilibrium holds only for the few billion years of the Earth's existence. Astronomers predict that eventually the sun will destroy the Earth, so that over a longer timescale, dynamic equilibrium

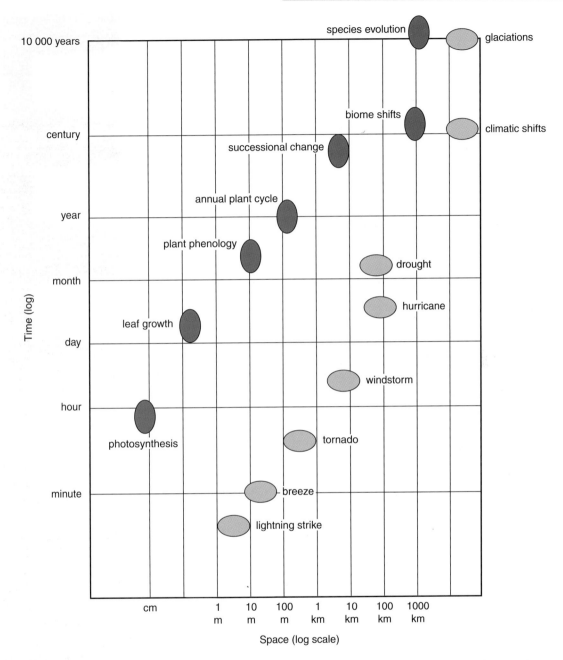

TIME AND SPACE SCALES

The key factors influencing natural events also vary at different combined spatial and temporal scales. Individual waves breaking on a beach constantly modify the beach profile, which is also affected by the daily pattern of tides dictating where on the beach the waves break. Individual storms alter the beach too, as do the types of weather associated with the seasons. However, all these influences are superimposed upon the effects of factors that operate over longer timescales and larger spatial scales, such as sediment supply and the sea level itself (Clayton, 1991).

Figure 1.13 The range of temporal and spatial scales at which ecosystem processes exist and operate (after Holling, 1995).

The range of temporal and spatial scales is illustrated for some biological and climatic processes in Figure 1.13. This emphasizes the fact that various processes in the natural environment (e.g. climatic changes, tornadoes) exist at specific scales, as do its elements (e.g. species, biomes). It is also important to note that no part of the physical environment is a closed, self-supporting system; all are a part of larger interacting systems.

The environmental issues in this book have arisen as a consequence of human activity conflicting with environmental systems. Resolution of such conflicts can only be based on an understanding of how natural systems work. For issues that stem from human impact upon the physical environment, as most do, we need to be able to rank the temporal and spatial scale of human impact in the natural hierarchy of influences on the natural system in question. Inevitably, we tend to focus on scales directly relevant to people, but we should not forget other scales, which may have less direct but no less significant effects. Indeed, successful management of environmental issues relies on the successful identification of appropriate scales and their linkages.

THE STATE OF OUR KNOWLEDGE

We already know a great deal about how the natural world works, but there remains a lot more to learn. We have some good ideas about the sorts of ways natural systems operate, but we remain ignorant of many of the details. Some of the difficulties involved in ascertaining these details include a lack of data and our own short period of residence on the Earth. Direct measurements using instruments are used in the contemporary era to monitor environmental processes. Historical archives, sometimes of direct measurements, otherwise of more anecdotal evidence, can extend these data back over decades and centuries. Good records of high and low water levels for the River Nile at Cairo extend from AD 641 to 1451, although they are intermittent thereafter until the nineteenth century, and continuous monthly mean temperature and precipitation records have been kept at several European weather stations since the early eighteenth century. Other types of written historical evidence date back to ancient Chinese and Mesopotamian civilizations as early as 5000 BP. The further back in time we go, however, the patchier the records become, and in some parts of the world historical records begin only in the last century.

These data gaps for historical time, and for longer time periods of thousands, tens of thousands and millions of years, can be filled in using natural archives. The geological timescale given in Table 1.2 is based on fossil evidence. Such 'proxy' methods are based on our knowledge of the current interrelationships between the different environmental spheres. Particular plants and animals thrive in particular climatic zones, for example, so that fossils can indicate former climates. The variability of climate during an organism's lifetime can also be inferred in some cases. Study of the width of the annual growth rings of trees gives an insight into specific ecological events that changed the tree's ability to photosynthesize and fix carbon. Essentially similar methods can be used to infer environmental variability from changes in the rate of growth of coral reefs. Other proxy palaeoenvironmental indicators include pollen types found in cores of sediment taken from lake or ocean beds, and the rate of sediment accumulation in such cores can tell us something about erosion rates on the surrounding land. Landforms, too, become fossilized in landscapes to provide clues about past environmental conditions. Examples include glacial and periglacial forms in central and northern Europe, indicating colder conditions during previous glaciations, and fossilized sand dunes in the Orinoco Basin of South America, also dating from periods of high-latitude glaciation, which indicate an environment much drier than that of today.

As with instrumental data and historical archives, natural archives used as proxy variables are patchy in both their spatial and temporal extent. Coral reefs grow only in tropical waters, ice accumulates only under certain conditions and not many trees live longer than 1000 years. Even instrumental data may not be perfectly reliable over long periods of time because methods and instrumentation can change, monitoring sites can be moved and external factors may alter the nature of the reading. The availability and limitations through time and space of some of the variables used to indicate temperature, a key palaeoenvironmental variable, in the Holocene period are shown in Table 1.3.

Variable	Spatial extent	Timescale		
		Interannual	Decades to centuries	Centennial and longer
Instrumental data	Europe from early 1700s, most other coastal regions during nineteenth century. Continental interiors by 1920s, Antarctica by late 1950s	Should be 'perfect' if properly maintained – changes assessable on daily, monthly and seasonal timescales	Site moves, observation time changes and urbanization influences present problems – changing frequency of extremes assessable	As previous, but rates of change to site, instrumentation and urbanization mean absolute levels increasingly difficult to maintain
Proxy indicators Contemporary written historical records (annals, diaries, etc.)	Europe, China, Japan, Korea, eastern N. America. Some potential in Middle East, Turkey and S. Asia and Latin America (since 1500s)	Depends on function of diary information (freeze dates, harvest dates and amounts, snowlines, etc.). Very difficult to compare with instrumental data	Depends on diary length and observer age. Lower frequencies increasingly likely to be lost due to human lifespan	Only a few indicators are objective and might provide comparable information (e.g. snowlines, rain days)
Tree-ring widths	Trees growing poleward of 30° or at high elevations in regions where cool season suspends growth	Generally dependent upon growing season months. Exact calendar dates determined by cross-dating	Standardisation method potentially compromises interpretation on longer timescales	Highly dependent on standardisation method. Likely to have lost variability, but difficult to assess
Ice-core melt layers	Coastal Greenland and high-latitude and high-altitude ice caps, where temperatures rise above freezing for a few days each summer	Depends on summer warmth. Unable to distinguish cold years that cause no melt. Rarely compared with instrumental records. Dating depends on layer counting – increasingly difficult with depth	May not respond to full range of temperature variability. Whole layer may melt if too warm; no melt layers if too cold	Increasingly depends on any flow model and layer compaction. Veracity can be assessed using other cores
Coral growth and isotopes	Tropics (between 30° N and S) where shallow seas promote coral growth	Response to annual and seasonal water temperature and salinity. Dating depends on counting. Rarely cross-dated	As coral head grows, low-frequency aspects may be affected by amount of sunlight, water depth, nutrient supply, etc.	Only achieved in a few cases. Veracity can be assessed by comparison with other corals

Source: after Jones et al. (1998: Tables 1 and 2).

TABLE 1.3 Spatial and temporal availability and limitations of instrumental data and some proxy variables for temperature in the Holocene

It is clear that our understanding of how environments change can be built up only slowly in a patchwork fashion, but the understanding gained from all these lines of evidence can then be used to predict environmental changes, incorporating any human impact, using models that simulate environmental processes. The accuracy of a model can be assessed by comparing its output with any monitored record and records reconstructed from proxy variables, developing the model as discrepancies are identified. The human impact may still provide further complications, however, because in many instances through prehistory, history and indeed in the present era, it can be difficult to distinguish between purely natural events and those that owe something to human activities (temperature readings at a town that becomes a city are an obvious example because urbanization affects temperature). It is the interrelationships between human activities and natural functions that form the subject matter of this book.

FURTHER READING

Begon, M., Townsend, C. and Harper, J.L. 2005 *Ecology: from individuals to ecosystems*, 4th edn. Oxford, Blackwell. This comprehensive textbook covers all the basics of ecology.

Goudie, A.S. 2001 *The nature of the environment*, 4th edn. Oxford, Blackwell. A good overview of physical geography, including the influence of geology and climatology, profiles of major world environments and the workings of landscapes and ecosystems.

Hamandawana, H., Eckardt, F. and Chanda, R. 2005 Linking archival and remotely sensed data for long-term environmental monitoring. *International Journal of Applied Earth Observation and Geoinformation* 7: 284–98. An illustration of how archival, historical and remotely sensed sources of data can complement each other for long-term environmental monitoring.

Inkpen, R. 2004 *Science, philosophy and physical geography*. London, Routledge. An accessible exploration of how study of the environment can vary with different scientific methods and philosophical perspectives.

Lovett, G.M., Burns, D.A., Driscoll, C.T., Jenkins, J.C., Mitchell, M.J., Rustad, L., Shanley, J.B., Likens, G.E. and Haeuber, R. 2007 Who needs environmental monitoring? *Frontiers in Ecology and the Environment* 5: 253–60. A cogent argument for long-term study as the basis for environmental science.

Melillo, J.M., Field, C.B. and Moldan, B. 2003 *Interactions of the major biogeochemical cycles: global change and human impacts*. Washington DC, Island Press. A series of papers on biogeochemistry in ecosystems covering theory, the lithosphere, the atmosphere, the hydrosphere and crosscutting issues.

Nicholls, K.E. 1997 Planktonic green algae in western Lake Erie: the importance of temporal scale in the interpretation of change. *Freshwater Biology* 38: 419–25. A cautionary illustration of how interpretation of data can vary according to the length of data sets.

Oldfield, F. 2005 *Environmental change: key issues and alternative approaches*. Cambridge, Cambridge University Press. A good overview of the significance of past and contemporary climatic and other environmental changes.

Thomas, M.F. 2004 Landscape sensitivity to rapid environmental change – a Quaternary perspective with examples from tropical areas. *Catena* 55: 107–24. An interesting assessment of environmental change including the effects of scales.

1920s and 1930s, the landscape of Machakos was badly degraded, with widespread loss of vegetation and severe gullying. Over the period 1930–90, the population of Machakos increased nearly six-fold, but changes in agricultural practices, such as the widespread construction of terraces to control erosion, have helped to transform the condition of the environment.

Political and economic forces also affect the ways in which people use or abuse their resources. The relationship between population and environmental degradation is further complicated by the fact that many human impacts are not direct: people living in a city, for example, have influence on resource use far from their immediate surrounds. A walk down a supermarket aisle in any city will indicate the great distances some products have been transported before they reach the urban consumer, an apt reflection of the globalization of the economy. Further investigation of the importance of human population numbers is made in Chapter 3.

Technology

Developments in technology have been closely associated with population growth. One view sees technological developments as a spur to growth, so that agricultural innovations provide more food per unit area and enable more people to be supported, for example. An opposite perspective sees technological change as a result of human inventiveness reacting to the needs created by more people (Boserüp, 1965). This latter view can be used to suggest that a growing human population is not necessarily bad from an environmental perspective. Any problems created by increasing population will be countered by new innovations that ease the burden on resources by using them more effectively. One illustration of this line of argument can be drawn from society's use of non-renewable fossil fuel resources. Since fossil fuel supplies will not last forever, and their current use is causing a range of environmental problems, such as global warming and acid rain, energy conservation is being promoted and alternative forms of renewable energy supplies are being developed (see Chapter 18).

However, many arguments can be presented to indicate that technological developments are responsible for much environmental degradation. Technology influences demand for natural resources by changing their accessibility and people's ability to afford them, as well as creating new resources (uranium, for example, was not considered a resource until its energy properties were recognized). The Industrial Revolution has been associated with high population growth and a greatly enhanced level of resource use and misuse; it has promoted urban development, improved transport and resulted in the globalization of the economy. But although these developments have undoubtedly increased the scale of human impact on the environment, this is not to say that pre-industrial technologies did not also allow severe impacts. Polynesians who reached the planet's last habitable areas, the Pacific islands, within the last 1000 to 4000 years, are thought to have exterminated more than 2000 bird species (some 15 per cent of the world total) with only Stone Age technology (Pimm et al., 1995; see also page 306).

Figure 2.2 A solar-powered kettle in Tibet illustrates a technology devised to relieve pressure on biological resources, since firewood is very scarce on the Tibetan Plateau.

Technology has a direct impact on resources, of course, and virtually every environmental issue can be interpreted as a consequence, either deliberate or inadvertent, of the impact of technology on the natural world. Advances in earth-moving and concrete technology, for example, have precipitated a marked escalation in the rate and scale of construction of big dams on rivers all over the world in recent times, and the adverse environmental impacts associated with these structures have attracted increasing public attention (see Chapter 9). The numerous examples of inadvertent impacts are usually the result of ignorance: a new technology being tried and tested and found to have undesirable consequences. The use of pesticides and fertilizers has helped to improve levels of food production, but they have also had numerous unintended negative effects on other aspects of the world in which we live (Conway and Pretty, 1991). On the other hand, technology is not environmentally damaging by definition (Fig. 2.2), since technological applications can be designed and used as a mitigating force, in many cases in response to a previous undesirable impact. Measures introduced to reduce harmful emissions from motor vehicles, such as the catalytic converter (see page 328), are just one illustration of this point. When and where technology is developed, used or abused is dictated by the nature of society and its organization.

Sociocultural organization

The influences of population and technology are intimately linked to the organization of human society. Economic, political and social values, norms and structures are a diverse set of driving forces that influence environmental change. They also underpin the mitigating forces that have been developed by societies to offset some of the damaging aspects of environmental issues. Dramatic transformations in population and technology have been associated with the two most significant changes in the history of humankind – the Agricultural Revolution of the late Neolithic period and the Industrial Revolution of the eighteenth and nineteenth centuries – but these changes have also been reflected in equally marked modifications to the ways that society is organized.

One of the most striking of these social changes is the rise of the city. Although cities have been a feature of human culture for about 5000 years, virtually the entire human species lived a rural existence just 300 years ago. Today, the proportion of the world's population living in cities is approaching 50 per cent, and individual urban areas have reached unprecedented sizes. In most cases, urban areas have much higher population densities than rural areas, and the consumption of resources per person in urban areas is greater than that of their rural counterparts. The environmental impacts of cities within urban boundaries are obvious, since cities are a clear illustration of the human ability to transform all the natural spheres, but the influence of cities is also felt far beyond their immediate confines.

The high level of resources used by city dwellers has been fuelled by extending their resource flows. Economic and political forces have developed to facilitate this extension, so that the world is now an integrated whole.

Although integrated, the world has also become a very unbalanced place in terms of human welfare and environmental quality. Much attention has been focused on how economic and political forces have produced global imbalances in the way human society interacts with the environment, not just between city and countryside, but between groups within society with different levels of access to power and influence (e.g. women and men, different political parties, ethnic groups). On the global scale, there are clear imbalances between richer nations and poorer nations. In general terms, the wealthiest few are disproportionately responsible for environmental issues, but at the other end of the spectrum the poorest are also accused of a responsibility that is greater than their numbers warrant. The motivations for these disproportionate impacts are very different, however. The impact of the wealthy is driven by their intense resource use, many say their overconsumption of resources. The poor, on the other hand, may degrade the environment because they have no other option (Fig. 2.3). Economic power is seen as a vital determinant: the wealthy have become wealthy because of their high-intensity resource use, and can afford to continue overconsuming and to live away from the problems this creates. The poor cannot afford to do anything other than overuse and misuse the resources that are immediately available to them, and as a consequence they are often the immediate victims of environmental issues. This difference in economic power is also manifested in political power: the wealthy generally have more influence over decisions that affect interaction with the environment than the poor, although when marginalized people are pushed to the edge of environmental destruction they may become active in forcing political changes (Broad, 1994). Some of the causes and manifestations of these global and regional imbalances are investigated further in the following sections.

Figure 2.3 The health of this argun tree in south-west Morocco is not improved by goats browsing in its canopy, but herders often have few options but to overuse the resources that are immediately available to them.

HUMAN-INDUCED IMBALANCES

Human society has created a set of sociocultural imbalances that is superimposed on geographical patterns of environmental resources on all spatial scales from the global to the individual. These patterns of uneven distribution have been developed by, and are maintained by, the processes and structures of economics, politics and society. These imbalance theories, combined with the human driving force theories outlined above, together make up a diverse set of explanations that have been put forward to explain the human dimension behind environmental issues (Table 2.3).

Theory	Explanation
Neo-Malthusian	Demographic pressure leads to overuse and misuse of resources
Ignorance	Ignorance of the workings of nature means that mistakes are made, leading to unintentional consequences
Tragedy of the commons	Overuse or misuse of certain resources occurs because they are commonly owned
Poor valuation	Overuse or misuse of certain resources occurs because they are not properly valued in economic terms
Dependency	Inappropriate resource use by certain groups is encouraged or compelled by the influence of more powerful groups
Exploitation	Overuse and misuse of resources is pursued deliberately by a culture driven by consumerism
Human domination over nature	Environmental issues result from human misapprehension of being above rather than part of nature

Source: after Barrow (1991).

TABLE 2.3 Some theories to explain why environmental issues occur

Ownership and value

Two interrelated theories that explain the underlying causes of imbalance between human activities and the environment stem from differential ownership of certain resources and the values put on them. Some environmental resources are owned by individuals while others are under common ownership. One theory argues that resources under common ownership are prone to overuse and abuse for this very reason – the so-called 'tragedy of the commons' (Hardin, 1968). The example often given to illustrate this principle is that of grazing lands which are commonly owned in pastoral societies. It is in the interest of an individual to graze as many livestock as possible, but if too many individuals all have the same attitude the grazing lands may be overused and degraded: the rational use of a resource by an individual may not be rational from the viewpoint of a wider society. The principle can also be applied to explain the misuse of other commonly owned resources, such as the pollution of air and water or catching too many fish in the sea.

It is important to note, however, that common ownership does not necessarily lead to overexploitation of resources. In many areas where resources are commonly owned, strong social and cultural rules have evolved to control the use of resources. In situations like this, resource degradation usually occurs because the traditional rules for the control of resource use break down for some reason. Reasons include migration to a new area, changes in ownership rights, and population growth. In examples like overfishing in the open oceans, by contrast, the tragedy of the commons applies because there is no tradition of rules developed to limit exploitation.

A related concept is the undervaluation of certain resources. Air is a good example. To all intents and purposes, air is a commonly owned continuous resource that, in practice, is not given an economic value. The owner of a windmill does not pay for the moving air the windmill harnesses, nor does the owner of a factory who uses the air as a sink for the factory's wastes. Since air has no economic value it is prone to be overused. A simple economic argument suggests that if an appropriate economic value were put on the resource, the workings of the market would ensure that as the resource became scarce so the price would increase. As the value of the resource increased, theory suggests that it would be managed more carefully.

Exploitation and dependency on the global scale

A complex series of economic, political and social processes has resulted in patterns of exploitation and dependency, which are associated with the misuse of resources. Inequalities exist between many different groups of people (see above) and can be identified on several different scales. Three levels are identified by Lonergan (1993): two spatial (international and national) and one temporal (intergenerational).

Some of the main structural inequalities of the global system are shown in Figure 2.4. They have evolved from colonial times to the point, today, where direct political control of empires has been superseded by more subtle control by wealthier countries over poorer ones. The economic dimension is particularly important, since it influences the rate of exploitation of natural resources in particular countries, the relative levels of economic development apparent in different countries, and the power of certain governments to control their own future.

The realities of global inequality in economic terms are stark. One billion people live in unprecedented luxury, while one billion live in destitution. Children in the USA even have more in pocket money (US$230 a year) than the half-billion poorest people alive (Durning, 1991). The gap between countries has also been widening in recent decades. In 1960, the richest 20 per cent of the world's population, who lived in high-income regions including western Europe, Japan, North America and Australia, absorbed 70 per cent of global income,

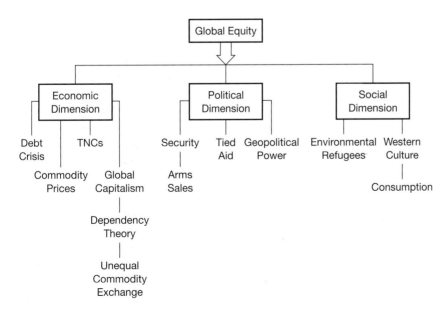

Figure 2.4 Structural inequalities in the global system (Lonergan, 1993).

about 30 times more than the world's poorest 20 per cent, who took just 2.3 per cent of global income (UNDP, 1993). By 2000, the richest 20 per cent of people accounted for 86 per cent of total private consumption, while the poorest 20 per cent accounted for only 1.3 per cent (UNFPA, 2001). On an individual level, a child born at the turn of the century in an industrialized country will add more to consumption and pollution over his or her lifetime than 30 to 50 children born in developing nations.

The structural aspects of this economic dimension have many facets, including the fact that many poorer countries are in debt to the countries and banks of the rich world (the so-called debt crisis), and many less-developed countries rely on a limited number of exports, which are usually primary products such as agricultural goods and minerals. Figure 2.5 illustrates this picture globally with regard to exports. A low index of commodity concentration of exports reflects a diverse export base, while a high index reflects a country's reliance on the export of a few agricultural or mineral resources. This pattern is maintained by terms of trade and prices for primary exports ('unequal commodity exchange'), which are set largely by the countries of the North that represent the major markets for these exports. Overexploitation of resources in poorer countries often occurs in response to the falling commodity prices that have been typical of recent decades, and the need to service debts.

Transnational corporations (TNCs), the very large majority of which have headquarters in the advanced capitalist regions, particularly Japan, North America and western Europe, also play an important role in the workings of global economics. Comparison of the annual turnover of TNCs with the gross national product (GNP) of entire nation states gives an indication of this role:

> By this yardstick, all of the top 50 transnational corporations – including the likes of Exxon, General Motors, Ford Motor Company, Matsushita Electronics, IBM, Unilever, Philips, ICI, Union Carbide, ITT, Siemens and Hitachi – carry more economic clout than many of the world's smaller peripheral nation-states; while the very biggest transnationals are comparable in size with the national economies of semi-peripheral states like Greece, Ireland, Portugal, and New Zealand.
>
> (Knox and Agnew, 1994: 38–9)

In development terms, investment by TNCs in developing countries has been portrayed as an engine of growth capable of eliminating economic inequality on the one hand, and as a major obstacle to development on the other. Some view such investment as a force capable of dramatically changing productive resources in the economically backward areas of the world, while others see it as a primary cause of underdevelopment because it acts as a major drain of surplus to the advanced capitalist countries (Jenkins, 1987).

The negative view has been illustrated by comparing the development paths of Japan and Java, which had a similar level of development in the 1830s. While Japan has subsequently developed much further, in spite of a poorer endowment of natural resources, Java has remained underdeveloped, despite a position on main trade routes and a good stock of natural resources, because few of the profits from resource use have been reinvested in the country (Geertz, 1963).

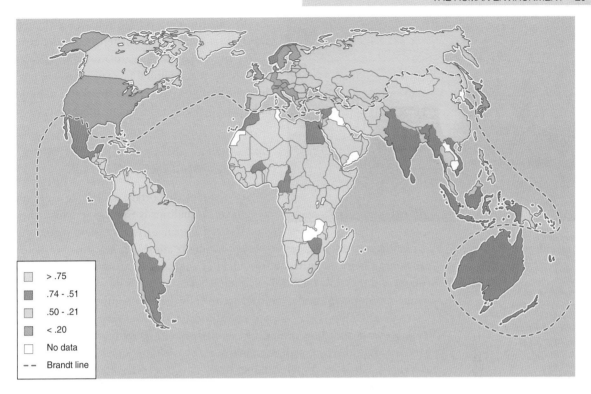

Figure 2.5 Index of commodity concentration of exports (Knox and Agnew, 1994). The Brandt line represents the division between countries of the more affluent 'North' and the poorer countries of the 'South'.

One aspect of these relationships, which some consider to be detrimental to the environment in poorer countries, is the movement of heavily polluting industries from richer countries that have developed high pollution-control standards, to poorer countries where such regulations are less stringent. TNCs may be particularly adept at relocating their production activities in this way if it means saving money otherwise spent on conforming to more stringent environmental requirements.

Fear of an increase in this trend of TNCs seeking so-called pollution havens was expressed during the negotiations for the Uruguay round of the General Agreement on Tariffs and Trade (GATT) and the establishment of the North American Free Trade Agreement (NAFTA) (Daly, 1993). Daly notes examples of 'maquiladoras', US factories which have located mainly in northern Mexico to take advantage of lower pollution-control standards and labour costs. However, not all assessments of the pollution haven hypothesis have been conclusive. A study by Eskeland and Harrison (2003), who analysed foreign direct investment across industries in Mexico, Venezuela, Morocco and Côte d'Ivoire, found little evidence in support of pollution havens. By contrast, Mani and Wheeler (1998) found clear confirmation of a pollution haven effect, even if they concluded that it has been transient in many countries.

Economic power is closely related to political power, which can be seen in the sale of arms and the giving of aid by richer countries to poorer ones. The workings of global capitalism also have social dimensions, including the spread of western cultural norms and practices (Fig. 2.6). The sale of western products can

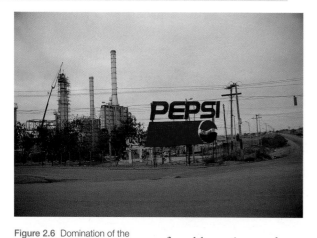

also be seen to reinforce the role of developing nations as suppliers of raw materials, as Grossman (1992) shows for the increasing use of pesticides on Caribbean agricultural plantations where produce is destined for export markets, a trend influenced by foreign aid, among other criteria.

Exploitation and dependency on the national scale

Figure 2.6 Domination of the world's poorer countries by their richer counterparts takes many forms, including what some term 'cultural imperialism', epitomized by this advertisement for Pepsi in Ecuador. Transfer of western technology is often in the form of polluting industries, as shown behind.

Perhaps the most important underlying aspect of the global inequalities is the way in which they combine to maintain a situation where a minority of wealthy nations and most of their inhabitants are able to live an affluent life consuming large quantities of resources at the expense of many more poorer nations and their inhabitants. Nevertheless, some countries do move up the economic development scale, and the terms 'North' and 'South' disguise much internal variability (Fig. 2.5). Structural inequalities also exist at the national level, however, and these inequalities similarly have implications for the ways in which people interact with the environment within countries. Some of the aspects of inequality on the national scale, categorized according to their economic, political and social dimensions, are shown in Figure 2.7.

Figure 2.7 Structural inequalities in national systems (Lonergan, 1993).

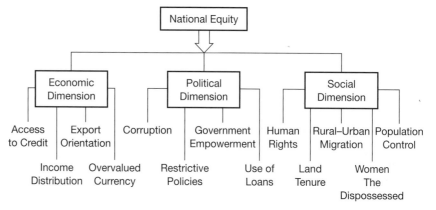

As at the global level, the national scene is often characterized by a small elite group that has more economic, political and social power than the majority of people in more marginal groups. In general terms, this pattern is often manifested in a rural/urban divide: cities are centres of power, although they also typically contain a poorer 'underclass' in both rich and poor countries. Outside the city in the South, most rural people do not have access to economic power: in Africa, Asia and Latin America, for example, more than 85 per cent of farmers are estimated to lack access to credit (Holmberg, 1991). Corruption and centralized control are all too frequent characteristics of political and economic management in developing countries, which often means that local communities lack power

determinism was widely accepted in western geographical thought in the late 1800s and early 1900s. The approach subsequently lost ground because of the way it was used by some as a justification for imperialism, colonial exploitation and racist views. Critics objected, for example, to the belief that bracing climates like that in Britain produced a generally energetic populace, whereas people born and brought up in places with hot, humid climates were inherently more lethargic.

Reactions to the ideas of environmental determinism have thrown up alternative views. Some of its critics have suggested that the environment never determines any particular way of life, but simply offers a number of different possibilities for society to follow. Supporters of this approach have pointed to the fact that different societies have maintained quite different relationships with similar environments.

Others simply reject altogether the idea that human society is reliant on the physical world, preferring to believe that social facts can only be explained by social causes, an approach variously referred to as cultural, economic or social determinism. But if some aspects of environmental determinism are today considered to be unacceptable or just plain wrong, it is equally foolish to dismiss environmental influences on society entirely.

THE NEED FOR CHANGE

The socio-economic system is just one part of the natural ecosystem in which materials are transformed and energy converted to heat (Fig. 3.1). The operation of the socio-economic system is dependent upon the ecosystem as a provider of energy and natural resources, and as a sink for wastes. The ecosystem also provides numerous 'environmental services' by virtue of its processes. These include provisioning, regulating and cultural services that directly affect people, plus various supporting services that are needed to maintain these other services (Fig. 3.2). This ecological, economic perspective emphasizes the fact that resource use and waste disposal take place in the same environment, and that both activities affect the life-support functions of the environment. Hence, the socio-economic system cannot expand indefinitely since it is limited by the finite global biosphere. Until recently, for example, the number of fish that could be sold at market was limited by the number of boats at sea; now it is limited by the number of fish in the sea. Through much of the history of human occupation of the planet, the socio-economic system has been small relative to the biosphere, so that resources were plentiful, the environment's capacity for assimilating wastes was large, and biospheric functions were relatively little affected by human impact. Today the situation is different. As Goodland *et al.* (1993a: 298) put it: 'now the world is no longer "empty" of people and their artefacts, the economic subsystem having become large relative to the biosphere'. As the socio-economic system has grown larger, fuelled by increased 'throughput' of energy and resources, its capacity for disturbing the environment has increased. Since this disruption ultimately feeds back on the operation of society itself, society's behaviour must conform more closely with that of the total ecosystem because otherwise it may destroy itself (Folke and Jansson, 1992).

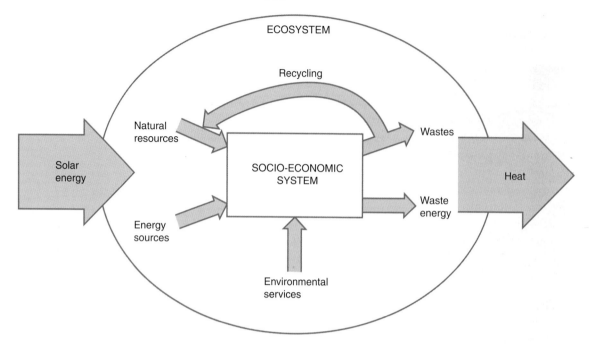

Figure 3.1 The socio-economic system as part of the global ecosystem (after Folke and Jansson, 1992; Daly, 1993).

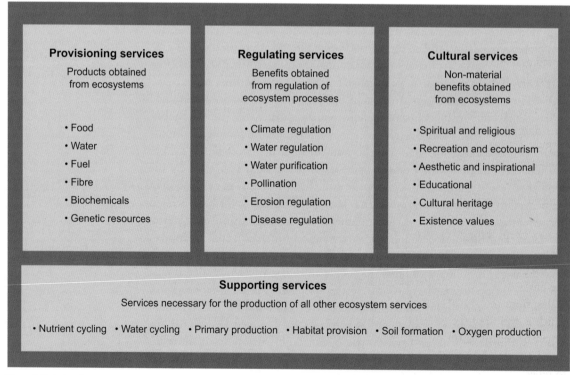

Figure 3.2 A classification of environmental or ecosystem services (after MEA, 2005).

Figure 3.3 The ruins at Palenque in southern Mexico, a reminder of the collapse of the Mayan civilization. No one is sure of the true reasons for the downfall of the Mayas, but one theory implicates human-induced environmental degradation as a key factor.

The potential for socio-economic degeneration and eventual collapse to occur when the human system operates too far out of harmony with the environment can be illustrated from both contemporary and historical examples, since although human activity has until recently been within the capacity of the environment on the global scale, breakdown has occurred on more local scales. Folke and Jansson (1992) note the recent, rapid, self-generated collapse of coastal shrimp industries in Taiwan and Thailand, within a decade of their beginnings, due to clearance of mangroves, which act as nursery and feeding areas for shrimps, and the deterioration of water quality through eutrophication and disease. A lack of harmony between the socio-economic system and the natural ecosystem has also been suggested as a cause of collapse for several ancient cultures. The decline of the Mayan civilization in Central America that began around AD 900 may have been due to excessive use of soils and an over-reliance on maize, which failed due to a virus (Fig. 3.3). Alternatively, some blame an inability to manage declining water supplies during a period of prolonged drought.

Similarly, the civilization that flourished in the tenth to twelfth centuries around Angkor Wat in present-day Cambodia was based on a sophisticated irrigation system, but forest clearance for cropland resulted in high silt loads, which clogged the canals in rainy-season floods. Irrigation channels were abandoned to become stagnant swamps where mosquitoes bred prolifically, and malaria epidemics swept through the city. This weakened Angkor Wat's capacity to adapt to change and the city was abandoned (McNeely, 1994).

A schematic representation of three ways in which human society interacts with the environment is shown in Figure 3.4. The model can be applied on various scales, from the global to the local, and across differing timescales. In cycle A, which is typical of the global economy in historical times, wealth is accumulated largely by degrading the environment. This wealth has brought numerous advances to most parts of the world, which reduce 'stress', a term used here in a wide sense to reflect the general well-being of society. Such advances include sanitation and other facilities, improved health and higher living standards. These improvements have promoted further inappropriate development to continue on cycle A.

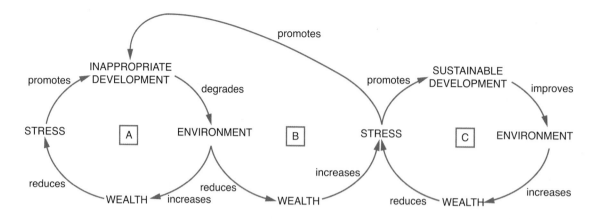

At some point in time, however, cycle A crosses an environmental threshold and the society may enter cycle B. The degraded environment begins to feed back on socio-economic wealth, and stress is increased. Increased stress in cycle B promotes further inappropriate development, particularly when the society in question has limited options as examples of poor, vulnerable groups quoted in this book show (e.g. accelerated soil erosion caused by farmers in Haiti and Ethiopia is discussed in Chapter 14), and on the national scale where rapid deforestation in many tropical countries has been pursued in response to the burden of debt and declining commodity prices (see Chapter 4). Continuing on cycle B can ultimately lead to socio-economic collapse, as in the examples of modern shrimp industries and ancient civilizations cited above.

Many people believe that, globally, we have now entered cycle B due to the sheer numbers of people on the Earth and the resulting scale of human impact on natural systems. There are numerous examples throughout this book which indicate that the productivity of many of the world's renewable resource-producing systems has reached its peak and in some cases is in decline. Currently, as much as 20–40 per cent of the potential global net primary productivity in terrestrial ecosystems is estimated to be diverted to human activities (Wright, 1990); about 20 per cent of atmospheric carbon dioxide results from human action; about 20 per cent of bird species on Earth have become extinct in the last two millennia, almost all due to human activities; more than 40 per cent of the planet's land surface has been transformed by human society; we use about 50 per cent of all accessible surface fresh water; 60 per cent of fixed nitrogen released each year owes its origin to human activity, and 66 per cent of marine fisheries are fully exploited, overexploited or depleted (Vitousek *et al.*, 1997b). Increased stress is manifested by, among other things, increasing levels of world poverty, fears over the effects of human-induced global warming and the depletion of the ozone layer.

Indeed, the impacts of human actions on the planet's biophysical systems have become so profound and widespread that many observers suggest we have entered a new planetary era best described as the 'Anthropocene' (Crutzen and Stoermer, 2000). As the name suggests, the defining feature of this era is the

The equation certainly has applications, but it also contains some flaws, and is based on assumptions that are not always valid. The effects of the driving forces on impacts are assumed to be strictly proportional, but we know that some environmental systems contain non-linear characteristics, including thresholds. Hence an ecosystem may be resilient under increasing pressure of human activity until a point is reached at which there is sharp, discontinuous change. The relationship also implies that a small human population with limited affluence and rudimentary technology has a small environmental impact, which may indeed be the case in many circumstances (Fig. 3.5), but not in all. There is persuasive evidence to suggest that in prehistoric times very small populations of hunter-gatherers may have been responsible for the extinction of several species of large mammal and wider-scale ecological change following the introduction of new fire regimes (Martin and Klein, 1984).

Some researchers argue that technological changes are far more significant than population or affluence in determining human-induced environmental change (e.g. Raskin, 1995). Indeed, absolute population numbers, density and growth rates are not always clearly related to degradation (see page 21). Although greater affluence, as defined above, can equate to greater environmental impact this is not necessarily so. In many cases, as affluence increases, so does a society's demand for environmental quality, with the consequent adoption of conservation measures and relatively 'clean' technologies. Similarly, population growth rates generally fall, sometimes even to negative values, with rising incomes.

Conversely, there is also a threshold below which decreasing affluence leads to greater degradation rather than less, as comments on the relationships between poverty and impact indicate (see page 25). Indeed, poverty is a key issue in the sustainability debate, an outcome of inequalities at the global and national scales. As a former executive director of the UN Environment Programme put it: 'The harsh fact remains: conservation is incompatible with absolute poverty' (Tolba, 1990: 10).

The $I = P \times A \times T$ equation (sometimes simply referred to as IPAT) also gives little recognition to such factors as beliefs, attitudes or politics, all important influences on a society's environmental impact. Another concern surrounds the geographical scale at which the equation can be applied. While the formula can be used to sum the human pressures on resources in a closed system, it does not indicate where within the system those pressures will be felt. Some environmental impacts will be local, of course, but others may involve degradation of a globally common resource such as the atmosphere, a sink for wastes such as greenhouse gases, which means that part of the impact is felt by others.

Figure 3.5 The Kombai of New Guinea rely on hunting for their main source of food, using traditional technology – spears and bows and arrows. Their environmental impact is minor, but elsewhere in earlier times small populations of hunter-gatherers are thought to have had considerable environmental impacts.

Some of the environmental effects of human activities may be displaced well away from the region of origin (Turner *et al.*, 1995). This means that an environmental impact made by the population of one country could be felt in a different country, as with some cases of acid rain. In addition to such environmental problems obviously crossing borders, trade and other economic relationships between societies may allow harmful effects to be 'exported' to another region in a less literal way. This could be because a poorer society is more willing to incur environmental damage in return for economic gain, or because it is less able to prevent it. The concept of an ecological footprint is one way of accounting for such displaced effects. It is an assessment of the total area required to sustain the population of a nation, region, city or community – or indeed an individual – and the associated level of resource consumption. This important geographical dimension is illustrated at the global scale by the view (Redclift, 1996) that it is the overconsumption of resources in the North that is primarily responsible for most environmental problems (Fig. 3.6).

Figure 3.6 This severely degraded landscape in Azerbaijan is an illustration of how environmental impacts are effectively exported from one place to another. Oil from the Caspian Sea coast has been exploited commercially in Azerbaijan for more than 100 years. Most of the oil has been exported to both eastern and western Europe, but the impact is clear to see in the region of origin.

Carrying capacity

Another facet of the I = PAT formula is its implicit acceptance of the concept of a finite carrying capacity. Carrying capacity is a term developed in ecology that formally means the point when the rate of growth of a population becomes zero (Caughley, 1979). However, the term has subsequently been widely used in many different areas of resource management, often meaning different things to different users. One of the most commonly used meanings is to indicate the point at which human use of an ecosystem can reach a maximum without causing degradation. In other words, carrying capacity is a threshold point of stability. If human activity occurs in a particular area at or below its carrying capacity, such activity can proceed in equilibrium with the environment, but if the carrying capacity of a particular area is exceeded, then the area's resources will be degraded. The important point is that the carrying capacity of an area is defined by the ecology of the area, not by people.

Three simple theoretical views of the relationship between carrying capacity and population are shown in Figure 3.7. Figure 3.7a illustrates a sustainable situation in which population numbers remain more or less stable and within the limits imposed by a fixed environmental carrying capacity. Figure 3.7b, by contrast, illustrates how carrying capacity declines when resources are degraded and human population declines as a consequence. The decline and fall of the Mayan civilization has already been mentioned as an example. Another often-quoted case is thought to have occurred on Easter Island, now known as Rapa Nui, where widespread deforestation probably took place principally for rollers to move the enigmatic statues found all over the island (Fig. 3.8). Deforestation resulted in accelerated soil erosion and falling crop yields leading to food shortages. The inability to erect more statues undermined belief systems and social organization, resulting in armed conflicts over remaining resources. This combination of effects led to a severe decline in human population (Bahn and Flenly, 1992). Subtropical trees and giant palms dominated Rapa Nui's vegetation when it was first colonized by people probably in about the year 1200 (Hunt and Lipo, 2006), but

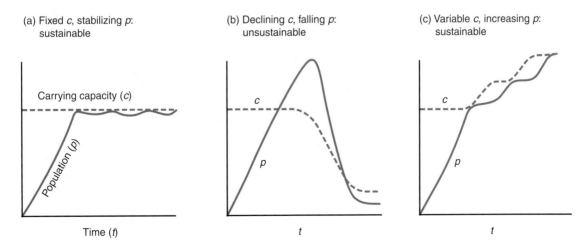

(a) Fixed *c*, stabilizing *p*: sustainable

(b) Declining *c*, falling *p*: unsustainable

(c) Variable *c*, increasing *p*: sustainable

Carrying capacity (*c*)

Population (*p*)

Time (*t*)

Figure 3.7 Three theoretical variations in carrying capacity and population totals.

when Dutch explorers landed on the island a few days after Easter Day in 1722, they found a barren landscape with a native society facing dwindling supplies of food and wood. Ever since, Rapa Nui has been considered a textbook example of a culture that doomed itself by destroying its own habitat. Rapa Nui is an extremely remote Pacific land mass, the nearest inhabited land being more than 2000 km distant, so effectively the island was a closed system. A parallel can be drawn with planet Earth isolated in an essentially uninhabitable universe.

This idea of a biologically defined carrying capacity underpins many notions of environmental degradation. It is inherent in Malthusian ideas of overpopulation (see below) and the tragedy of the commons (Fig. 3.7b), and is directly related to the idea of maximum sustainable yield (Fig. 3.7a). This idea that human society is subject to natural biological laws strikes right at the heart of the sustainable development debate. Some believe that human ingenuity puts us above the laws of nature. The situation in Figure 3.7c is also sustainable, but human population grows because carrying capacity is not fixed; it is actually increased because of new technologies and new resource perceptions (see also below). Meanwhile, some ecologists suggest that the carrying capacities of some natural environments are naturally variable, because the environments are not in equilibrium. Such environments are constantly dynamic, varying in time and space, rendering the idea of carrying capacity meaningless (see page 12).

Figure 3.8 Ancient statues on the deforested Rapa Nui (formerly known as Easter Island) in the Pacific Ocean. Many believe that widespread clearance of trees exceeded the island's carrying capacity, eventually resulting in a collapse of the island's human population.

Population

Population is regarded by many as the key to the whole sustainable development issue. Some very influential ideas about the relationship between the size of human population and the availability of natural resources were developed at the end of the eighteenth century by Thomas Malthus (1798). Malthus based his theory on two central principles: that without any checks, human population can grow at a geometric rate; and that even in the most favourable circumstances agricultural production can only increase at an arithmetic rate. Hence, at some point the size of human population will become too large for the food available. Malthus proposed that two sorts of check might act to keep the human population at a manageable size. These were 'preventive checks' such as delaying the age of marriage, which would reduce the fertility rate, and 'positive checks' such as famine, disease and warfare, which would increase the death rate.

Several authors have invoked the Malthusian argument in recent times to suggest that essentially there is a limit to the size of human population on this planet (e.g. Ehrlich, 1968) and that this limit is imposed by the planet's finite resources (e.g. Meadows *et al.*, 1972; 2004). Examples of Malthus' preventive and positive checks are still plain to see, of course (Fig. 3.9). However, needless to say, not everyone agrees with so-called neo-Malthusian scenarios. The opposing

found that incorporating the area that is selectively logged doubles previous esti-mates of the total amount of forest degraded by human activities in this area (Asner *et al.*, 2005).

Estimates, from numerous sources, of the annual rate of deforestation of closed forests in the humid tropics (tropical moist forest, which includes two main types: tropical rain forest and tropical monsoon/seasonal forest) have varied from 11 to 15 million hectares for the early 1970s, 6.1 to 7.5m ha for late 1970s, and 12.2 to 14.2m ha for the 1980s (Grainger, 1993b). This author suggests that the uncertainties are primarily the result of lack of attention to remote sensing measurements, and overconfidence in the use of expert judgement. One of the most recent assessments of the rates of change of forest cover by country, which has been prepared by the FAO, is shown in Fig. 4.1. This map shows clearly that while forest cover in the high latitudes is generally stable or increasing, virtually all tropical countries are experiencing a loss. This survey estimated the deforesta-tion rate in all tropical forests for the period 1990–2000 to be 14.2m ha a year (FAO, 2001). The overall annual global loss of all tropical moist forests over the period 1981–90 was estimated at 13.1m ha (FAO, 1995).

CAUSES OF DEFORESTATION

A concise summary of the causes of deforestation in the humid tropics is no easy task, since cutting down trees is the end result of a series of motivations and driv-ing forces that are interlinked in numerous ways. On a worldwide basis, the people who actually cut down the trees can generally be agreed upon. They are:

- agriculturalists
- ranchers
- loggers.

However, a proper understanding of the deforestation process requires a deeper investigation of the driving forces behind these agents. Access to forests is an important aspect, for example, and this is usually provided by road networks. Hence, construction of a new road, whether it be by a logging company or as part of a national development scheme, is an integral part of deforestation. Another part of the equation is the role played by the socio-economic factors that drive people to the forest frontier: poverty, low agricultural productivity and an unequal distribution of land are often important, while the rapid population growth rates that characterize many countries in the tropics also play a part. The role of national government is another factor in encouraging certain groups to use the forest resource, through tax incentives to loggers and ranchers, for example, or through large-scale resettlement schemes. On the global scale, international mar-kets for some forest products, such as lumber and the produce from agricultural plantations, must also be considered.

The importance of these factors varies from country to country and from region to region, and may change over time. Table 4.1 is an attempt to identify the prime factors that lie behind deforestation in the major forest regions of the tropics, based on a review of the large literature on the subject. A later review indicates how the nature of deforestation changed from being a process largely

TABLE 4.1 Important factors influencing deforestation in the tropics, by major world region

Region	Main factors
Latin America	Cattle ranching, resettlement and spontaneous migration, agricultural expansion, road networks, population pressure, inequitable social structures
Africa	Fuelwood collection, logging, agricultural expansion, population pressure
South Asia	Population pressure, agricultural expansion, corruption, fodder collection, fuelwood collection
South East Asia	Corruption, agricultural expansion, logging, population pressure

Source: after Kummer (1991).

initiated by the state to one driven by private enterprise in the last decades of the twentieth century (Rudel, 2007). During the 1970s state-run road building and colonization programmes opened up regions for settlement and deforestation throughout the tropics. By the 1990s these programmes had all but disappeared, to be replaced by enterprise-driven processes that had expanded and diversified since the 1970s.

The scale of clearance that has occurred in some countries, and the influence of external factors, can be illustrated by the experience of Viet Nam, a country that in pre-agricultural times was almost entirely covered in forests but that has lost more than 80 per cent of its original forest area, much of it during the second half of the last century (Fig. 4.2). Clearance of the coastal plains and valleys for agriculture took place over the last few centuries, and during the French colonial period when large areas in the south were cleared for banana, coffee and

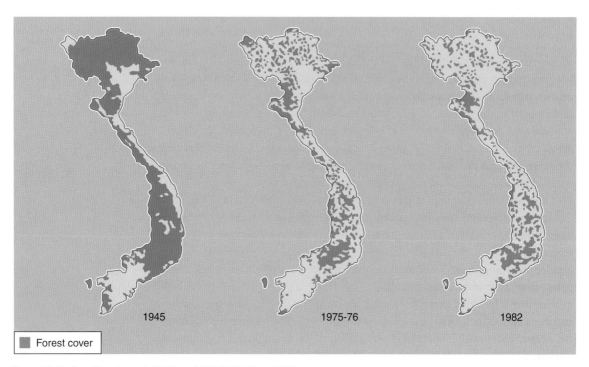

1945   1975-76   1982

Forest cover

Figure 4.2 Decline of forest cover in Viet Nam, 1945–82 (Viet Nam, 1985).

rubber plantations, but 45 per cent of the country was still forested in the 1940s. That proportion had fallen to about 17 per cent in the late 1980s as extensive zones were destroyed during the Viet Nam War (see Chapter 20), and still greater areas have since been destroyed by a rapidly growing population rebuilding after the war.

The forces of international economics that are integral to many areas of deforestation have played a central role in West Africa, where in most countries there is hardly any stretch of natural, unmodified vegetation left. A classic example is Côte d'Ivoire. Virtually every study of deforestation in the tropics has concluded that Côte d'Ivoire has experienced the most rapid forest clearance rates in the world, at 2800–3500 km^2 per year for the past 40 years.

Like most African governments, Côte d'Ivoire has viewed the nation's forests as a source of revenue and foreign exchange. However, given the country's high external debt, and declining international prices received for agricultural export commodities, the country has been faced with little alternative but to exploit its forests heavily. In 1973, logs and wood product exports provided 35 per cent of export earnings, but this figure had fallen to 11 per cent by the end of that decade due to the rapidly declining resource base. In the late 1970s, about 5.5 million m^3 of industrial roundwood was extracted annually, but this production had fallen below 3 million m^3 by 1991. In 1997 Côte d'Ivoire introduced restrictions on the export of logs with the aim of increasing its income by processing them at home. This has resulted in increased log milling and increased manufacture of wood products, but also in lower log prices for forest owners, devaluation of the forest resource and negative impacts on forest management (FAO, 2000). Industrial roundwood production in 2004 was 1.7 million m^3. Deforestation has also been fuelled by a population that grew from 5 million in 1970 to nearly 15 million in 2000, uncontrolled settlement by farmers, and clearance for new coffee and cacao plantations encouraged by government incentives.

Logging and agriculture have also been the primary agents of deforestation in the Philippines since the 1940s, and the series of factors that lie behind the loggers and agriculturalists, as interpreted by Kummer (1991), is shown graphically in Figure 4.3. Forest cover in the Philippines declined from 70 per cent of the national land area to 50 per cent between 1900 and 1950, and declined further to below 25 per cent in the early 1990s, by which time lowland forest had virtually disappeared. Natural forests were estimated to cover just 17 per cent of the national land area in 2000 (FAO, 2001).

The most common pattern of events has been the conversion of primary forest to secondary forest by logging, followed by clearance of the secondary forest for the expansion of agriculture. Both activities are preceded by the construction of roads, built by provincial and national governments for general development purposes, or by loggers to access their concessions. Kummer suggests that the granting of logging concessions has occurred to foster development, but also as political favours to Filipino elites and foreign-based transnationals. Much of the financial gain has also flowed to a small number of well-connected individuals. This concentration of the benefits from the Philippines' forest resource has been partly responsible for widespread and increasing poverty in the country, with no improvement in the living standards of

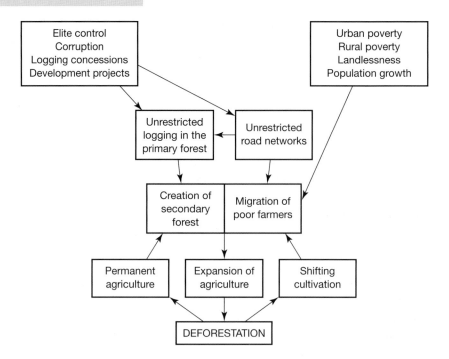

Figure 4.3 Factors affecting deforestation in the Philippines (Kummer, 1991).

the bottom 50–75 per cent of the population over the past 40 years. Most of the agriculturalists who clear the secondary forests are subsistence farmers, spurred on by poverty, a rising population and a lack of land.

The role of government policy and practice has also been central to the deforestation of the Amazon Basin in Brazil, which began on a large scale in the mid 1970s with a concerted effort to develop the country's tropical frontier. Agricultural expansion was the most important factor responsible for forest clearance at this time, both by smallholders and large-scale commercial agriculturalists, including ranchers producing beef for the domestic market. The Brazilian government's view of the Amazon as an empty land rich in resources spurred programmes of resettlement, particularly in the states of Rondônia and Pará under the slogan 'people without land in a land without people' (Moran, 1981), along with agricultural expansion programmes and plans to exploit mineral, biotic and hydroelectric resources.

The various agents of deforestation in the Brazilian Amazon have been summarized by Fearnside (1990). Cattle ranching has been encouraged by government subsidies and has been additionally attractive as a means of storing wealth, both in land and cattle, during periods of high inflation. Slash-and-burn agriculture practised by pioneer farmers arriving from outside the Amazon, as opposed to the shifting cultivation long practised by the indigenous peoples of the region, is another serious cause of deforestation, as it has long been in the Amazonian parts of Peru and Ecuador. Pioneers' slash-and-burn occurs at too great a human density of population, often leaves insufficient fallow periods and/or follows an initial crop with pasture planting, making it unsustainable. The construction of hydroelectric dams, with the inundation of reservoirs, has the potential for further major impacts to follow on from some of those existing, such as the Tucuruí and Balbina dams. The destruction caused by mining is also important, although usually on a local scale. In the case of the Grande Carajás Programme in the state of Pará, however, the proposed development of iron ore, bauxite, copper and manganese involves local smelting, a new railway and highway network, and a very large agricultural scheme. Lumbering is rapidly increasing in importance; agribusiness, until now a minor cause of deforestation in Brazil, could expand significantly, and the military bases being constructed along the Brazilian Amazon's northern frontier under the Calha Norte Programme pose another serious threat.

The broader set of dynamic circumstances underlying this policy of frontier development in Brazil has been highlighted by Turner *et al.* (1993), who trace them back to the OPEC (Organization of Petroleum Exporting Countries) oil crisis of the 1970s, which resulted in a large transfer of economic wealth from industrial countries to oil producers who, in turn, deposited these revenues in US and European banks. Large-scale lending of these monies to Brazil, among other developing countries, allowed development programmes to be financed. In Brazil, agricultural modernization took much of this finance and was channelled into export crops such as wheat, soybeans and coffee. Soybean production was boosted particularly, because relative to coffee the international market for soybeans was much more dependable, and this expansion was concentrated in two states: Rio Grande do Sul and Paraná. However, widespread replacement of coffee cultivation, a labour-intensive crop, with soybean, which is more capital and energy intensive, has resulted in large-scale emigration, particularly from Paraná. Large numbers of migrants went to new opportunities on the forest frontier in Rondônia, practising small-scale slash-and-burn agriculture along the World Bank-financed Highway BR-364, as it was extended into the state (Fig. 4.4).

Figure 4.4 The distinctive herringbone pattern of tropical forest clearance by slash-and-burn agriculturists along transport routes in Rondônia, Brazil. Dark areas in this space shuttle photograph are remaining forest. Roads are 4–5 km apart.

CONSEQUENCES OF DEFORESTATION

Deforestation in the tropics, like deforestation anywhere, occurs because people want to use the forests' resources. Hence, tropical deforestation provides human societies with many benefits, such as food, timber and other raw materials, as well as jobs and income to numerous countries, many of them relatively poor. However, the loss of forests may also degrade some of their ecosystem services, and much of the concern over the issue of tropical deforestation stems from the perturbation it represents to the forests' role as part of human life-support systems, by regulating local climates, water flow and nutrient cycles, as well as their role as reservoirs of biodiversity and habitats for species. The numerous deleterious environmental consequences resulting from the loss of tropical forests range in their scale of impact from the local to the global. Human clearance is by no means

Figure 4.5 A fallen tree in Central Africa's Congo forest. This natural form of disturbance is often caused by lightning in the Congo Basin where satellite data indicate an average of 50 lightning strikes per square kilometre a year, higher than anywhere else in the world.

the only form of disturbance that forests experience, however, since the forest landscape is in a state of dynamic equilibrium. Gaps are continually formed in the forest canopy as older trees die, are struck by lightning or are blown over (Fig. 4.5). Regrowth occurs continually in such gaps so that small areas are in a state of perpetual flux while the landscape as a whole does not appear to change, prompting the description of tropical rain forests as a shifting mosaic steady state (Bormann and Likens, 1979).

Natural perturbations also occur on much larger scales. A tropical cyclone, for example, can cause tremendous damage over huge areas, while volcanic eruptions, earthquakes and associated landslides are frequent in some tectonically active areas such as Indonesia, New Guinea and Central America. Fire has been confirmed as a natural disturbance in the Amazon Basin (Sanford *et al.*, 1985), while on the upper tributaries of the Amazon in Peru violent annual flooding causes frequent changes in the rivers' courses, eroding banks and depositing fresh sediment on which primary succession occurs (Salo *et al.*, 1986). These disturbances result in a markedly striped pattern in the forest canopy representing different species composition at various stages of succession. These continual disturbances, evident across about one-eighth of the Peruvian Amazon forests, mean that climax is never reached. Through geological time, the global extent of tropical forests has probably also varied with climate and is thought by some to have been much smaller than its current extent during periods of glacial maxima (e.g. Endler, 1982). Nevertheless, palaeoclimatological and palaeoecological data suggest that the Amazon rain forest has been remarkably resilient through geological time and has been a permanent feature of South America for at least the last 55 million years (Maslin *et al.*, 2005).

The human impact on tropical forests has a long history too. In practice it can be difficult to distinguish in the field between primary forest and secondary forest that is the result of human impact sometimes dating back over long periods. For instance, large areas of tropical forest in the Yucatan Peninsula in Mexico and in neighbouring Guatemala (Fig. 4.6), long believed to be primary forest, are now considered to be secondary forest managed by the Mayan people more than 1000 years ago (Gómez-Pompa *et al.*, 1987). To the casual observer, secondary forests more than 60–80 years old are often indistinguishable from undisturbed primary forests and are, in fact, treated as primary forests in the FAO assessments of tropical forests. Secondary forests less than 60–80 years of age are extensive in the tropics, making up about 40 per cent of the total forest area (Brown and Lugo, 1990). Indeed, palaeoenvironmental evidence now indicates that measurable human impacts on equatorial forests can be traced back as far as 3500 years BP in the Amazon and Congo basins, and 8000 BP in South East Asia (Willis *et al.*,

2004). However, although humans have registered an impact on tropical forests over many centuries, which cumulatively has affected great areas, the intensity, speed and relative permanence of clearance by human populations in the modern era puts this form of disturbance into a different category.

The effects of deforestation on hydrology have been widely discussed and an example of the multiple impacts upon aquatic habitats in the rivers of Madagascar is described in Chapter 8 (see Fig. 8.1). Deforestation generally leads to an increase in runoff and stream discharge, a causal relationship demonstrated in studies of small watersheds (< 10 km^2) throughout the tropics (Sahin and Hall, 1996). Larger river systems are probably affected in the same way.

A particular concern stems from recognition of the forests' role in regulating the flows of rivers and streams from upland catchments. The feared type and scale of regional impact on natural systems consequent upon deforestation is well illustrated in the Himalayas, where the theory that widespread deforestation since 1950 has been responsible for increased flooding of the Ganges and Brahmaputra plains has been widely accepted. The theory has not been without its critics, however, who, upon looking at the evidence, have shown that there is, in fact, little reliable data with which to support the proposed link between deforestation and increased flooding (Ives and Messerli, 1989). Although there is clearly a need to conserve forest cover on catchments, quantitative evidence of the role deforestation plays in flooding has been difficult to establish. However, an assessment made for developing countries by Bradshaw *et al.* (2007) found clear relationships between flood frequency and natural forest area loss after making adjustments for rainfall, slope and degraded landscape area. Several measures of flood severity (duration, people killed and displaced, and total damage) also showed detectable, though weaker, correlations to natural forest cover and loss.

A less controversial effect is that on sediment loads in rivers due to enhanced runoff and erosion (Fig. 4.7). High sediment loads have been the cause of problems, particularly in reservoirs – shortening their useful lives as suppliers of energy and irrigation water, for example, and requiring costly remediation (see Chapter 9). Another facet of hydrology likely to be affected by deforestation is local water tables. When deep-rooted trees are replaced by shallow-rooted crops or grasses the increased recharge of aquifers can lead to a rise in the water table. This effect has been reported from the uplands of north-eastern Thailand where local forest clearance for kenaf and cassava cultivation has resulted in salinization problems on lower slopes and valley floors due to rising saline groundwater (Löffler and Kubinok, 1988).

Figure 4.6 Secondary tropical forest surrounding ancient Mayan monuments in Guatemala's Tikal National Park. The extent of deforestation during the Mayan period was probably much larger than was once thought.

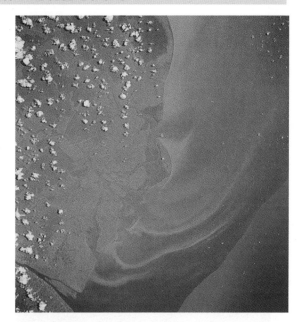

Figure 4.7 Plumes of sediment and vegetable matter in the rivers and coastal seas of Kalimantan Barat province in Borneo, Indonesia. Deforestation in this area has been caused by settlers encouraged to emigrate from the main Indonesian island of Java by the government. The lighter, deforested coastline is distinguishable from the darker, undisturbed patches of dense rain forest.

Soil degradation – including erosion, landslides, compaction and laterization – is a common problem associated with deforestation in any biome, but is often particularly severe in the tropics. Rainfall in the humid tropics is characterized by large annual totals, it is continuous throughout the year and highly erosive. Hence, clearance of protective vegetation cover quickly leads to accelerated soil loss, although the rate will vary according to what land use replaces the forest cover (see Chapter 14). Reviewing work in South East Asian forests, Sidle et al. (2006) conclude that the highest levels of soil loss per unit impacted area generally come from roads and trails, but losses from converted forest lands are high in mountainous areas if sites are heavily disturbed by cultivation and/or when crops or plantations have poor overall ground cover. These authors also note that most of the soil loss studies do not include estimates of landslide erosion, which over the long term may contribute comparable levels of sediment in steep terrain. The probability of landslides does not increase substantially until several years after forest conversion and may then persist indefinitely if weaker rooted crops or plantations continue.

Soil erosion can also be exacerbated by compaction caused by heavy machinery, trampling from cattle where pasture replaces forest, and exposure to the sun and rain. A compacted soil surface yields greater runoff and often more soil loss as a consequence. Laterization, the formation of a hard, impermeable surface, was once feared to be a very widespread consequence of deforestation in the tropics, but is probably a danger on just 2 per cent of the humid tropical land area (Grainger, 1993a).

The poor nutrient content of many tropical forest soils is a factor that tends to limit the potential of many of the land uses for which forest is cleared (Haynes and Williams, 1993). In parts of the Amazon Basin, for example, the available phosphorus and other nutrients in the soil initially peaks after the burning of cleared vegetation, giving relatively high yields and consequently high incomes for farmers. But nutrient levels often decline thereafter due to leaching, and are insufficient to maintain pasture growth in less than ten years. Soil nutrient depletion, compaction and invasion by inedible weeds quickly depletes the land's usefulness as pasture. There comes a time when beef cattle ranching is no longer profitable and the land will be abandoned (Fig. 4.8).

Similarly, unsustainable shifting cultivation quickly depletes soil nutrients, and, as with the degraded pastures, rapidly diminishing yields from inappropriate land uses encourage settlers to move on and clear further forest areas in a process of positive feedback. Some of the other major constraints for two of the most dominant soil orders found in the Amazon Basin are shown in Table 4.2.

- stop highway construction in Amazonia
- abolish subsidies for cattle pastures
- end energy subsidies in Amazonia
- ensure proper protection for natural forest reserves and stop reneging on previous commitments to reserves whenever the land is wanted for another purpose.

While these proposals might seem sensible from one perspective, the needs of national economic development cannot be denied. For Brazil to cease development of its largest sovereign natural resource is clearly neither desirable nor feasible. In practical terms, too, the fact that such suggestions often come from developed countries that have previously all but destroyed their own forests in the course of their development can quickly be interpreted as 'ecoimperialism'. There are many parallels between today's developing countries and the past experience of those that have developed further. In Britain, for example, almost the entire land area was covered by forest about 5000 years ago, about the time that human activity began to have an impact on the landscape. Today, the UK is one of the least-wooded countries in Europe. Woodland covers just 8 per cent of England and Wales, but most of this is recent plantings. The area covered by ancient woodland is about 2.6 per cent (Spencer and Kirby, 1992); most of the lost forests have been converted into farmland, which occupies some 72 per cent of the total land area today, and many wildlife species have become extinct in Britain as a result of this destruction of habitat, which made them more susceptible to hunters (see Table 15.2).

Outsiders can make a positive contribution to controlling the poor use of forest resources, although direct pressure on governments from well-intentioned individuals abroad can backfire. Improvements in the environmental performance of such players as commercial banks and other investors can be called for, and moves made to tighten their financial approach to reduce the temptation of borrowing countries to run up heavy debts and promote short-sighted land use policies to pay them back, as in the case of investment in soybean production in southern Brazil. Criticism of the World Bank for its association with wasteful and illegal deforestation, such as the aforementioned Highway BR-364 in Brazil's Rondônia state, led to the Bank changing its approach towards forests in 1991. The World Bank stopped financing major infrastructure investments that were likely to harm forests and introduced a ban on the financing of commercial logging (World Bank, 2000). Debt-for-nature swaps have also proved to be a successful approach in several countries, making a positive contribution to conservation and developing countries' debt burdens (see Chapter 22), while the links between tropical deforestation and global warming may provide another source of economic incentive to conserve forests via the international markets in carbon created by the Kyoto Protocol and the European Union's emissions trading system (see Chapter 11).

A pragmatic approach to the problems of deforestation cannot seriously obstruct all extension of cultivated lands or all clearance of forest to provide new industrial or urban sites. But this process requires surveys, inventories and evaluation to ensure that each hectare of land is used in the optimum way, to meet both the needs of today and those of future generations. A series of questions that should be answered in deciding whether or not to alter a tropical forest has been proposed by Poore and Sayer (1987):

- What are the dominant ecological and social constraints in the tropical forest area in question? Soil analysis is essential; many tropical forest lands (especially on poor, wet soils) can sustain nothing but an intact tropical forest cover.
- Is there degraded, altered – or at least non-primary – tropical forest available that could also sustain the required enterprise? Such land usually supports fewer species, provides fewer ecological benefits, is nearer to settlements and infrastructure, and can be rehabilitated by development. A notable example is timber production from old secondary tropical forest, which often yields a much higher proportion of desirable species than primary tropical forest.
- Are there ways in which the enterprise could be sustained within the existing tropical forest? In other words, can this be done without altering the forest structure?
- If the tropical forest were to be cleared and a new use established, what would be the net change in costs and benefits (including all tropical forest values, such as watershed protection)?

These authors suggest that the full range of ecological processes and species diversity of tropical forests can only be maintained if large undisturbed areas are established in perpetuity for conservation. Designating legal protection is not necessarily a guarantee of non-disturbance, as the example cited above in the Indonesia's Sunda Shelf demonstrates, but there are some more positive examples. In the Brazilian Amazon, more than a third of the forest is legally protected, in indigenous lands and other types of protected areas, and both inhabited and uninhabited reserves appear to be successful in reducing both deforestation and the occurrence of fire, the standard processes heralding conversion of forest to agriculture (Nepstad *et al.*, 2006).

However, totally protected areas can never be sufficiently extensive to provide for the conservation of all ecological processes and all species. In this case, the obvious avenues to explore are ways in which a natural forest cover can be used sustainably, to harvest products without degrading the forest. In this case, sustainable forestry means to harvest forest in a way that provides a regular yield of forest produce without destroying or radically altering the composition and structure of the forest as a whole. In other words, sustainable operations need to mimic natural ecosystem processes.

The obvious product in this respect is timber, but attitudes towards the logging industry have become polarized, with some people suggesting that it is essentially a primary cause of tropical deforestation and that the international trade in tropical timber should therefore be banned. In practice, however, logging in the tropics almost always involves the removal of selected trees rather than the clear-felling that is much more common in temperate forestry operations. Some damage to other trees also occurs even during selective logging, but less damaging techniques are available and if well enforced can greatly reduce smashing and other forms of degradation. The introduction of strict silvicultural rules in Queensland, Australia, in 1982 proved this point (Fig. 4.10).

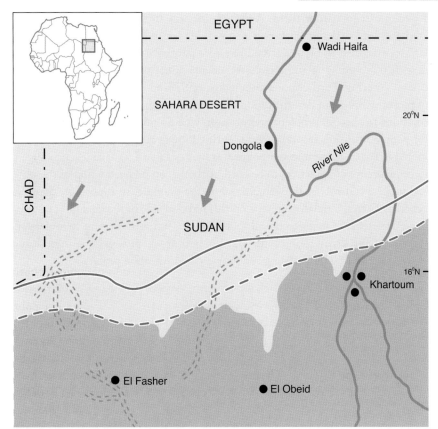

desert was mapped by reconnaissance in 1975 and then compared to the boundary drawn from another survey carried out in 1958. The two boundaries indicated that the desert's southern margin had advanced by 90–100 km between the two dates (Fig. 5.2), at an average rate of advance of 5.5 km per year over 17 years.

An immediate criticism can be made of the methodology used for the study in that given the inherent variability of drylands, two snapshot surveys can only be of very limited use in determining significant changes in vegetation, particularly since the 1970s was a period of drought in the Sudan while the 1950s was a decade characterized by above-average rainfall. Reliable conclusions can only be drawn after long-term monitoring that takes into account seasonal and year-to-year fluctuations in vegetation cover. When Lamprey's conclusions were scrutinized by Swedish geographers they were found to be inaccurate. It transpired that the 1958 desert vegetation line was not based on a ground survey but followed the 75 mm isohyet, and satellite imagery and ground survey data compiled over several years did not confirm Lamprey's findings (Hellden, 1988).

CAUSES OF DESERTIFICATION

The methods of land use that are applied too intensively and, hence, contribute to desertification are widely quoted and apparently well known. They can be classified under the headings of intensive grazing, overcultivation and over-exploitation of vegetation. Salinization of irrigated cropland is often viewed as a separate category from these. Although the way in which these inappropriate land uses lead to desertification is also well known in theory, in practice, particular areas deemed to be desertified due to a particular cause have often been so described according to subjective assessments rather than after long-term scientific monitoring. Furthermore, although specific land uses have been the subject of most interest from desertification researchers, it can be argued that permanent solutions to specific problem areas can only be found when the deeper reasons for people misusing resources are identified. Such reasons, many of which are rooted in social, economic and political systems (Table 5.2), enable, encourage or force inappropriate practices to be used. Although an understanding of the physical processes involved in overcultivation, for example, is important, there has generally been too much emphasis on this physical side of the equation, resulting in an over-reliance upon technical solutions. It is just as important to understand the underlying driving forces, the amelioration of which is of equal significance in the quest to find long-lasting solutions to desertification problems.

TABLE 5.2 Suggested root causes of land degradation

Natural disasters
Degradation due to biogeophysical causes or 'acts of God'
Population change
Degradation occurs when population growth exceeds environmental thresholds (neo-Malthusian) or decline causes collapse of adequate management
Underdevelopment
Resources exploited to benefit world economy or developed countries, leaving little profit to manage or restore degraded environments
Internationalism
Taxation and other forces interfere with the market, triggering overexploitation
Colonial legacies
Trade links, communications, rural–urban linkages, cash crops and other 'hangovers' from the past promote poor management of resource exploitation
Inappropriate technology and advice
Promotion of wrong strategies and techniques, which result in land degradation
Ignorance
Linked to inappropriate technology and advice: a lack of knowledge leading to degradation
Attitudes
People's or institutions' attitudes blamed for degradation
War and civil unrest
Overuse of resources in national emergencies and concentrations of refugees leading to high population pressure in safe locations

Source: Thomas and Middleton (1994).

Intensive grazing

The overuse of pastures, caused by allowing too many animals or inappropriate types of animals to graze, has been the cause of degradation over the largest areas of desertified land on the global scale according to the estimates produced by UNEP. Of the 3592 million hectares estimated in 1992 to be suffering from desertification, no less than 2576m ha, just under 72 per cent, were considered to be experiencing degradation of vegetation. Intensive grazing can result in both the actual removal of biomass by grazing animals and other effects of livestock such as trampling and consequent compaction. A common consequence of heavy grazing pressure is a decrease in the vegetative cover, leading to increased erosion by water or wind.

Another widespread effect of intensive grazing is the encroachment of unpalatable or noxious shrubs into grazing lands. Long-term grazing of semi-arid grasslands can typically lead to an increase in the spatial and temporal heterogeneity of water, nitrogen and other soil resources, which promotes invasion by desert shrubs, in turn leading to a further localization of soil resources under shrub canopies in a process of positive feedback. In the barren area between shrubs, soil fertility is decreased by erosion and gaseous emissions (Schlesinger *et al.*, 1990). Increased runoff and erosion result in stripping of the soil surface layer, the formation of desert pavement in intershrub areas, and the development of rills. This degradation of the plant resource, in turn, reduces the number of livestock that are able to graze the area.

Traditional herders, for whom larger numbers of livestock represent greater personal wealth and social standing, have often been seen as the culprits in this process in the developing world. Such arguments have been used as a reason for encouraging settlement of nomadic pastoralists in many dryland countries of Africa, the Middle East and Asia. Intensive grazing problems have also been identified on commercial ranches in North America and Australia.

In practice, the reasons for increased grazing pressure on pastures are numerous and complex. They include competition for land as cultivated areas increase, pushing herders into more marginal pastures. In many parts of the Sahel, expanding areas of sorghum and millet cultivation have been primary factors responsible for a major decrease in the availability of range, as Ringrose and Matheson (1992) have identified. The position of herders at the margins of society in the eyes of many central governments has often meant that they are situated at the end of a chain of events that sees the expansion of irrigated land for cash cropping displacing rainfed subsistence cultivators who encroach into traditional grazing grounds, forcing herders into smaller ranges. This situation is described by Janzen (1994) in southern Somalia where expansion of irrigated agriculture on the Jubba and Shabelle rivers has forced small farmers to clear large areas of bushland for cultivation. For nomadic herders, this savanna zone and the river valleys themselves were important grazing lands during the dry season. Resultant intensification of grazing pressure into smaller areas has also been driven by the sedentarization of some nomadic groups, a trend encouraged by government policy in the 1970s, and accelerated more recently by drought. The issue of government-sponsored sedentarization continues in many other countries in Africa and elsewhere.

Sinking boreholes to provide new and more reliable water supplies has also led to increased grazing pressures across much of the Sahel and in the Kalahari of Botswana where, between 1965 and 1976, livestock numbers and the accessible grazing resources were increased by about two and a half times (Sandford, 1977). In some parts of the world, degradation has been seen as the result of a change in the approach to pasture use: from a flexible strategy typical of traditional pastoralists in which the natural dynamism of dryland vegetation is used by regular movement of herds and maintaining several different animal species (Fig. 5.3), to a less flexible westernized approach in which the pasture may be fenced off and only cattle are grazed.

Figure 5.3 Mixed herds are traditionally kept by herders in drylands, as here in Mongolia's Gobi Desert. Different animals eat different types of vegetation and have different susceptibilities to moisture availability.

Although these ideas on intensive grazing problems have been followed by many scientists and policy-makers, recent thinking on the nature of dryland vegetation and ecology has questioned much of this conventional view. Distinguishing between degradation of vegetation and other forms of vegetation change is very difficult, and the importance of intensive grazing as a cause of desertification has probably been exaggerated in many areas.

One commonly quoted situation considered to be typical of desertified areas is the loss of vegetation around wells or boreholes, bare areas that supposedly grow and coalesce. In fact, several studies have failed to show that these 'piospheres' expand over time (e.g. Hanan *et al.*, 1991). Halos of bare, compacted soil 50–100 m in circumference caused by grazing and trampling are undoubtedly characteristic of many rangeland watering holes (Fig. 5.4). But such areas are also typified by higher levels of soil nutrients than surrounding areas thanks to regular inputs from dung and urine (Barker *et al.*, 1990), which may balance out any negative effects of possible soil loss by erosion. Piospheres are perhaps best interpreted as 'sacrifice zones' in which the loss of the vegetation resource is outweighed by the advantages of a predictable water supply (Perkins and Thomas, 1993). However, despite this reassessment of piospheres, the areas beyond the sacrifice zone around these types of focal point in the landscape can become desertified by bush encroachment. High cattle densities are thought to encourage invasion by thorny bushes as described above. Although cows will browse from bushes as well as graze on grasses, they tend to avoid some species because of the thorns, and these species become more abundant as a result. A thick cover of thorny bushes deters grass growth and prevents cows from entering thickets. This type of bush encroachment

Figure 5.4 Cattle around a waterhole in Niger. Such 'piospheres' are typically devoid of vegetation, but the soil has a high nutrient content.

has led to a significant reduction in the extent of high-quality rangeland in Botswana (Moleele *et al.*, 2002).

Other ideas about the effects of grazing on rangeland vegetation are also being substantially revised. Formerly, most claims that a particular area was being 'overgrazed' were based on the idea that the area had a fixed carrying capacity, or theoretical number of livestock a unit area of pasture could support without being degraded. This idea in turn was based on Clements' (1916) model of vegetation succession and ecological stability. But current thinking depicts semi-arid ecosystems as seldom, if ever, reaching equilibrium. Rather they are in a state of more or less constant flux, driven by disturbances such as drought, fire and insect attack. Hence, while calculation of a carrying capacity is possible in relatively unchanging environments, it is difficult to apply to non-equilibrium environments like dryland pastures because the number of animals an area can support varies on several timescales: before and after a rainy day, between a wet season and a dry season, and between drought years and wet years. Grazing the number of livestock appropriate for a wet year on the same pasture during a drought could result in degradation, but several studies cited by Warren and Khogali (1992) show that such disastrous concentrations of livestock are rarely reached because, under conditions of environmental stress, the animals are often the first component of the system to fail, by dying. Traditional pastoralists have also developed social and economic mechanisms for coping with such occurrences, as McCabe (1990) has documented for the Turkana in East Africa.

In the light of these changes in our understanding of rangeland ecology, the relative importance of intense grazing and natural stresses is being reassessed. One study of open woodlands in north-west Namibia, an area long thought to have been desertified by local herders overgrazing, found very little evidence of degradation (Sullivan, 1999). This study concluded that previous assessments of the area's ecological health have been based more on perceptions than scientific assessment. These perceptions have been clouded by an adherence to ideas of a fixed carrying capacity based on rangelands as equilibrium systems, and remnants of a colonial ideology that views traditional communal herding as environmentally degrading.

Many authorities now believe that rainfall variability is a more important determinant of the health of rangeland and its soils than overgrazing (Behnke *et al.*, 1993). This change in understanding of dryland ecology is an important development because if natural environment factors are the major determinant of available rangeland resources, this has major implications for pastoral management (Scoones and Graham, 1994).

Overcultivation

Several facets of overcultivation are commonly quoted. Some stem from intensification of farming, which can result in shorter fallow periods, leading to nutrient depletion and eventually reduced crop yields. Soil erosion by wind and water is another result of the overintensive use of soil, resulting from a weakened soil structure and reduced vegetation cover. Monocultures can lead to all these forms of soil degradation as data from 27 years of monitoring on cropland in the semi-arid pampa of Argentina show (Buschiazzo *et al.*, 1999). Long-term cultivation of millet was demonstrated to have the most deleterious effects on both the physical and chemical properties of soils, leading to decreases in dry aggregate stability (by 10 per cent), soil organic matter (30 per cent), and available nutrients such as phosphorus (44 per cent), iron (20 per cent) and zinc (90 per cent). The depletion of nutrients means that greater amounts of fertilizers have to be applied to maintain crop yields, while the declines in organic matter and soil stability have meant a greater susceptibility to erosion.

In many cases, erosion has also been caused by the introduction of mechanized agriculture with its large fields and deep ploughing, which further disturbs soil structure and increases its susceptibility to erosive forces. Similar outcomes have also been noted in areas where cultivation has expanded into new zones that are marginal for agricultural use because they are more prone to drought, or are made up of steeper slopes that are more prone to erosion. Some classic examples of overcultivation, their root causes, inappropriate land uses and resulting degradation, are shown in Table 5.3. The wind erosion resulting in the Great Plains and the Virgin Lands is discussed on page 288.

Overexploitation of vegetation

Clearance of forested land is undertaken for a number of reasons, but most commonly to make way for the expansion of grazing or cultivation and/or to provide fuelwood. Such action is a degradation of vegetation resources and also reduces the protection offered to soil by tree cover. Accelerated erosion may result, and over the longer term soil is deprived of inputs of nutrients and organic matter from decomposing leaf litter. Both of these processes can lead to the degradation of soil structure and fertility. Water tables may also be affected.

In many areas, vegetation clearance has a long history. In northern Argentina, the semi-arid Chacoan forests have been exploited for more than 100 years, initially because the wood made excellent railway sleepers, but more recent clearance has been for agricultural expansion, prompted by high grain prices and positive rainfall balances since the 1970s (Margarita and Loyarte, 1996). In African drylands, more or less complete removal of the vegetation cover is occurring in many parts of the Sahel region. The expansion of agriculture is a prime cause of deforestation in Burkina Faso, where an estimated 50 000 ha of woodland was being cleared every year in the early 1980s. Similarly, widespread replacement of tree savanna by cultivation has been reported over the period

TABLE 5.3 Examples of overcultivation

Area (date)	Root causes	Land use	Environmental response
US Great Plains (1930s)	Pioneer spirit	Deep ploughing for cereals	Wind erosion
Former USSR's Virgin Lands (1950s)	Political ideology, food security	Deep ploughing for cereals	Wind erosion
Niger (1950s and 1960s)	Colonial influence, cash crops	Extensification of groundnut cultivation	Nutrient depletion

1957–87 from the Nara area on the Mali/Mauritania border, where the agricultural area virtually doubled over the period (IGN, 1992).

Overexploitation for domestic purposes (particularly fuelwood and charcoal making) does not usually lead to the complete removal of all vegetation, but it represents the use of vegetation to a degree that is beyond its natural capability to renew itself and thus results in a degraded vegetation cover. As trees are removed, villagers may supplement wood for fires with dried animal dung that would otherwise be left on the soil to provide valuable nutrients. One study in Ethiopia estimated that the economic value of manure diverted from this fertilizing role to the cooking stove was US$123 million annually, which could increase grain harvests by 1–1.5 million tonnes a year (Newcombe, 1984). An expanding human population is the ultimate driving force behind this form of desertification.

In Pakistan, the few remaining stands of tropical thorn forests that once covered the Punjab Plains, largely cleared for irrigated agriculture, are under continuing pressure for their long-standing use as a source of fuelwood (Khan, 1994). Fuelwood collection around many urban centres in India has significantly reduced forested areas in their hinterlands in recent decades, as the urban poor have been forced to turn increasingly to fuelwood by rising prices of kerosene, coal and charcoal. One study of major Indian cities, using satellite imagery (Bowonder *et al.*, 1988), has shown that more than half of the closed forest cover within a 100 km radius around many dryland cities was lost in the ten years to 1982 (Table 5.4).

In the 1970s and 1980s, the environmental problems caused by fuelwood collection were thought to be so acute in Sahelian Africa that a 'fuelwood crisis' was feared. The World Bank (1985) estimated that sustainably harvested fuelwood could support just two-thirds of the human population in the Sahel. However, this regional environmental disaster has not materialized and in the late 1990s the fuelwood situation in the Sahel was being reassessed. The methods used, comparing current woodfuel consumption with current stocks, annual tree growth and annual population growth, has been criticized by some (e.g. Leach and Mearns, 1988). Poor survey data, the importance of replacement fuels such as crop residues and dung, and the effect of increasing woodfuel prices as local supplies dwindle are highlighted as making the situation more complex than was previously proposed. Overall, it seems that the surveys conducted in the 1970s

Urban centre (state)	Closed forest cover (km^2)		Loss (%)
	1972–82	1972–75	1980–82
Ajmer (Rajasthan)	259	124	52
Amritsar (Punjab)	208	111	47
Bhavnagar (Gujarat)	112	9	92
Bhopal (Madhya Pradesh)	3031	1417	53
Gwalior (Madhya Pradesh)	1353	515	62
Hyderabad (Andhra Pradesh)	40	26	35
Indore (Madhya Pradesh)	3770	1070	71
Jaipur (Rajasthan)	1534	786	49

TABLE 5.4 Loss of closed forest cover around selected dryland urban centres in India

Source: after Bowonder et al. (1988).

and 1980s underestimated the amount of fuelwood available in the Sahel (World Bank, 1996).

Although the predicted fuelwood crisis in the Sahel has not taken place on the scale once feared, environmental degradation has occurred in some areas. Much of this form of desertification is concentrated around urban areas that have expanded very rapidly since the late 1960s as rural migrants fled the effects of drought. Denuded areas susceptible to enhanced erosion have been reported from numerous Sahelian cities, including Khartoum, Dakar, Ouagadougou and Niamey.

However, the complexity of the fuelwood issue can be illustrated by the case of Kano in northern Nigeria, where Nichol (1989) found that tree density had increased in recent times in the immediate vicinity of the city as the transport of fuelwood by donkey had been displaced by the use of long-distance trucks. A decline in tree density was recorded in the zone 70–250 km from Kano. This view is confirmed in an analysis presented by Mortimore and Turner (2005), who also show diminishing areas of natural woodland since the 1950s in several areas that serve the Kano fuelwood market. However, these authors are not convinced that this trend should necessarily be equated to a degradation problem since 'pollarding selected, mature trees in mixed woodland stimulates regeneration, and may be regarded as a form of rotation; moreover, rates of regeneration have been grossly under-estimated' (Mortimore and Turner, 2005: 584). They also point out that if a 'fuelwood gap' were opening up between demand and supply, the price of fuelwood should increase in consequence, but stable real retail prices of wood fuel in the cities of northern Nigeria suggest the opposite.

Salinization

Salinization is a form of soil degradation most commonly encountered in dry climatic regions, although it also occurs in more humid environments. Natural, or 'primary', salt-affected soils are widespread in drylands because the potential evaporation rate of water from the soil exceeds the input of water as rainfall, allowing salts to accumulate near the surface as the soil dries. While these primary salt-affected soils are found extensively under natural conditions, salinity problems of particular concern to agriculturalists arise when previously productive soil becomes salinized as a result of poor land management, so-called 'secondary' salinization. Secondary, or human-induced, salt-affected soils cover a smaller area than primary salt-affected soils (Oldeman *et al.*, 1990), but secondary salinization represents a more serious problem for human societies because it mainly affects cropland. Major agricultural crops have a low salt tolerance compared to wild salt-tolerant plants (halophytes), so salinization rapidly leads to declines in yields. Consequently arable land, a scarce and valuable resource in dryland regions, is frequently abandoned when it becomes salinized, due to the very high cost of remediation.

The human activities that lead to desertification through the build-up of salts in soils are well documented and are summarized into five groups in Table 5.5; secondary salinization occurs under a number of circumstances but is most commonly associated with poorly managed irrigation schemes. One estimate suggests that nearly 50 per cent of all the irrigated land in arid and semi-arid regions is

pests, the farming methods used and economic forces. Distinguishing the effects of these various factors is, in practice, very difficult, quite apart from the fact that data on crop productivity are often unreliable and many measurements of soil erosion are also open to question (see Chapter 14). While the theory linking desertification to food production is basically sound, it is often oversimplified and deserves further careful research.

The link between desertification and famine is even more difficult to make. This is not the case in theory, since food shortages stem from reduced harvests and thinner or even dead animals, although such shortages are also caused by factors of the natural environment, particularly drought. In practice, however, famines typically occur in areas that are characterized by a range of other factors such as poverty, civil unrest and war. Several authors have emphasized the social causes of severe food shortages (e.g. Sen, 1981; Wijkman and Timberlake, 1984). In the African context, Curtis *et al.* (1988: 3) suggest that 'social, not natural or technological, obstacles stand in the way of modern famine prevention' (see also the food security section on page 273).

Mass starvation is probably more a function of poor distribution of food, and people's inability to buy what is available, than desertification, although desertification, drought and many other natural hazards may act as a trigger. This tentative conclusion is supported by one of the few studies that specifically aimed to assess the relative importance of these factors, in the Sudanese famine of 1984/85 (Olsson, 1993). Millet and sorghum yields in the provinces of Darfur and Kordofan, the worst affected areas, were reduced to about 20 per cent of pre-drought levels, largely due to climatic factors – the amount and timing of the rains. Desertification, by contrast, was calculated to account for just 10–15 per cent of the variation in crop yields. While drought was undoubtedly a trigger for ensuing famine, the profound causes were different. As fears of crop failures mounted, the price of food in Darfur and Kordofan soared to levels that most rural people were unable to afford. While food was available at the national level, the distribution network was inadequate and famine followed.

UNDERSTANDING DESERTIFICATION

Appropriate solutions to desertification problem areas can only be found after more long-term studies of specific areas. Monitoring is necessary to identify where desertification is happening, how it works and why it is occurring. It must also attempt to distinguish between natural environmental fluctuations and impacts that can be attributed to human action, since it is the human aspects we have the ability to alter. Monitoring programmes also need to combine scientific measurements with an understanding of how social systems are related to the environment, an aspect of the desertification issue that has been relatively neglected until recently. Although, to date, there have been few such long-term investigations, work from two areas illustrates the approach.

The US Great Plains

The Dust Bowl of the 1930s on the North American Great Plains is one of the best-known dryland environmental disasters in history. Over a period of 50 years, grasslands were turned into wheat fields by a culture set on dominating and exploiting natural resources using ploughs and other machinery developed in western Europe (Worster, 1979). When, in the 1930s, drought hit the area, as it periodically does, wind erosion ensued on a huge scale. The most severe dust storms, so-called 'black blizzards', occurred between 1933 and 1938. These huge events carried soil dust northwards as far as Canada and eastwards to New York and out over the Atlantic Ocean. At Amarillo, Texas, at the height of the Dust Bowl period, one month had 23 days with at least ten hours of airborne dust, and one in five storms had zero visibility (Choun, 1936). By 1937, the US Soil Conservation Service estimated that 43 per cent of a 6.5m ha area at the heart of the Dust Bowl had been seriously damaged by wind erosion. The large-scale environmental degradation, combined with the effects of the Great Depression, ruined the livelihoods of hundreds of thousands of American families.

However, although the lessons learned from the Dust Bowl years inspired major advances in soil conservation techniques, the environmental health of the area has continued to decline. Continued degradation is believed to account for a significant part of declining yields of sorghum and kafir over 30–40 years in the Texas Panhandle (Fryrear, 1981), and soil erosion during the drought in the 1970s was on a comparable scale to that in the 1930s (Lockeretz, 1978). Investigation of the soil losses of the 1970s illustrates some important underlying causes, indicating that political and economic considerations overshadowed the need for sustainable land management. Large tracts of marginal land had been ploughed for wheat cultivation in the early 1970s, driven by high levels of exports, particularly to the then USSR. To encourage farmers to produce, a federal programme was set up that guaranteed them payment according to the area sown, so that the disincentive to plough marginal areas was removed: the farmers were paid whether these areas yielded a crop or not. At the same time, new centre-pivot irrigation technology was widely adopted to water the new cropland, but the use of the rotating irrigation booms required that windbreaks, planted to protect the soil, be removed (McCauley et al., 1981).

The increasing use of irrigation has also resulted in a new form of desertification on the Great Plains: groundwater depletion. Water pumped from the Ogallala aquifer, which stretches across parts of eight Great Plains states from South Dakota southward to Texas, is essentially a non-renewable resource, since recharge of the aquifer is negligible. However, in the 1960s when water levels in irrigation wells began to decline, farmers did not act to conserve dwindling supplies, but actually increased pumping because those who reduced their consumption still experienced declining water tables as others continued to irrigate, a clear example of the tragedy of the commons. Projections indicate that, over the next 20 years or so, up to half the land irrigated today may have to be withdrawn due to water depletion (Opie, 1993). Despite the booms and busts Great Plains farmers have experienced throughout the last century, they are still not farming in a sustainable manner.

The Sahel

The important role of external factors in the degradation equation can also be illustrated from work on the Sahel catastrophe of the 1970s and 1980s, events that sparked worldwide interest in desertification. Rainfall varies greatly across the Sahel, being patchy in space and fluctuating from year to year and from decade to decade. Sahelian societies have adapted to this variability in numerous ways to insure themselves during times of hardship caused by drought, which can be applied equally to desertification, as Mortimore (1987) has shown in northern Nigeria. However, these adaptive systems were put under a greater burden than they could cope with by two main driving forces: the increasingly dry episode that started in the Sahel in the late 1960s and the changing political economy of the region.

The recent desiccation of the Sahelian climate provides the clearest and most dramatic example of climate variability that has been measured anywhere in the world to date (Hulme, 2001): averaged over 30-year periods, annual rainfall in the region declined by between 20 per cent and 30 per cent between the decades (1930s to 1950s) leading to political independence for Sahelian countries and the decades since (post-1960s). The resultant impact on traditional adaptations was combined with stresses from deteriorating regional political and global economic conditions, which illustrate the changing scene faced by inhabitants of many dryland communities in the developing world.

The possibilities for grain storage have been diminished by a number of circumstances, including a growing population and land scarcity. The imposition of taxes payable in currency, the monetization of the economy and poor terms of trade, changes that began during colonial times, have also encouraged people to produce cash crops in place of subsistence crops.

The generation of savings from activities away from the fields also suffered under changing political policies. Agriculturalists who had moved to urban areas to work in the informal sector were forcibly sent back to the land by the government, while cash savings were further eroded by inflation and sudden devaluations in the national currency.

The desiccation in climate, combined with continued population growth, reduced the effectiveness of social insurance, as people who could previously have been relied upon to help out their poorer relations did not have enough to feed themselves. The traditional advantages of ecological insurance have also been eroded as colonial and subsequent governments have encouraged moves towards specialization in crop production and discouraged traditional pastoralism, which is inconsistent with modern political policies and boundaries.

A loss of autonomy over their affairs lies at the heart of the consequent problems faced by farming and pastoral communities in developing-country drylands. The absorption of such communities into centralized economies has undermined the traditional ways in which they have coped with environmental stress, increasing

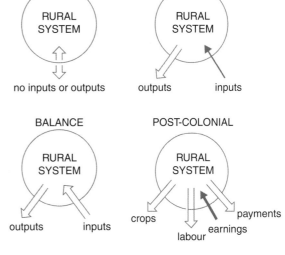

Figure 5.7 Model for the incorporation of rural systems into the market (after Mortimore, 1987).

their vulnerability (Fig. 5.7). While government welfare or private economic insurance is available to inhabitants of richer countries, such safety nets are seldom available in the so-called Third World, and it is in these regions where the need to more fully comprehend the nature and extent of desertification is the most pressing.

FURTHER READING

Boone, R.B. 2005 Quantifying changes in vegetation in shrinking grazing areas in Africa. *Conservation and Society* 3: 150–73. Using an ecosystem model to quantify the effects of land subdivision and sedentarization on vegetation in South Africa and Kenya. (Open access journal: www.conservationandsociety.org/cs-3-1_9_iboone.pdf).

Herrmann, S.M., Anyamba, A. and Tucker, C.J. 2005 Recent trends in vegetation dynamics in the African Sahel and their relationship to climate. *Global Environmental Change* 15: 394–404. A long-term assessment of vegetation using remote-sensing data.

Kettle, N., Harrington, L. and Harrington, J. 2007 Groundwater depletion and agricultural land use change in the High Plains: a case study from Wichita County, Kansas. *The Professional Geographer* 59: 221–35. Unsustainable use of groundwater from the Ogallala aquifer.

Latz, P. 1995 *Bushfires and bushtucker: Aboriginal plant use in Central Australia.* Alice Springs, IAD Press. A good assessment of environmental management and change which includes a large compendium of desert plants and their numerous uses.

Reed, M.S., Dougill, A.J. and Taylor, M.J. 2007 Integrating local and scientific knowledge for adaptation to land degradation: Kalahari rangeland management options. *Land Degradation and Development* 18: 249–68. This paper shows how local and scientific knowledge can be combined to develop rangeland management strategies in response to degradation.

Reynolds, J.F. and Stafford Smith, D.M. (eds) 2002 *Global desertification: do humans cause deserts?* Dahlem Workshop Report 88. Berlin, Dahlem University Press. An effective collection of practical and theoretical contributions from both biophysical and socio-economic perspectives.

Sivakumar, M.V.K. 2007 Interactions between climate and desertification. *Agricultural and Forest Meteorology* 142: 143–55. A review of the literature on this important subject.

Thomas, D.S.G. and Middleton, N.J. 1994 *Desertification: exploding the myth.* Chichester, Wiley. This book focuses on the political aspects of the desertification issue and highlights many of the difficulties of identifying desertification in the field.

Warren, A. 2005 The policy implications of Sahelian change. *Journal of Arid Environments* 63: 660–70. A thoughtful article that rounds off a special issue on the Sahel.

Xu, J. and Liao, J. 2007 Original and secondary high-frequency sandstorm zones in the loess plateau region, China. *Geografiska Annaler* 89A: 121–7. An assessment of human mismanagement enhancing wind erosion in a very fertile part of China.

River management

River modification and management are rooted in society's view of rivers both as hazards to be ameliorated and resources to be maximized. There are numerous ways in which people have modified rivers: by constructing dams, building levees, widening, deepening and straightening channels (Table 8.3; see also Chapters 9 and 21). The beginnings of direct river modification in the UK, for example, can be traced back to the first century AD with fish ponds and water mills, and changes to facilitate transportation and to effect land drainage (Sheail, 1988). Severe pollution in the mid nineteenth century led to an organized system of river management. A marked east–west rainfall gradient, combined with an uneven population distribution (a high proportion live in eastern and south-eastern England where the rainfall is low at 600–700 mm/year) means that many rivers in central and southern England, and many urban rivers throughout the UK, are overexploited. Today, most towns and cities rely on interbasin water transfers, and virtually all the major rivers in the UK are regulated directly or indirectly by mainstream impoundments, interbasin transfers, pumped storage reservoirs or groundwater abstractions (Petts, 1988).

TABLE 8.3 Selected methods of river channelization and their US and UK terminologies

Method	US term	UK equivalent
Increase channel capacity by manipulating width and/or depth	Widening/deepening	Resectioning
Increase velocity of flow by steepening gradient	Straightening	Realigning
Raise channel banks to confine flood waters	Diking	Embanking
Methods to control bank erosion	Bank stabilization	Bank protection
Remove obstructions from a watercourse to decrease resistance and thus increase velocity of flow	Clearing and snagging	Pioneer tree clearance; control of aquatic plants; dredging of sediments; urban clearing

Source: after Brookes (1985).

Ideally, river management should pursue four objectives (Mellquist, 1992):

1 balancing between users' interests
2 optimization of resource use
3 inclusion of environmental interests and those of the general public when exploiting water resources
4 cleaning up after past abuses.

In practice, these objectives can be conflicting, and the relative weight given to each by decision-makers is affected by a wide range of influences that include economic, political and environmental considerations. River management is no different from any other natural environmental management issue in that it involves compromises. Some conservationists, for example, argue that river regulation and environmental conservation are intrinsically incompatible since regulation modifies the natural environment in which original communities of organisms became established (e.g. Hellawell, 1988). Indeed, in some cases the ecological requirements of organisms are destroyed or modified beyond the limits of adaptations and the organisms are unable to survive.

Other conservationists, however, adopt a different view of the situation. Moore and Driver (1989) point out that in England and Wales there are more than 500 water supply reservoirs, with a total water surface of 20 000 ha, much of which flooded in the twentieth century. Waterfowl, amphibious and aquatic wildlife have all benefited from this change, one that is especially important after so much wetland has been drained and ploughed for increased agricultural production. The general importance of reservoirs to wildlife conservation is indicated by the designation of 174 reservoirs as Sites of Special Scientific Interest (SSSIs). Modern reservoirs include landscaping and conservation in their planning, construction and operation, while protection from recreational activity, a use of resources that is potentially damaging to wildlife, is an essential part of management at these sites.

The importance of ecological good health in river systems has been increasingly recognized in recent times, both from the purely moral standpoint and from the point of view of human society's use of their resources. There are numerous ways in which damage done in the past can be rectified, many of which are not new in themselves. In 1215, the Magna Carta demanded the removal of numerous weirs along the River Thames so that migratory Atlantic salmon and sea trout could pass upstream to their spawning grounds. There was, however, little response to this edict nor to similar statutes issued in the fifteenth century. The Thames Water Authority has installed fish passes on navigation weirs as part of a salmon rehabilitation programme initiated in 1979 (Mann, 1988). Extensive damage to migratory salmonid fish stocks has also occurred in Finland, caused by the dredging of rivers and brooks both to facilitate boat traffic and, increasingly during the last century, for timber-floating. Timber-floating has now almost completely ceased and Finnish water legislation obliges water authorities to make good any damage caused by dredging. The restoration of rapids and their restocking have been increasingly used to rehabilitate damage caused by dredging (Jutila, 1992).

A critical final point to make with regard to river management, however, is the simple fact that management of the channel alone is usually insufficient. It is important to realize that rivers are an integral part of the landscapes through which they flow. Rivers affect the land in their drainage basins and vice versa. Hence, management of human activities in the entire basin is both logical and sensible. The importance of making this connection between the channel and its basin is not in itself new. Governmental regulation of timber harvesting along mountain streams so as to maintain channel stability dates back to AD 806 in Japan, for example (Wohl, 2006). In more contemporary parlance, the approach is embodied in 'catchment management plans', as Burt (1993) points out in the UK context. Should a river's basin lie in more than one area of jurisdiction, however, impacts will produce transboundary environmental changes. Agreement on an appropriate plan for a river that flows through more than one country, for example, enters the realm of international politics (Fig. 8.6).

Figure 8.6 The Mekong River basin drains parts of six countries. Hydropower development and the improvement of river navigation, in China particularly, are producing impacts downstream. Long boats using this stretch of the Mekong in Laos are unlikely to be affected, but fisheries from the village in the background are expected to be adversely impacted by the ecological changes.

LAKES

Lacustrine degradation

As with rivers, human use of fresh water from lakes has led to numerous impacts. In some cases, entire lakes have dried up as rivers feeding them have been diverted for other purposes. Owens Lake in California is a case in point. Levels began to drop in the second half of the nineteenth century due to offtakes for irrigated agriculture, but an accelerated decline in water levels occurred with the construction of a 360 km water export system by the Los Angeles Department of Water and Power during the first 20 years of the last century. The lake, which was 7.6 m deep in 1912, had disappeared by 1930. In its place, the dry bed of lacustrine sediments covering 220 km² is a source of frequent dust storms, which are hazardous to local highway and aviation traffic, often exceed California State standards for atmospheric particulates and have increased morbidity among people suffering from emphysema, asthma and chronic bronchitis (Reinking *et al.*, 1975). From 1930 the Los Angeles system was extended northwards and began to tap streams flowing into the saline Mono Lake in 1941. By 1990, Mono Lake had fallen by 14 m, doubled in salinity, and lost a number of fresh-water habitats, such as delta marshes and brackish lagoons that formerly provided lakeside habitats for millions of birds. A repeat of the Owens Lake story was avoided in 1994 when the Los Angeles Department of Water and Power was ordered to ensure protection for Mono Lake and its streams and to effect some restoration of the damaged habitats. Since then the lake's level and salinity have been slowly improving (Fig. 8.7) towards a lake level of 1948 m as ordered by the California Supreme Court.

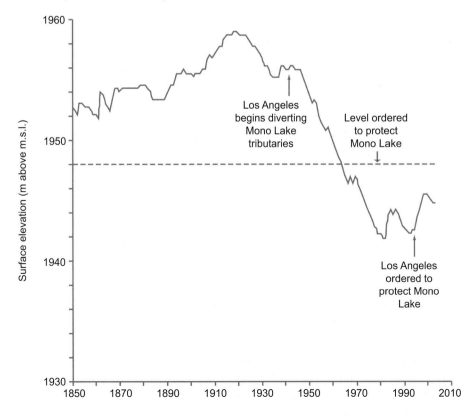

Figure 8.7 The level of Mono Lake, USA, 1850–2006 (data from www.monolake.org/ accessed August 2007).

Similar offtakes, in this case for agriculture, have had dramatic consequences for the Aral Sea in Central Asia. Diversion of water from the Amu Darya and Syr Darya rivers to irrigate plantations, predominantly growing cotton, has had severe impacts on the inland sea since 1960. Expansion of the irrigated area in the former Soviet region of central Asia, from 2.9 million ha in 1950 to about 7.2 million ha by the late 1980s, was spurred by Moscow's desire to be self-sufficient in cotton. As a result, the annual inflow to the Aral from the two rivers, the source of 90 per cent of its water, had declined by an order of magnitude between the 1960s (about 55 m^3/year) and the 1980s (about 5 m^3/year).

Changes in the level of the Aral Sea have occurred naturally throughout its history, and sea level variations of up to 36 m are thought to have occurred during the Quaternary due to climatic, geomorphological and tectonic influences (Middleton, 2002). Human use of water resources in the Aral Sea basin dates back more than 3000 years, but the unprecedented intensity of water use dating from about 1960 has clearly been responsible for the falling sea levels since then.

In 1960 the Aral Sea was the fourth largest lake in the world, but since that time its surface area has more than halved (Fig. 8.8), it has lost two-thirds of its volume, and its water level has dropped by more than 20 m. The average water level in the Aral Sea in 1960 was about 53 m above sea level (asl). By early 2003, it had receded to about 30 m asl, a level last seen during the fourteenth to fifteenth centuries, but in those days for predominantly natural reasons (Boroffka *et al.*, 2006). In some parts, the Aral Sea's remaining waters are more than two times saltier than seawater in the open ocean.

These dramatic changes have had far-reaching effects, both on-site and off-site. The Aral Sea commercial fishing industry, which landed 40 000 tonnes in the early 1960s, had ceased to function by 1980 (Fig. 8.9) as most of its native organisms died out (Williams and Aladin, 1991). The delta areas of the Amu Darya and Syr Darya rivers have been transformed due to the lack of water, affecting flora, fauna and soils, while the diversion of river water has also resulted in the widespread lowering of groundwater levels (Khakimov, 1989). The receding sea has had local effects on climate, and the exposed seabed has become a dust bowl from which an estimated 43 million tonnes of saline material is deposited on surrounding areas each year. This dust contaminates agricultural land up to several hundred kilometres from the sea coast, and is suspected to have adverse effects on human health. The irrigated cropland itself has also been subject to problems of in situ salinization and waterlogging due to poor management, with consequent negative effects on crop yields (Smith, 1992). Drainage water from these schemes is characterized by high salinity and is contaminated by high concentrations of fertilizer and pesticide residues, which have also been linked to poor human health in the region (Glazovsky, 1995).

The declining water levels led to a split in the sea in 1989/90, creating a small northern lake in Kazakhstan fed by the Syr Darya and a much larger southern lake, divided between Kazakhstan and neighbouring Uzbekistan, fed by the Amu Darya. The southern Large Aral has continued to shrink but the size of the northern Small Aral stabilized in 1996. Since completion in 2005 of a concrete dam blocking a narrow spillway linking the two water bodies, the Small Aral has actually managed to increase its water content for the first time in half a century.

(a)

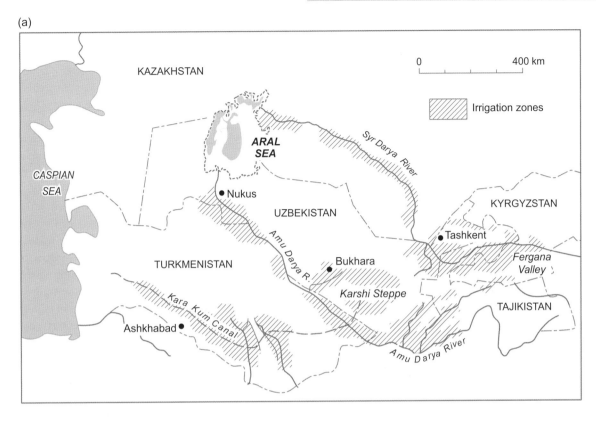

(b)

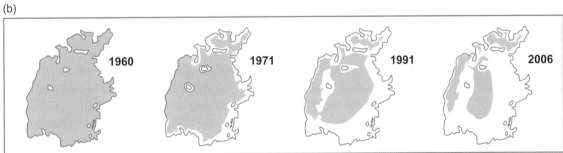

Figure 8.8 (a) Irrigated areas in central Asia (after Pryde, 1991) and (b) changes in the surface area of the Aral Sea (UNEP, 1992b; Micklin, 2007).

Figure 8.9 Abandoned trawlers near the former Aral Sea fishing village of Zhalangash, Kazakhstan, victims of perhaps the most extreme example of human-induced environmental degradation in the modern era.

The ecological demise of the Aral Sea and its drainage basin is one of the late twentieth century's foremost examples of human-induced environmental degradation. But it was not the result of ignorance or lack of forethought, since anecdotal or informal projections of disaster were made in some Soviet quarters well before the situation became serious. Seemingly it is the result of an unspecified cost–benefit analysis in which environmental and health impacts were given little consideration (Glantz *et al.*, 1993). The desire to be self-sufficient in textiles, combined with the Soviet belief that human society was capable of complete domination over nature, overrode any fears of the associated environmental implications. It is an example of the dangers of an extreme technocentric approach to the environment and a complete rejection of the precautionary principle.

The introduction of non-native species to lakes is another way in which, often unwittingly, the human impact has caused serious ecological change (see the case study of the North American Great Lakes on page 322). Deliberately introducing fish species to lakes to provide employment and additional sources of nutrition was a common aspect of economic development projects during the 1950s and 1960s. Predatory species such as largemouth, bass and black crappie, introduced into the oligotrophic Lake Atitlan in Guatemala, succeeded in wiping out many of the smaller fish that had previously been used by indigenous lakeside people. Similar dramatic effects on the pelagic food web resulted from the introduction of the Amazonian peacock bass to Gatun Lake in the Panama Canal. One serious consequence of this predator's elimination of the lake's smaller native fishes was a dramatic increase in malaria-carrying mosquitoes, since the minnows that had previously occupied the shallower lakeside waters had fed off mosquito larvae (Fernando, 1991).

The relative merits, or otherwise, of ecological changes forced by exotic introductions also depend to a degree on the stance taken towards environmental issues. In East Africa's Lake Victoria, the predatory Nile perch, introduced in the early 1960s, has consumed to very low numbers (probably in many cases to extinction) most of the lake's endemic open-water *Haplochromine cichlid* species. Before the introduction of the Nile perch, Lake Victoria contained about 300 cichlid species, but in just 30 years an estimated 200 of these have become extinct (Goldschmidt, 1996). This clear example of a human-induced mass extinction is inexcusable from an ecocentric perspective. However, the Nile perch has brought considerable benefits, expanding an artisanal fishery into a multimillion-dollar export industry for Nile fillets, while improving the incomes and welfare of lakeside communities. Annual fish landings rose from about 40 000 tonnes in the early 1970s to peak at around 550 000 tonnes in the late 1980s, and although they have declined since, they remained between 400 000 and 500 000 tonnes throughout the 1990s (Njiru *et al.*, 2005). The loss of some species may be the price that has to be paid for these social benefits. If this more technocentric view is adopted, however, it is sad to note that the Nile perch is already being exploited at its maximum sustainable yield, and with more processing plants planned it looks set to become overexploited, a fate that afflicts virtually all such new commercial fisheries. Lack of finance prevents the countries concerned from supporting adequate fishery regulatory bodies. One of the main lessons to be learned from Lake Victoria's experience, therefore, is that if a radical change is forced upon an ecosystem, the human component of it requires proper management to keep in step with that forced change.

Another range of problems common to many lakes are those stemming from the introduction of plant species, particularly waterweeds. The water hyacinth is a frequent culprit, growing very fast, covering the water surface (so reducing light and oxygen for other plants and for fish), increasing evaporation, blocking waterways, presenting a serious threat to hydroelectrical turbines and providing a suitable habitat for dangerous organisms such as snakes and disease-carrying mosquitoes. The water hyacinth became a major problem in Lake Victoria after its introduction there in 1988.

There are numerous examples of lakes being degraded inadvertently, many of which are due to lacustrine sensitivity to pollutants. Some examples of problems caused by pollution, particularly acidification from industrial and mining activity, are covered in Chapters 12 and 19. One of the world's most pervasive water pollution problems, and one that is widespread in all continents, is the eutrophication of standing water bodies (Ryding and Rast, 1989). Eutrophication is a natural phenomenon in lakes, brought on by the gradual accumulation of organic material through geological history. But human activity can accelerate the process, so-called cultural eutrophication, by enriching surface waters with nutrients, particularly phosphorus and nitrogen. Such increased nutrient concentrations in lakes have been attributed to wastewater discharge, runoff of fertilizers from agricultural land and changes in land use that increase runoff.

Eutrophication is an important water quality issue that causes a range of practical problems. These include the impairment of the following: drinking water quality, fisheries and water volume or flow. The main causes of these problems include algal blooms, macrophyte and littoral algal growth, altered thermal conditions, turbidity and low dissolved solids. Health problems range from minor skin irritations to bilharzia, schistosomiasis and diarrhoea.

Monitoring of Lac Léman (Lake Geneva) indicates how the build-up of nutrient pollutants can be rapid (Fig. 8.10). Water quality deteriorated from its relatively clean state during the 1950s as concentrations of phosphorus increased, primarily from point-source discharges, to reach a critical stage in the late 1970s. In this case the situation has improved following the introduction of tertiary wastewater treatment plants and a ban on the use of phosphates in detergents in 1986 (Rapin *et al.*, 1989).

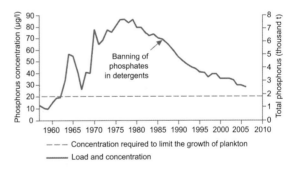

Figure 8.10 Phosphorus concentrations in Lake Léman, Switzerland, 1957–2006 (data from www.cipel.org/ accessed June 2007).

Lake management

The restoration and protection of lakes presents all sorts of problems for policy-makers and environmental managers, and the management experience of the North American Great Lakes illustrates the difficulties well. A major restoration effort has been in progress throughout the Great Lakes Basin since the US and Canadian governments committed themselves to the Great Lakes Water Quality Agreement, first signed in 1972 and renewed in 1978. The agreement adopted an ecosystem approach, which incorporates the political and economic interests of the 'institutional ecosystem' as well as elements of the natural ecosystem, after two previous management strategies had failed to address fully the dangers faced by the lakes (Hartig and Vallentyne, 1989). Current efforts are focused on reducing pollution entering the lakes, incorporating the 'critical loads' approach adopted in studies of acid rain pollution (see page 241). Serious pollutants include volatile organic compounds (VOCs), heavy metals, and industrial and agricultural chemicals, which come from both point and non-point sources such as municipal and industrial effluent, rainfall and snowmelt. Special and immediate attention has been given to 43 severely degraded so-called Areas of Concern. Collingwood Harbour, on the Canadian side of Lake Huron, was the first of these 43 sites to be removed from the list of Areas of Concern, in 2000, following successful restoration and protection efforts.

The importance of integrating the ecological needs with those of the lake's users – which are, of course, intimately related – is most acute in lakes that support high population densities. However, the balance of interests also depends upon the nature of the lake and the type of overall regulatory body involved. The example of Lake Baikal in eastern Siberia, the deepest and volumetrically the largest freshwater lake in the world and home to 800 species of plant and 1550 species of animal life, most of which are endemic to its particularly pure waters, illustrates the point well. Theoretically, the state ownership and centralized decision-making of the former USSR was the ideal structure for successfully integrating ecological and user interests on such a unique freshwater body. In practice, however, as numerous examples of environmental problems quoted in this chapter and elsewhere in this book illustrate, the ecological side of the equation was too often given inadequate consideration.

Efforts to protect Lake Baikal against pollution, a struggle that dates from the mid 1960s, was the first major issue in the rise of public environmental awareness in the former USSR (Pryde, 1972). Although there have been small logging and industrial processing operations on the shores of the lake for several decades, concern was raised at the proposal to establish two large wood-processing plants. Great debates occurred over the possible effects of effluents from the plants and the effects of soil erosion resulting from deforestation of the lake shore to supply the plants. Public outcry succeeded in forcing the introduction of new measures to protect the lake's waters, including a ban on logging on surrounding steep slopes, the establishment of several protected areas around the lake, and the eventual conversion of one of the processing plants to a less-damaging manufacturing role. Wastewater from the Baikalsk Pulp and Paper Plant (BPPP), on the lake's southern shoreline, has been a concern since the plant was built in 1966. Although effluents from the BPPP are treated by mechanical, chemical and biological means before being discharged into the lake, they remain a potential source of pollution and hence a focus for research and monitoring (Efremova *et al.*, 2002).

WETLANDS

The term wetland covers a multitude of different landscape types, located in every major climatic zone. They form the overlap between dry terrestrial ecosystems and inundated aquatic ecosystems such as rivers, lakes or seas. The Ramsar Convention (see below) uses a very broad definition, which has been widely accepted:

Wetlands are areas of marsh, fen, peatland or water, whether natural or artificial, permanent or temporary, with water that is static or flowing, fresh, brackish or salt, including areas of marine water the depth of which at low tide does not exceed six metres.

This definition encompasses coastal and shallow marine areas (including coral reefs, which are covered in Chapter 7), as well as river courses and temporary lakes or depressions in semi-arid zones.

It is only in the past 30 years or so that wetlands, which currently cover about 6 per cent of the Earth's land surface, have been considered as anything more than worthless wastelands, only fit for drainage, dredging and infilling. But an increasing knowledge of these ecosystems in academic and environmentalist circles has yielded the realization that wetlands are an important component of the global biosphere, and that the alarming rate at which they are being destroyed is a cause for concern.

Wetlands perform some key natural functions and provide a wealth of direct and indirect benefits to human societies (Table 8.4). Wetlands form an important link in the hydrological cycle, acting as temporary water stores. This function helps to mitigate river floods downstream, protects coastlines from destructive erosion and recharges aquifers. Chemically, wetlands act like giant water filters, trapping and recycling nutrients and other residues. This role is partly a function of the very high biological productivity of wetlands, among the highest of any world ecosystem (see Table 1.1). The importance of this function is indicated by the fact that the 6.4 per cent global wetland area is estimated to contribute 24 per cent of global terrestrial primary productivity (Williams, 1990a). As such, wetlands provide habitats for a wide variety of plants and animals. All these functions provide benefits to human societies, from the direct resource potential provided by products such as fisheries and fuelwood, to the ecosystem value in terms of hydrology and productivity, up to a value on the global level in terms of the role of wetlands in atmospheric processes and general life-support systems (Odum, 1979).

Hydrology
    Flood control
    Groundwater recharge/discharge
    Shoreline anchorage and protection
Water quality
    Wastewater treatment
    Toxic substances
    Nutrients
Food-chain support/cycling
    Primary production
    Decomposition
    Nutrient export
    Nutrient utilisation
Habitat
    Invertebrates
    Fisheries
    Mammals
    Birds
Socio-economic
    Consumptive use (e.g. food, fuel)
    Non-consumptive use (e.g. aesthetic, recreational, archaeological)

Source: Sather and Smith (1984).

TABLE 8.4 Wetland functions

Wetland destruction

Estimates of the global area of wetlands drained vary considerably, but a total of 1.6 million km^2 by 1985 is considered by Williams (1990a) to be a reasonable figure. Nearly three-quarters of this total has occurred in the temperate world, and the prime motivation has been to provide more land to grow food. The wetlands of Europe have been subject to human modification for more than 1000 years. In the Netherlands, where particularly active reclamation and drainage

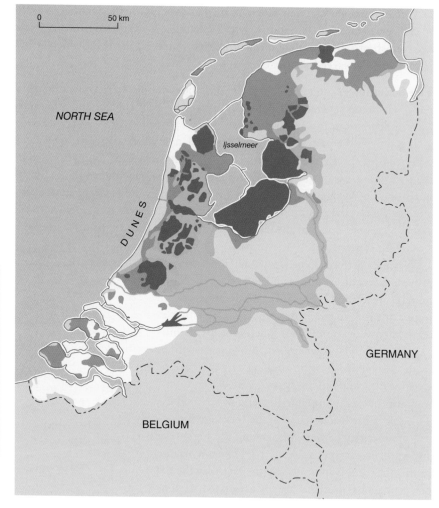

NORTH SEA

Ijsselmeer

D U N E S

GERMANY

BELGIUM

Reclaimed Land

River flood plains,
mainly before 1600

Peat, mainly
after 1600

Lakes, mainly
after 1600

Intertidal lands,
before 1300

Intertidal lands,
after 1300

Figure 8.11 Reclamation of
wetland types in the Netherlands
(after de Jong and Wiggens,
1983).

periods occurred in the seventeenth, nineteenth and twentieth centuries, more
than half of the national land area is now made up of reclaimed wetlands (Fig.
8.11), and Dutch drainage engineers have hired out their skills to neighbouring
countries for more than 300 years.

In the USA, where wetlands are very largely concentrated in the east of the
country, with major areas around the Great Lakes, on the lower reaches of the
Mississippi River, and on the Gulf of Mexico and Atlantic seaboard south of
Chesapeake Bay, about half of the pre-settlement area of wetlands had been lost
by 1975 (Williams, 1990b). Agriculture has been the major beneficiary from the
drainage operations in the USA, while urban and suburban development, dredging and mining account for much of the rest.

Although the rich soils of former wetland areas often provide fertile agricultural
lands, conversion to cropland is not always successful. Drainage of the extensive
marshlands around the Pripyat River in Belarus during the post-war Soviet period,
for example, was largely unsuccessful. The low productivity of reclaimed areas
necessitated the application of large amounts of chemical fertilizers, and some
former wetland zones also became prone to wildfires (Pryde, 1991).

There have been numerous other reasons for wet-land reclamation. On the national scale, in Albania, where about 9 per cent of the country was drained in the period 1946–83, reclamation was as much driven by the fight against malaria as the desire to increase food output, although most of the former marshes were converted to irrigated agriculture (Hall, 1993). Urban sprawl has been a major cause in many areas. Mexico City, for example, was surrounded by five shallow lakes when the Spanish first arrived in 1519, but as the city has expanded since then, all but one small wetland area have been desiccated for their water and land. The remaining area at Xochimilco is threatened by the city's declining water table (Fig. 8.12). In southern Sudan, the Jonglei Canal Project was designed to utilize the large proportion of the White Nile's discharge that currently feeds the Sudd Swamps. The 360 km artificial channel, designed to bypass and effectively drain the swamps, would provide much-needed additional water to the dryland countries of Sudan and Egypt if it is ever completed – the project has been hindered by civil war in the region. Plans to utilize the water resources of wetlands also threaten other sites, such as the inland Okavango Delta in semi-arid northern Botswana. The general well-being of the Okavango is also under increasing pressure from cattle encroaching into the lush grazing of the delta, a threat currently held at bay by a 300 km cordon fence; but the lure of resources other than water and land has proved to be a serious cause of wetland degradation in many areas.

Figure 8.12 Mexico City's last remaining area of wetland at Xochimilco, which is in danger of drying up due to the continuing need for water from the world's largest city.

The fuel resources harboured in wetlands represent perhaps the most important reason in this respect. In many developing countries fuelwood collection is a prime cause of degradation. It is the major threat to wetlands in Central America, as it is in many coastal mangrove swamps in Africa and Asia (see pages 134–5). In more temperate latitudes, particularly above 45° N, peat is the most important organic fuel of the wetland habitat. Hand-cutting of peat has been practised in rural communities in northern Europe for centuries, and continues today in remote parts of Ireland, Scotland, Scandinavia and Russia, but since the 1950s peat has been cut from much larger areas with machines. Worldwide production reached 100 million tonnes in the late 1970s (Kivinen and Pakarinen, 1981), most for fuel but with exploitation for horticultural purposes particularly important in some countries. In 1999, when global production was just over 100 million m^3, Finland, Ireland and Russia were the world's largest producers (IPS, 2001). The Finnish peatlands, covering a total area of some 89 000 km^2, are some of the most important in Europe and Finland has the highest proportion of wetlands of any country in the world. In Ireland, by contrast, 94 per cent of raised bogs and 86 per cent of blanket bogs have been lost, inspiring urgent conservation measures for remaining areas. Raised bogs only occur in eight countries, all in Europe, and while the habitat is close to extinction in the Netherlands and Germany, Eire still has about half of the world's remaining area of oceanic raised bogs worthy of conservation. Their conservation under the EU Habitats Directive is thus a priority (Irish Peatland Conservation Council, 1998).

The arguments in favour of preserving peatlands take in all the reasons for wetland preservation in general (Table 8.4), and the importance of peatlands for global-scale stability is increasingly being realized. There is a growing body of evidence to suggest that peatlands play a key role in the initiation of ice ages, through feedbacks with geomorphology, surface albedo, atmospheric moisture and the concentration of greenhouse gases (Franzen, 1994). Another possible role of peatlands lies in their important relationship with nearby marine ecosystems. A link has been suggested whereby vital nutrients are exchanged between coastal marine ecosystems and adjacent peatlands. The biological productivity of oceans tends to be limited by a lack of key nutrients, particularly iron. Runoff from peat is rich in iron and probably makes an important contribution to marine productivity in many coastal areas. Productivity in peat ecosystems is often limited by a lack of sulphur, and sulphur from the oceans reaches peat wetlands through the atmosphere (Klinger and Erickson, 1997). One possible feedback resulting from the loss of peatlands is, therefore, decreased marine productivity, and since human populations derive most of their fisheries from coastal waters the consequences for society are clear.

Wetland protection

Realization of the value of wetlands to human and animal populations has prompted moves to protect this threatened landscape in recent decades, although in many cases conservationists still face a difficult task in protecting wetlands from destructive development projects. In the case of the Göksu Delta on the south coast of Turkey, threatened by a proposed tourist complex, airport and shrimp farm, the Turkish Society for the Protection of Nature enlisted international help in publicizing the danger to the delta, and successfully lobbied the Turkish Government, which in 1990 declared the delta a Protected Special Area. The Göksu Delta is a key European site for migrant and wintering birds, holding important populations of no less than 12 globally threatened species, and its beaches are among the main nesting sites for the two Mediterranean species of sea turtle. Following the designation of the delta as a protected area, studies are under way to develop a management plan for the area, but the threats to the Göksu Delta have not all disappeared, since its ecology will be altered significantly by the Kayraktepe dam.

A comprehensive national effort towards wetland conservation has been made in the USA, where numerous state and federal laws have a bearing on wetland protection. An attempt is also being made to reverse the loss with the Wetlands Reserve Program (WRP), established in 1990, which seeks to restore 405 000 ha of privately owned freshwater wetlands that have been previously drained and converted to cropland. The WRP aims to improve environmental quality without significantly impacting the agricultural production or the economic well-being of the regions concerned by paying compensation to farmers who take part in the scheme and by allowing certain other money-making activities, such as hunting and fishing, in their wetland areas.

On the international front, one of the earliest attempts to protect a major world biome was the Ramsar Convention, designed to protect wetlands of international importance. Formally known as the Convention on Wetlands of

electricity, no less than 83 per cent of national production is consumed in Panama City and Colón, so that the dam is reinforcing the concentration of wealth in the urban areas.

Hence it is clear that the undoubted benefits of big dams are not always gained solely by the country where the dam is located, and that within the country concerned, the demands of urban populations can outweigh those of rural areas. Many of the drawbacks of such structures, however, are borne by the rural people of the country concerned. Despite the success of many big dams in achieving their main economic aims, their construction and associated reservoirs create significant changes in the pre-existing environment, and many of these changes have proved to be detrimental. It is the negative side of environmental impacts that have pushed the issue of big dams to a prominent position in the eyes of environmentalists and many other interest groups.

ENVIRONMENTAL IMPACTS OF BIG DAMS

The environmental impacts of big dams and their associated reservoirs are numerous, and Goodland (1990) has outlined the main areas that they influence (Table 9.2). The temporal aspect of environmental impacts within a certain area is also important. The river basin itself can be thought of as a system that will respond to a major change, such as the construction of a dam, in many different ways and on a variety of timescales. While the creation of a reservoir represents an immediate environmental change, the permanent inundation of an area not previously covered in water, the resulting changes in other aspects of the river basin, such as floral and faunal communities, and soil erosion, will take a longer time to readjust to the new conditions.

The range of environmental impacts consequent upon dam construction, and their effects on human communities, can be considered under three headings that reflect the broad spatial regions associated with any dam project: the dam and its reservoir; the upstream area; and the downstream area.

1. The catchments contributing to the reservoir or project area and the area below the dam to the estuary, coastal zone and offshore
2. All ancillary aspects of the project such as power transmission corridors, pipelines, canals, tunnels, relocation and access roads, borrow and disposal areas and construction camps, as well as unplanned developments stimulated by the project (e.g. logging or shifting cultivation along access roads)
3. Off-site areas required for resettlement or compensatory tracts
4. The airshed, such as where air pollution may enter or leave the area of influence
5. Migratory routes of humans, wildlife or fish, particularly where they relate to public health, economics, or environmental conservation.

Source: Goodland (1990).

TABLE 9.2 Areas of influence of dam and reservoir projects

The dam and its reservoir

The creation of a reservoir results in the loss of resources in the land area inundated. Flooding behind the Balbina Dam north of Manaus, Brazil has destroyed much of a centre of plant endemism, for example. In some cases the loss of wilderness areas threatened by new dam projects has raised considerable debate, both nationally and internationally. A case in point was the Nam Choan Dam Project on the Kwae Yai River in western Thailand, first proposed in 1982. The suggested reservoir lay largely within the Thung Yai Wildlife Sanctuary, one of the largest remaining relatively undisturbed forest areas in Thailand, containing all six of the nation's endangered mammal species. Debate over the destructive impact of the project resulted in it being shelved indefinitely in 1988 (Dixon *et al.*, 1989).

Some resources, such as trees for timber or fuelwood, can be taken from the reservoir site prior to inundation, although this is not always economically feasible in remote regions. There are dangers inherent in not removing them, however. Anaerobic decomposition of submerged forests produces hydrogen sulphide, which is toxic to fish and corrodes metal that comes into contact with the water. Corrosion of turbines in Surinam's Brakopondo reservoir has been a serious problem. In a similar vein, decomposition of organic matter by bacteria in the La Grande 2 reservoir in Quebec, Canada, has released large quantities of mercury by methylation. Mercury has bioaccumulated in reservoir fish tissue to levels often exceeding the Canadian standard for edible fish of 0.5 mg/kg (Harper, 1992).

Reservoirs formed by river impoundment typically undergo significant variations in water quality in their first decade or so, before a new ecological balance is reached. Biological production can be high on initial impoundment, due to the release of organically bound elements from flooded vegetation and soils, but declines thereafter. Hence the initial fish yield from Lake Kariba in 1964, its first year of full capacity, was more than 2500 tonnes but by the early 1970s the annual yield had stabilized at around 1000 tonnes (Marshall and Junor, 1981).

Figure 9.3 The Temple of Philae, which has been moved to higher ground to avoid inundation by Lake Nasser.

Blooms of toxic cyanobacteria, a type of microscopic algae, may be another facet of the nutrient enrichment that often follows impoundment of new reservoirs, particularly in tropical, subtropical and arid regions of the world. These cyanobacterial toxins are potentially dangerous to humans and animals if consumed in sufficient quantities. A range of gastrointestinal and allergenic illnesses can affect people exposed to the toxins in drinking water, food or during swimming, but the most severe case of human poisoning due to cyanobacterial toxins occurred when inadequately treated water from a reservoir was used for patients in a kidney dialysis clinic in the Brazilian city of Curaru in 1996. More than 50 people died due to direct exposure of the toxin to their bloodstream during dialysis (Chorus and Bartram, 1999).

Cultural property may also be lost by the creation of a reservoir – 24 archaeological sites dating from AD 70–1000 were inundated by the Tucuruí Dam reservoir in Brazil, for example – although in some cases such property is deemed important enough to be preserved. Lake Nasser submerged some ancient Egyptian monuments, but major ones – including the temples of Abu Simbel, Kalabsha and Philae – were moved to higher ground prior to flooding (Fig. 9.3).

Big dams often necessitate resettlement programmes if there are inhabitants of the area to be inundated, and the numbers of people involved can be very large. Global estimates suggest that 40–80 million people have been displaced by reservoirs in the last 50 years (World Commission on Dams, 2000). Some of the biggest projects in this respect have been in China. The Sanmen Gorge Project on the Huang Ho River involved moving 300 000 people, and the Three Gorges Dam on the Yangtze River involves planning for the displacement of up to 1.4

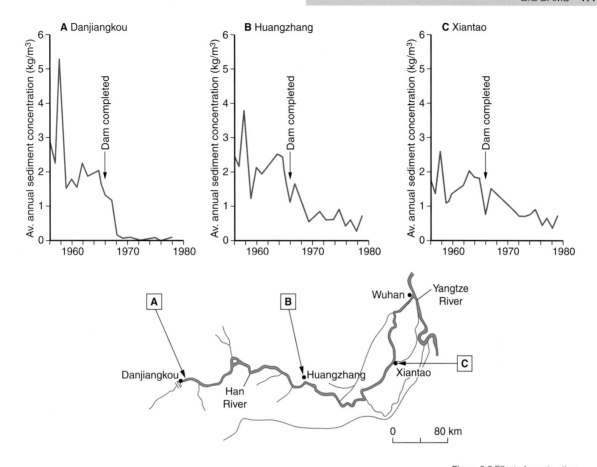

Figure 9.5 Effect of construction of the Danjiangkou Dam on sediment loads of the Han River, China (after Chien, 1985).

Affected area (thousand ha)	
1966–73	344
1979	464
1989–91	578
1994–95	890

Source: Saheed (1995).

TABLE 9.6 Increase in area affected by salinity in Bangladesh

Dams can also affect marine and lake fish populations through the barrier they create, which effectively cuts off access to spawning grounds. This effect has been evident on salmon and aloses in the River Garonne and its tributaries in south-western France since the Middle Ages (Décamps and Fortuné, 1991). In the twentieth century, decline in the landed catches of Caspian Sea sturgeon, the source of caviar, from 40 000 tonnes early in the century to just 11 000 tonnes in the 1970s, is attributable primarily to large hydroelectric dams on the Volga and the consequent loss of spawning grounds. Although catches had largely recovered to pre-dam levels in the early 1980s with the establishment of new sturgeon

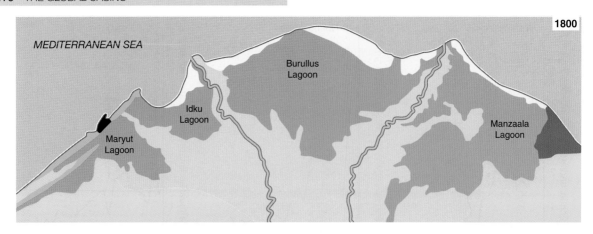

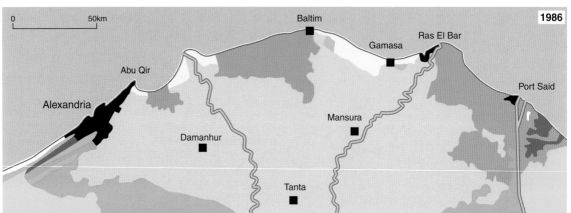

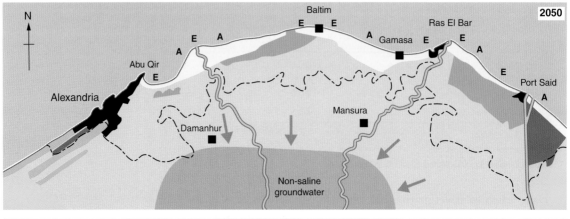

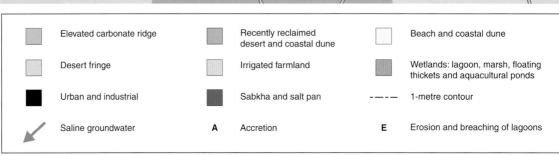

Figure 9.6 Nile delta changes from Stanley and Warne, reprinted with permission from AAAS.

hoods, recognizing entitlements and sharing benefits, ensuring compliance and sharing rivers for peace, development and security

- criteria and guidelines for good practice related to the strategic priorities, ranging from life-cycle and environmental flow assessments to impoverishment risk analysis and integrity pacts.

A late twentieth-century trend relating to large dams noted by the Commission is that of decommissioning dams that no longer serve a useful purpose, are too expensive to maintain safely, or have unacceptable levels of impacts in today's view. The desire to restore rivers to their pre-dam ecological state has accelerated in many countries in recent years, particularly in North America. Indeed, in the USA the decommissioning rate for large dams has overtaken the rate of construction since 1998. Decommissioning dams can enable the restoration of fisheries and riverine ecological processes as experience in North America and Europe has shown, but the removal of dams needs to be preceded by careful planning. Environmental problems are also inherent in the removal of such large-scale structures. These include negative impacts on downstream aquatic life due to a sudden flush of the sediments accumulated in the reservoir.

A less dramatic approach to the problems associated with big dams involves attempting to restore natural flow regimes and associated ecosystem health and services by modifying dam operations in some way. This strategy is referred to as 're-operation' by Richter and Thomas (2007), who contend that significant environmental benefits can be gained through a careful reassessment of how river water is used and by modifying the uses through more conservative management. However, although decommissioning is progressing in some areas and re-operation may help to alleviate problems in others, big dams are still being built in many parts of the world. Appropriate design (Table 9.10) and management will hence continue to be important for many years to come.

TABLE 9.10 Characteristics of good and bad dams from an ecosystem standpoint

Good dam	Bad dam
Reservoir with relatively small surface area (often in a narrow gorge)	Reservoir with large surface area
Reservoir that is deep and silts slowly	Relatively shallow reservoir (which sometimes equates to relatively short useful life)
Little loss of wildlife and natural habitat	Considerable flooding of natural habitat and consequent loss of wildlife
Little or no flooding of forests	Submerged forests that decay and create water quality problems
River that is relatively small, with little aquatic biodiversity	Large river with much aquatic biodiversity
No problem with large floating aquatic plants	Serious problem with large floating aquatic plants
Many unregulated downstream tributaries	Few or no downstream tributaries
No tropical diseases (i.e. high elevation or mid to high latitudes)	Location in the lowland tropics or subtropics, conducive to the spread of vector-borne disease

Source: after Ledec et al. (1997).

The building of dams on rivers flowing through more than one country brings international political considerations on to the agenda of big dam issues. Such considerations are particularly pertinent in dryland regions where rivers represent a high percentage of water availability to many countries. The main issues at stake here are those of water availability and quality.

In several international river basins, peaceful cooperation over the use of waters has been achieved through international agreement. One such agreement, between the USA and Mexico over use of the Rio Grande, was signed in 1944 and is operated by the International Boundary and Water Commission. This body ensures equal allocation of the annual average flow between the two countries. Similarly, an international treaty between Egypt and Sudan governs the volume of Nile water allowed to pass through the Aswan High Dam, although none of the other eight Nile Basin countries has an agreement over use of the Nile's waters. India and Bangladesh signed a water-sharing accord for the Ganges in 1996. It specifies water allocation in normal and dry periods after 20 years of wrangling over the effects of the Farakka Barrage.

Such agreements to resolve disputes over water resources have a very long history. The beginnings of international water law can be traced back at least to 4500 BP, when the two Sumerian city states of Lagash and Umma reached an agreement to end a dispute over the water resources of a tributary of the River Tigris in the Middle East (Wolf, 1998). Wrangles over water are still a significant potential source of conflict in the Tigris–Euphrates Basin due to a lack of agreements in the contemporary era. While there is currently a water surplus in this region, the scale of planned developments raises some concern (Agnew and Anderson, 1992). Turkey's Southeastern Anatolian Project, a regional development scheme on the headwaters of the two rivers, centres on 22 dams. In early 1990, when filling of the Ataturk Dam reservoir (Fig. 9.8) commenced, stemming the flow of the

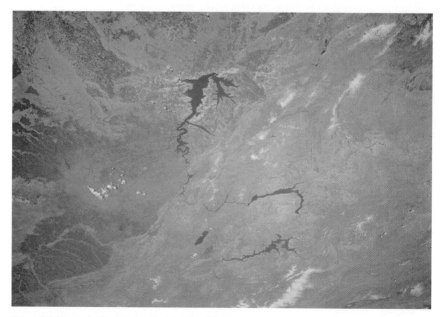

Figure 9.8 Space shuttle photograph of the River Euphrates flowing through south-eastern Turkey. The largest of the three reservoirs in this picture is that behind the Ataturk Dam, completed in 1992. Concern at the scale of water use in Turkey's Southeastern Anatolian Project, which has contributed to the decline of the Tigris–Euphrates marshlands in Iraq, has heightened political tensions in this part of the Middle East.

Euphrates, immediate alarm was expressed by Syria and Iraq, despite the fact that governments in both countries had been alerted and discharge before the cut-off had been enhanced in compensation. Syria and Iraq nearly went to war when Syria was filling its Euphrates Dam. Full development of the Southeastern Anatolian Project, expected in about 2030, could reduce the flow of the Euphrates by as much as 60 per cent, which could severely jeopardize Syrian and Iraqi agriculture downstream. The three Tigris–Euphrates riparians have tried to reach agreements over the water use from these two rivers, and the need for such an agreement is becoming ever more pressing.

FURTHER READING

Bunn, S.E. and Arthington, A.H. 2002 Basic principles and ecological consequences of altered flow regimes for aquatic biodiversity. *Environmental Management* 30: 492–507. A thorough overview of the literature.

Cummings, B.J. 1990 *Dam the rivers, damn the people*. London, Earthscan. The story of two major hydroelectric developments in the Amazon, and the conflicts between them and local environments and populations.

Fearnside, P.M. 2005 Brazil's Samuel Dam: lessons for hydroelectric development policy and the environment in Amazonia. *Environmental Management* 35: 1–19. A typical case study from the tropics.

Gupta, H.K. 2002 A review of recent studies of triggered earthquakes by artificial water reservoirs with special emphasis on earthquakes in Koyna, India. *Earth-Science Reviews* 58: 279–310. Just as it says.

Hornig, J.F. (ed.) 1999 *Social and environmental impacts of the James Bay Hydroelectric Project*. Montreal, McGill-Queen's University Press. Insights from a variety of disciplines on the controversies surrounding the first mega-scale hydroelectric project in the subarctic, on the La Grande River in Canada.

McCully, P. 2001 *Silenced rivers: the ecology and politics of large dams*. London, Zed Books. Tracing the history of dam building worldwide and the growth of the anti-dam movement.

Palmieri, A., Shah, F. and Dinar, A. 2001 Economics of reservoir sedimentation and sustainable management of dams. *Journal of Environmental Management* 61: 149–63. An economic appraisal of managing dams in a sustainable manner.

Scudder, T. 2006 *The future of large dams*. London, Earthscan. Examination of the social, environmental, institutional and political issues by a former member of the World Commission on Dams.

World Commission on Dams 2000 *Dams and development: a new framework for decision-making*. London, Earthscan. Report of the world body set up to review the environmental, social and economic impacts of large dams.

Yuefang, D. and Steil, S. 2003 China Three Gorges Project resettlement: policy, planning and implementation. *Journal of Refugee Studies* 16: 422–43. An appraisal of the resettlement issue in China's largest dam project.

WEBSITES

www.dams.org/ official site of the World Commission on Dams.
www.sandelman.ottawa.on.ca/dams/ the Dam and Reservoir Impact and Information Archive.
www.irn.org/ the International Rivers Network site has information, campaigns and publications (e.g. *World Rivers Review*) on many riverine issues.
www.nwcouncil.org/ documents, journals and related information on the management of the Columbia River Basin in North America.
www.narmada.org/ site that aims to present the perspective of grass-roots people's organizations on the construction of large dams on the River Narmada in central India.
www.recovery.bcit.ca/ River Recovery – Restoring Rivers Through Dam Decommissioning. This project seeks to restore the ecological health of British Columbia's rivers by identifying dams that require alteration or removal.

POINTS FOR DISCUSSION

- On the whole, do you consider big dams to be good or bad things?
- Are any of the environmental impacts of big dams irreversible?
- Is hydroelectricity a sustainable form of power generation?
- Outline the possible environmental impacts of decommissioning a large dam.

10 Urban Environments

TOPICS COVERED

Transformation of nature, Surface water resources, Groundwater, The urban atmosphere, Garbage, Hazards and catastrophes, Towards a sustainable urban environment

KEY WORDS

megacity, urban sprawl, flashy discharge regime, subsidence, urban heat island, post-industrial city

Large numbers of people have lived in close proximity to each other in cities for thousands of years. The first urban cultures began to develop about 5000 years ago in Egypt, Mesopotamia and India, but the size of cities and their geographical distribution expanded dramatically after the Industrial Revolution of the previous millennium. This expansion accelerated into the twentieth century which began with 13 per cent of the world's population living in cities and ended with a figure of nearly 47 per cent. This global urban population reached 1 billion in 1960, 2 billion in 1985, and 3 billion in 2002. By 2030 it is expected to near 5 billion (UNDESA, 2006).

This is not to say that all cities have grown inexorably through the ages. Some of the world's large urban areas have a long history of continuous occupancy and importance, but others have not adjusted successfully to changing circumstances. Baghdad, Cairo and Istanbul (formerly Constantinople) ranked among the world's largest cities at both the beginning and end of the second millennium. Other cities of major importance in AD 1000 have now faded from prominence (e.g. Nishapur, Persia; Córdoba, Spain) or have been abandoned altogether (e.g. Angkor, Khmer Empire).

Nonetheless, growth rates in many of today's major world cities have been unprecedented in recent decades. In 1950, two urban areas – New York-Newark and Tokyo – had a population of more than 10 million people. These were joined by a third so-called megacity – Mexico City – within the next 25 years, but 25 years after that, in the year 2000, the number of megacities had reached 18 (Fig. 10.1).

Many cities in the industrializing world experienced remarkable growth in the last 30–50 years of the twentieth century. The populations of Mexico City, São Paulo, Karachi and Seoul grew by more than 800 per cent in the second half of the twentieth century. The urban area of Mexico City, which is probably the largest conurbation in the developing world, expanded from 27.5 km^2 in 1900 to cover 1450 km^2 in 2000. The phenomenal growth of some cities, and the high concentrations of people they represent (the urban density of Mexico City in 2000 was 12 559 people/km^2), has created some acute environmental problems both outside and within the city limits.

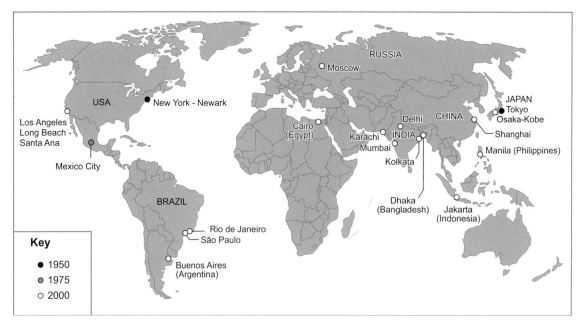

Figure 10.1 Urban agglomerations with 10 million inhabitants or more in 1950, 1975 and 2000 (from data in UNDESA, 2006).

By contrast in the more prosperous countries, large cities such as New York and London grew little in the second half of the twentieth century. These urban areas now face different challenges, including generally unplanned incremental development, characterized by a low-density mix of land uses on the urban fringe. Such 'urban sprawl' is classically a North American phenomenon, but is now also commonly seen throughout Europe where city structure has traditionally been much more compact (EEA, 2006).

Cities represent a completely artificial environment; they absorb vast quantities of resources from surrounding areas and create high concentrations of wastes to be disposed of. The degree to which cities impinge on their hinterlands, their ecological footprint, is indicated by a few examples. About 10 per cent of prime agricultural land has been lost to urbanization in Egypt. The twentieth-century growth of São Paulo was fuelled by the expansion of coffee plantations in southeast Brazil, which reduced the forest cover of São Paulo State from 81 per cent in 1860 to 6 per cent in the late 1980s (Monteiro, 1989). The demand for water in Tehran spurred the construction of a series of dams and canals in the early decades of the last century, to bring water 50 km from the River Karaj to the west, reducing the water available for rural agriculture. By the 1970s, supplies were again running low, so water was diverted more than 75 km from the River Lar to the north-east (Beaumont *et al.*, 1988). In Rio de Janeiro's Guanabarra Bay, pollution from two oil refineries, two ports, 6000 industries, 12 shipyards, 16 oil terminals, sewage and garbage dumps has reduced commercial fishing by 90 per cent and mangrove cover by 90 per cent, led to outbreaks of water-borne diseases such as infectious hepatitis and typhoid, and is silting the bay by 81 cm/100 years (Kreimer *et al.*, 1993).

The acute environmental problems that occur within many cities, particularly in the developing world, their underlying reasons, and the scale of the clean-up task faced by urban authorities are well summarized in the case of Manila Metro, capital of the Philippines. A 1990 population of 8 million had risen to 10.7 million by 2005. All the city's rivers are biologically dead. Each day, 2000 tonnes of solid waste is left uncollected, to be burnt, thrown into waterways or to moulder on the ground. Much of the garbage collected is dumped on 'Smokey Mountain', a 23 ha open tip, which represents a severe health hazard to the 20 000 people who reside on its fringes and earn a living by scavenging from the dump (Jimenez and Velasquez, 1989).

About 65 per cent of the country's 1500 recognized industrial enterprises are located in the Manila Metro area, and only one-third to one-half of them are thought to comply with minimal air and water pollution emission standards. One million vehicles, more than half the country's total, operate in the Manila Metro area. Just half of these vehicles are thought to meet even minimal emission standards. The annual cost to the economy due to congestion alone is estimated to be more than US\$50 million, which is low by the standards of other Asian capitals, while the economic burden of air pollution may be an order of magnitude higher (Table 10.1).

TABLE 10.1 Some estimates of the annual cost of congestion and air pollution in selected Asian cities

| City | Cost (US$ million/year) | |
	Congestion	Air pollution
Bangkok Metropolitan Area (1989)	272	380–580
Bangkok Metropolitan Region (1993)	400	1300–3100
Seoul	154	–
Manila	51	–
Jakarta	68	400–800

Source: after Brandon and Ramankutty (1993).

The basic cause of Manila Metro's severe environmental problems is that more than 10 million people are using infrastructure, much of which dates from the US colonial period, estimated to be adequate for about 2 million people, at most. A large proportion of the solid and liquid wastes are simply inaccessible for collection by virtually any means due to the density of squatter settlements, inappropriate collection systems and the simple lack of services such as septic tank desludging. The problems of physical infrastructure are exacerbated by the government's inability to stop polluters, largely a function of serious understaffing at the metropolitan regulation agency (World Bank, 1989).

TRANSFORMATION OF NATURE

The growth of cities inevitably occurs at the expense of the natural environment. This modification of nature for urban development takes many forms, affecting the lithosphere, biosphere, hydrosphere and atmosphere. Often deliberate, sometimes inadvertent, these alterations range from the total and dramatic transformation of a landscape to the subtle, partial change in the behaviour of an animal. Overall, cities represent such a dramatic transformation of nature that effectively they can be treated as a type of physical environment in their own right. The scale of ecological change can be illustrated by the growth of a relatively small and new city: Singapore. In 1819 the island of Singapore was almost entirely covered in primary forest, but most of the trees had been removed by the end of the nineteenth century to make way for the cultivation of cash crops. Since the 1930s, agricultural land has gradually been replaced by the spread of the urban area, which occupied about 50 per cent of the island by the beginning of the twenty-first century, with another 45 per cent of the land area modified in other ways for human use.

Singapore's two centuries of ecological transformation have involved signifi-cant losses of the island's original biota (Corlett, 1992; Brook *et al.*, 2003). Local extinctions of a wide range of terrestrial and freshwater species have been recorded, but since the first reliable species records were made only in the 1870s, it is likely that many other, unrecorded species have also disappeared.

Less than 100 ha of primary rain forest survives, while a further 1600 ha is covered in tall secondary forest (Corlett, 1992), and most of these remaining forest fragments now lie within nature reserves. In 2003 these protected areas constituted 4.8 per cent of the national land area, which has itself been enlarged through a programme of land reclamation.

A concerted effort to expand the country's terri-tory around its coastline for residential, commercial and industrial use followed independence in 1959, although the history of reclamation in Singapore dates back to the late nineteenth century. Singapore's national land area grew by about 100 km², an increase of more than 15 per cent, in the last four decades of the twentieth century (Table 10.2).

This programme of land reclamation has occurred at the expense of adjacent coastal ecology, while remaining marine ecosystems, including coral reefs (Dikou and van Woesik, 2006), have been subjected to persistent disturbance in the form of increased sediment loads from the reclamation and dredging activities, as well as shipping, oil-related industries, recreation and the dumping of urban wastes.

Year	Total land area (km²)
1966	581.5
1970	586.4
1975	596.8
1980	617.8
1985	620.5
1990	633.0
1995	647.5
2000	682.7
2005	699.4

Source: Yearbook of Statistics Singapore, various years.

TABLE 10.2 The increase in Singapore's land area due to reclamation since the 1960s

SURFACE WATER RESOURCES

Urbanization can result in numerous impacts on waterways by altering their hydrology, affecting stream morphology, water quality and the availability of aquatic habitats (Table 10.3), effects that are often continuous and synergistic. In hydrological terms, urban areas are typified by 'flashy' discharge regimes caused by the increased area of impervious surfaces such as tarmac and concrete, and networks of storm drains and sewers. The timelag between rainfall and peak dis-charge of a river is decreased and the peak discharge itself is increased as a result of these impervious surfaces, which has a significant impact on the volume, fre-quency and timing of floods. Many urban rivers have been subject to structural measures to reduce the flood hazard, such as channel straightening and channel-ization, the building of levees and the stabilization of banks (see Chapter 21).

One of the most important environmental issues that stems from urban modi-fications to the hydrological cycle is that of poor water quality. Runoff from developing urban areas is usually choked with sediment during construction phases, when soil surfaces are stripped of vegetation, and a finished urban zone greatly increases runoff. This drastically modified urban drainage network feeds large amounts of urban waste products into rivers and ultimately into oceans.

Many rivers that flow through urban areas are biologically dead, thanks to heavy pollution. Hardoy *et al.* (1992: 73) sum up the state of urban rivers in developing countries as follows: 'Most rivers in Third World cities are literally large open sewers.' They go on to point out that of India's 3119 towns and cities, only 209 have partial sewage treatment facilities and just 8 have full facilities. India's Jamuna River, for example, contains 7500 coliform organisms per 100 ml of water on entering New Delhi, a figure that rises to 24 million coliform organisms per 100 ml after flowing through the city. For comparison, the World Health Organization (WHO) guidelines for such microbiological pollution are 10 coliform organisms per 100 ml for drinking water and 1000 per 100 ml for irrigation purposes. Industrial effluents combine with this domestic source of riverine pollution to make urban rivers the most polluted freshwater sources on Earth.

All the rivers flowing through Jakarta, Indonesia, are heavily polluted from numerous, mostly untreated, discharge sources: household drains and ditches, overflows and leaks from septic tanks, commercial buildings and industries. Water-related diseases such as typhoid, diarrhoea and cholera increase in frequency downstream across the metropolitan area (Hardoy *et al.*, 1992). Untreated sewage and discharge from the 20 000 classified water-polluting industries that feed into Bangkok's canal system have created a distinct sag in the dissolved oxygen profile of the Chao Phraya where the canals feed the river (Phantumvanit and Liengcharernsit, 1989). Although the example of the Thames at London (see Fig. 8.4) shows how such near-anaerobic river conditions can be improved, neither the money nor the political will are currently as forthcoming in Thailand.

The local hydrological impact of the Saudi capital, Riyadh, provides a very contrasting example to the depressing catalogue of riverine disaster areas typically associated with large, rapidly growing cities. Discharge of Riyadh's wastewater feeds the Riyadh River, which scarcely existed 20 years ago, but now flows throughout the year down what was the seasonal Wadi Hanifa. The water, which is originally derived from desalinated Gulf sea water, is partially treated before being released to flow down the steep-sided wadi and enter open countryside, eventually disappearing 70 km from Riyadh. The new flow has created an attractive valley lined by tamarisk trees and phragmites, which is becoming an important recreational site for Riyadh's 4.9 million population. Beyond the wadi, significant irrigated agriculture has grown up, drawing on the groundwater

Change in stream characteristics	Effects
Hydrology	Increased magnitude and frequency of severe floods
	Increased annual volume of surface runoff
	Increased steam velocities
	Decreased dry weather baseflow
Morphology	Channel widening and down cutting
	Increased erosion of banks
	Stream enclosure or channelization
Habitat and ecology	Changes in diversity of aquatic insects
	Changes in diversity and abundance of fish
	Destruction of wetlands, riparian buffers and springs
Water quality	Massive sediment pulses
	Increased pollutant washoff
	Nutrient enrichment
	Bacterial contamination
	Increased organic carbon loads
	Higher levels of toxics, trace metals, hydrocarbons
	Increased water temperature
	Trash/debris jams

Source: after Baer and Pringle (2000).

TABLE 10.3 Major impacts of urbanization on waterways

around the river. This unique new feature is, however, under some threat from needs to further recycle the much-needed water resource (Meynell, 1993).

Indeed, the quantity of water available is another critical environmental issue for many cities, as the situation in Tehran mentioned above indicates. Nearly half of the 640 major cities in China face water shortages, with 100 experiencing severe scarcities. The quantity and quality of water resources are related, of course, and severe pollution of many urban stretches of rivers in China reduces the options for their use. Testing of 135 urban river sections in 1994 found 54 to be of such low quality that the water was deemed unsuitable even for industrial or agricultural use (NEPA, 1997).

Different types of environmental problem are encountered in permafrost areas where surface water and soil moisture is frozen for much, and in some places all, of the year. Frozen rivers and lakes mean that many of the uses such water bodies are commonly put to at more equable latitudes, such as sewage and other waste disposal, are not always available. The low temperatures characteristic of such regions also mean that biological degradation of wastes proceeds at much slower rates than elsewhere. Hence the impacts of pollution in permafrost areas tend to be more long-lasting than in other environments.

The nature of the permafrost environment also presents numerous environmental challenges to the construction and operation of settlements – challenges that have been encountered in urban developments associated with the exploitation of hydrocarbons and other resources in Alaska, northern Canada and northern Russia. Disturbance of the permafrost thermal equilibrium during construction can cause the development of thermokarst (irregular, hummocky ground). The heaving and subsidence caused can disrupt building foundations and damage pipelines, roads, railtracks and airstrips. Terrain evaluation prior to development is now an important procedure in the development of these zones, following expensive past mistakes. Four main engineering responses to such problems have been developed: permafrost can be neglected, eliminated or preserved, or structures can be designed to take expected movements into account (Johnston, 1981). Preservation of the thermal equilibrium is achieved in numerous ways, such as by insulating the permafrost with vegetation mats or gravel blankets, and ventilating the underside of structures that generate heat (e.g. buildings and pipelines; see Fig. 10.2).

GROUNDWATER

The water needs of urban population and industry are often supplemented by pumping from groundwater, and pollution of this source is another problem of increasing concern in many large cities. Seepage from the improper use and disposal of heavy metals, synthetic chemicals and other hazardous wastes such as sewage, is a principal origin of groundwater pollution. Some of the major pollutants involved in a selection of cities are shown in Table 10.4. The quantity of such compounds reaching groundwater from waste dumps in Latin America, for example, is thought to be doubling every 15 years (World Bank, 1992a). A serious threat to groundwater quality in Bermuda is posed by those parts of the urban area without sewage systems. Unsewered sanitation provisions, consisting

Figure 10.2 Buildings that disturb the thermal equilibrium of permafrost can lead to heaving and subsidence, as seen on the left. One solution is to raise buildings and pipelines up above the ground surface on stilts, so ventilating heat-generating structures (right). Both photographs were taken in Yakutsk, eastern Siberia.

of septic tanks and pit latrines, leak bacteria and nitrogen compounds from excreta. High concentrations of nitrates in groundwater are closely correlated with population density in unsewered areas of Bermuda (Thomson and Foster, 1986). Another regular source of contamination in snow-belt regions of Europe and North America is de-icing agents, usually sodium chloride, applied to roads. Salts washed away from urban highways accumulate in soils as well as groundwater (Howard and Haynes, 1993). Contamination of groundwater beneath any city is a serious long-term issue since aquifers do not have the self-cleansing capacity of rivers and, once polluted, are difficult and costly to clean.

A frequent outcome of overusing groundwater is a lowering of water-table levels and consequent ground subsidence, an issue confronted by many urban areas (Table 10.5). Mexico City is one of the most dramatic examples where use of subterranean aquifers for 100 years and more has caused subsidence in excess of 8 m in some central areas, greatly increasing the flood hazard in the city and threatening the stability of some older buildings, notably the sixteenth-century cathedral. The rate of surface lowering in Mexico City has varied since 1900, accelerating from 30 mm/year up until 1920 to peak at a remarkable 260 mm/year

City/region	Country	Major pollutants
Merida	Mexico	Bacteria
Milwaukee	USA	Cl, SO_4, bacteria
Birmingham	UK	Majors, metals, B, P, Si, CN, organics
Narbonne	France	SO_4, NO_3
Cairo	Egypt	NO_3, majors, metals
Bermuda	Bermuda	Micro-organisms, Cl, NO_3

Source: after Lerner and Tellam (1993: 324, Table 1).

TABLE 10.4 Some examples of urban groundwater pollution

in the early 1950s. Since groundwater pumping was banned in downtown Mexico City in the 1960s, the rate in central parts of the city has slowed to less than 100 mm/year, but water is still drawn from more recent wells sunk on the outskirts of town in the late 1970s and early 1980s, and subsidence at some sites near the newer wells has exceeded 300 mm/year (Ovando-Shelley *et al.*, 2007).

TABLE 10.5 Some examples of subsidence due to groundwater extraction in urban areas

City	Country	Period	Total subsidence (m)	Subsidence rate (mm/yr)
Taipai	Taiwan	1970–2000	2.5	100
Osaka	Japan	1935–70	2.9	80
Mexico City	Mexico	1900–99	>8.0	80
Manila	Philippines	1991–2003	>1.0	50–90
Shanghai	China	1921–65	2.6	60
Tokyo	Japan	1895–1970	4.4	59
Bangkok	Thailand	1978–2003	1.0	40
Houston	USA	1906–95	>3.0	34
Tianjin	China	1981–2003	0.6	27
Jakarta	Indonesia	1982–99	2.6	9–27
Ravenna	Italy	1897–2002	>1.0	10

Source: Rodolfo and Siringan (2006); Teatini *et al.* (2005); Ovando-Shelley *et al.* (2007); IGES (2006).

Marked episodes of subsidence have also occurred in Japanese cities reflecting phases of economic and industrial growth. The problem was first identified in Tokyo's Koto Ward in the southern part of the Kanto Plain in the decade after 1910 as industrial activity grew after the First World War. Rapid industrial use of groundwater also saw marked subsidence in the early 1940s in Osaka, but the process came to a halt for some years in the late 1940s in both cities following the destruction of industries in the Second World War which greatly reduced the industrial use of groundwater (TMG, 1985; see Fig. 10.3). Renewed industrial activity during the Korean War accelerated the subsidence process once more, but the trend was slowed in the late 1960s with the introduction of pumping regulations, and subsidence has been virtually halted since these regulations were strengthened in 1972, although an intense drought in 1994 saw a fresh intensification of subsidence in areas such as the northern part of the Kanto Plain.

In other coastal cities, depletion of aquifers has created problems of seawater intrusion. Israel's coastal aquifer, which extends 120 km along the Mediterranean coast, has been heavily exploited for half a century. Overpumping of groundwater in the Tel Aviv urban area depleted groundwater levels to below sea level over an area of 60 km^2 in the 1950s, requiring a programme of freshwater injection along a line

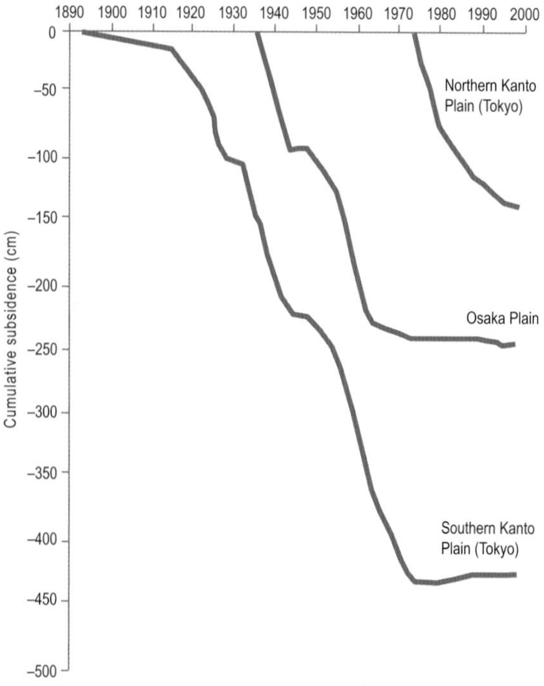

Figure 10.3 Ground subsidence in Tokyo and Osaka (after www.env.go.jp/en/water/ accessed June 2007).

	Carbon dioxide (CO_2)	Methane (CH_4)	Nitrous oxide (N_2O)	Chlorofluroro-carbons (CFCs)	Tropospheric ozone (O_3)	Water vapour (H_2O)
Greenhouse role	Heating	Heating	Heating	Heating	Heating	Heats in air; cools in clouds
Effect on stratospheric ozone layer	Can increase or decrease	Can increase or decrease	Can increase or decrease	Decrease	None	Decrease
Principal natural sources sources	Balanced in nature	Wetlands	Soils; tropical forests	None	Hydrocarbons	Evapo-transpiration
Principal anthropogenic sources	Fossil fuels; deforestation	Rice culture; cattle; fossil fuels; biomass burning	Fertiliser; land-use conversion	Refrigerants; aerosols; industrial processes	Hydrocarbons (with NOx) biomass burning	Land conversion; irrigation
Atmospheric lifetime	50–200 years	10 years	150 years	60–100 years	Weeks to months	Days
Pre-industrial concentration (1750–1800) at surface (ppb)	278 000	715	270	0	10	Unknown
Present atmospheric concentration in parts per billion (ppb) by volume at surface	379 000	1774	319	CFC-11: 0.25 CFC-12: 0.54 CFC-113: 0.08	20–40*	3000–6000 in stratosphere
Present annual rate of increase	0.5%	0.9%	0.3%	4%	0.5–2.0%	Unknown
Global warming potential	1	11	270	3400–7100	–	–
Relative contribution to the anthropogenic greenhouse effect	60%	15%	5%	12%	8%	Unknown

*Northern hemisphere
Source: after Earthquest (1991)

TABLE 11.3 Atmospheric trace gases that are significant to global climatic change

The effectiveness of these gases in causing climatic change is assessed in terms of their so-called radiative forcing, a measure of how the energy balance in the Earth–atmosphere system is influenced when factors that affect climate are changed. The contributions to radiative forcing from the key greenhouse gases and other important factors are indicated in Figure 11.2 which shows the total forcing relative to the start of the industrial era, which is put at 1750. When radiative forcing from a factor is positive, the energy of the Earth–atmosphere system ultimately increases, leading to warming. A negative radiative forcing, by contrast, means the energy will ultimately decrease, leading to a cooling of the system. As Figure 11.2 indicates, the only increase in natural forcing of any significance between 1750 and 2005 occurred in solar radiation. Human activities are considered to have had much greater influence and although some are thought to have contributed to global cooling since 1750, these have been outweighed by other actions that have produced a net global warming effect.

Most interest has focused on carbon dioxide as the most important greenhouse gas to have been increased by human action since it has the greatest radiative forcing. Atmospheric concentrations of carbon dioxide have risen by 25 per cent over the last 100 years, with about half of this increase occurring in

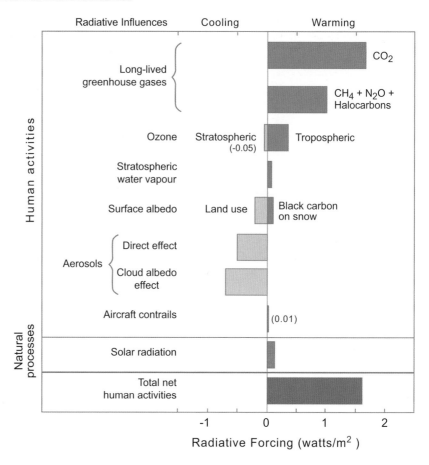

Figure 11.2 Principal causes of global warming since 1750 (after Forster *et al.*, 2007, Fig. 2.20).

the past 25 years. The burning of fossil fuels is the most significant source of human additions to atmospheric carbon dioxide (Fig. 11.3), while cement manufacture and land use changes such as deforestation and biomass burning are also important. Global carbon dioxide emissions from fossil fuel combustion and cement manufacture are responsible for more than 75 per cent of the increase in atmospheric carbon dioxide concentration since pre-industrial times. North America and Europe are by far the largest sources of these industrial emissions. Until the mid twentieth century most deforestation also occurred in temperate latitudes, but more recently a greater carbon dioxide contribution has come from deforestation in tropical regions. Estimates of the carbon dioxide due to forest conversion vary because of the problems of assessing deforestation rates in the tropics (see Chapter 4).

Figure 11.3 Coal-fired power stations like this one at Cottam in central England are major contributors to the human-induced increase in global atmospheric carbon dioxide concentrations.

The rapid rise in the atmospheric concentration of methane, which is today more than double its pre-industrial concentration, is linked to both industrialization and increases in world food supply. Estimates of the global methane budget indicate that methane emissions associated with human activity (produced by anaerobic bacteria in the standing waters of paddy fields and the guts of grazing livestock by so-called enteric fermentation, plus biomass burning and waste) exceed the total natural production, an output dominated by rotting vegetation in wetlands. Like carbon dioxide emissions, industrial sources of methane also contain an important fossil fuel element.

CFCs and other halocarbons are compounds that do not occur naturally. Their development, which dates from the 1930s, was for use as aerosol propellants, foam-blowing agents and refrigerants, and their release into the atmosphere has been inadvertent. Although national regulations on the use of CFCs in aerosol sprays during a time of economic recession in the developed world led to a fall in CFC emissions in the late 1970s and early 1980s, emissions climbed again subsequently as economies improved. While aerosol propellants accounted for almost 70 per cent of the market for CFCs in the mid 1970s, by the late 1980s refrigerants and foam-blowing agents accounted for 60 per cent of the market (McFarland, 1989). Concentrations of these compounds are far lower than those of other greenhouse gases, but the greenhouse warming properties of CFCs are several thousand times more effective than carbon dioxide. Production of eight halocarbons, including the most abundant CFC-11 and CFC-12, has been severely curtailed by the Montreal Protocol adopted in 1987 (see below), and the radiative forcing of stratospheric concentrations of chlorine (the CFC breakdown product that actually destroys ozone) peaked in 2003.

Further indication of the relative importance of human influence on the atmospheric concentrations of greenhouse gases can be gauged from the fact that the contemporary concentrations of the two gases with greatest radiative forcing, carbon dioxide and methane, are both very likely to be much higher than at any time in at least the last 650 000 years. The recent rate of change in concentration is dramatic and unprecedented; increases in carbon dioxide never exceeded 30 ppm in 1000 years, yet in the most recent times carbon dioxide has risen by 30 ppm in less than 20 years (Forster *et al.*, 2007).

GLOBAL WARMING

The theory relating increased atmospheric concentrations of greenhouse gases and global warming is strongly supported by proxy evidence from ice-core data, which show that natural fluctuations in the atmospheric concentrations of greenhouse gases through geological time have oscillated in close harmony with global temperature changes over the past 150 000 years, indicating that the two are almost certainly related (Lorius *et al.*, 1990). Evidence gleaned from a range of other proxy indicators suggests that the twentieth century was the warmest of the last millennium (Jones *et al.*, 1998), and the changes in global mean temperature measured instrumentally since the mid nineteenth century are shown in Figure 11.4, which indicates that, overall, the planet has warmed at the surface by about 0.74 °C over the past 100 years – between 1906 and 2005 (Trenberth *et al.*, 2007). Although it is possible that this recent warming trend reflects the end of the Little Ice Age (see Fig. 11.1b), most researchers think that the trend shown in Figure 11.4 is very unlikely to be entirely natural in origin. In part, it reflects the operation of an enhanced greenhouse effect due to human activities, most importantly pollution of the atmosphere.

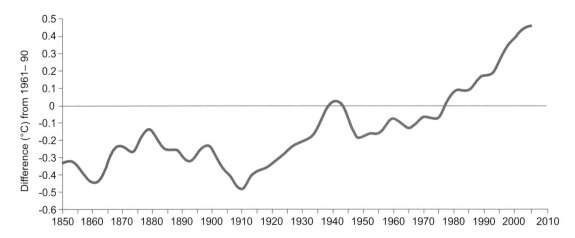

Indeed, in recent years, atmospheric scientists have become increasingly confident about the contribution of humans to this contemporary warming. The Intergovernmental Panel on Climate Change (IPCC), an international body of scientists set up especially to look into the issue of global warming, concluded in their first assessment that the observed increase in global temperatures could be due to human influence, but could equally be largely due to natural variability. This first assessment was published in 1990. By the time of the IPCC's fourth assessment, published in 2007, the panel's statements were much more decisive. By this time, the increase in anthropogenic greenhouse gas concentrations was considered to be very likely to have caused the observed increase in globally averaged temperatures since the mid twentieth century. Table 11.4 traces the IPCC's increasing confidence in its assessment of the human contribution to contemporary global warming, a confidence based on longer and improved records and our better scientific understanding of the processes involved in global temperature change.

TABLE 11.4 The growing confidence in the IPCC's assessment of the human contribution to global warming

IPCC assessment	Attribution of cause
First (1990)	'The size of this warming is broadly consistent with prediction of climate models, but it is also of the same magnitude as natural climate variability. Thus the observed increase could be largely due to this natural variability'
Second (1995)	'The balance of evidence suggests a discernible human influence on the climate'
Third (2001)	'Most of the observed warming over the last 50 years is likely to have been due to the increase in greenhouse gas concentrations'
Fourth (2007)	'Most of the observed increase in globally averaged temperatures since the mid-20th century is very likely due to the observed increase in anthropogenic greenhouse gas concentrations'

Nevertheless, the warming trend over the past 14 or 15 decades has not been continuous through either time or space. Two periods of relatively rapid warming (from 1910 to the 1940s, and again from the mid 1970s to the present) contrast preceding

floods are also likely to have significant consequences for food production beyond the impacts due to changes in average conditions, creating the possibility for unexpected changes in yields (Easterling *et al.*, 2007).

Relatively small changes in climate can also influence the availability of fresh water. Consequent problems would be particularly acute in semi-arid regions and more humid areas where demand or pollution has already created water scarcity (Fig. 11.5). The Mediterranean Basin is one example here (Smith, 1997). Decreasing trends in precipitation totals have been identified in western-central parts of the basin in recent decades, as well as marked changes in seasonality. A clear tendency for rainfall to be concentrated into a shorter period of the year has been noted in the Alentejo region of southern Portugal, with the proportion of annual precipitation falling in autumn and winter increasing at the expense of spring totals. Springtime rainfall has also been decreasing in southern Spain (Corte-Real *et al.*, 1998). In north-eastern Spain, an increase in precipitation in winter and summer has been recorded since the 1920s, along with a generally higher number of extreme events separated by longer dry periods (Ramos and Martínez-Casasnovas, 2006). These authors note the changes in rainfall distribution have had negative effects on the availability of water for crops and have contributed to accelerated erosion in the area. Such changes in the seasonality and intensity of rainfall may also be expected to have an impact on the flood regimes of rivers. Work on a number of the world's large drainage basins has already identified a significant rising trend in the risk of great floods (those with a return period of 100 years) in the twentieth century (Milly *et al.*, 2002).

Figure 11.5 A hoarding urging the residents of Praia, capital of Cabo Verde, to conserve water. Supplies are limited on all of the country's islands due to their arid climate and are likely to become less reliable with the effects of global warming.

High latitudes have long been recognized as areas where global greenhouse warming is likely to be greatest and surface air temperatures north of 65 °N have increased at almost twice the global average rate in the past 100 years (Trenberth *et al.*, 2007). Significant changes are projected in glacial and periglacial processes, affecting glacier ice, ground ice and sea-ice, which, in turn, would affect vegetation, wildlife habitats, and human structures and facilities. A prediction of the pattern of changes around the Arctic Circle in northern Canada is shown in Figure 11.6. There is a strong possibility that the Arctic Ocean's ice cover will disappear, facilitating marine transport and oil and gas exploration on the one hand, but also increasing the dangers from icebergs. In fact, the rate of decline in Arctic sea-ice since the 1950s has been faster than most GCMs predict, averaging nearly 8 per cent per decade for September, the end of the melt season, over the 1953–2006 period (Stroeve *et al.*, 2007). The disappearance of sea-ice has feedback implications because the ice has a high albedo, reflecting a large proportion of sunlight back into space and so providing a cooling effect. The darker areas of open water, which are expanding, absorb greater amounts of solar radiation and increase temperatures. This positive feedback contributes to the increasingly rapid loss of ice.

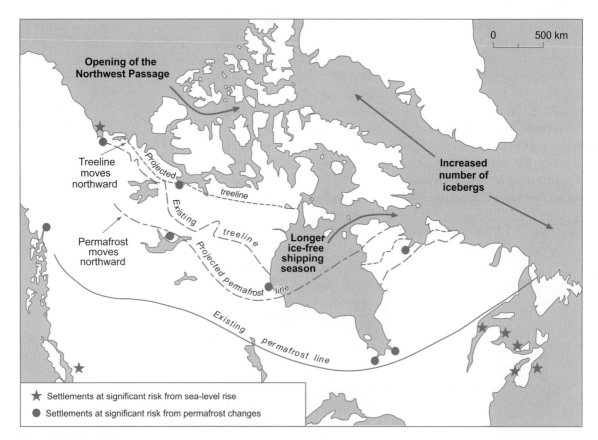

Figure 11.6 Projected changes in northern Canada following climate warming (after Slaymaker and French, 1993; Nelson *et al.*, 2002).

On land, the northward movement of the permafrost line envisaged in Figure 11.6 would have many implications for roads, buildings and pipelines now constructed on permafrost, necessitating reinforcement, and new engineering design and construction techniques. A serious feedback aspect of high-latitude permafrost melting is the consequent release of methane, a greenhouse gas, although the net outcome of such changes is uncertain given that other trends will offset this methane release at least to some extent. For example, the higher temperatures, longer growing seasons and northward movement of vegetation are all likely to increase the capture and storage of carbon by photosynthesis. Twentieth-century warming in Alaska has already been accompanied by a widespread advance of boreal forest trees into tundra ecosystems where analysis of satellite images indicates that the length of the growing season has increased by three days per decade (Hinzman *et al.*, 2005).

The warming trend documented for the Antarctic Peninsula since the 1940s has already affected the frequency of extensive sea-ice in the Southern Ocean. Cold winters with extensive sea-ice cover occurred on average in four out of five years in the middle of the last century, but have decreased to just one or two years in five since the mid 1970s. One function of this trend appears to be a decline in the abundance of krill in the Southern Ocean (Loeb *et al.*, 1997; see also Chapter 6). Warmer air temperatures are also having a predictable effect on glaciers – melting and retreat – in Antarctica and most other parts of the world. Glaciers are receding particularly fast in the Himalaya (Fig. 11.7), generating worries about long-term water supplies for hundreds of millions of people in China, India and Nepal who rely on rivers fed by glacial meltwater.

Another soil-related positive feedback appears to be under way in mid latitudes. A study of soils in England and Wales from more than 5600 sample sites found that the carbon content had declined by an average of 13 million tonnes a year over the

Figure 11.7 Himalayan glacier in retreat in Nepal's Lang Tang national park. Many glaciers in Asia and elsewhere have been retreating over the last 100 years or so, probably due to global warming.

period 1978–2003 (Bellamy *et al.*, 2005). Since the carbon stored in the soil appeared to be released regardless of how the soil was used, the authors concluded that the main cause must be climate change, with higher average temperatures over the period having increased the rate at which organic matter decayed and the carbon within it released. The results are particularly worrying since soils were previously thought to act as a 'sink' for increased atmospheric carbon that would absorb more carbon from the atmosphere as carbon dioxide levels increased, acting as a sort of buffer to the effects of global warming. However, this research suggests that much, if not all, of this benefit is offset by enhanced activity in the soil which processes carbon and releases some of it back into the atmosphere.

Numerous effects of global climatic change on geomorphological processes can be expected. These would occur through the direct effects of warming, and as a consequence of related changes in precipitation and temperature regimes, and their impacts on such geomorphologically significant variables as vegetation. In many semi-arid areas, for example, soil moisture is predicted to be reduced by larger losses to evapotranspiration and decreased summer runoff, and increased rates of soil erosion by wind can be expected as a consequence. Modelling studies of southern Africa by Thomas *et al.* (2005) suggest that during the present century most of the sand dunes in the Kalahari Desert, which have been immobile throughout the Holocene, will become reactivated and mobile due to the combined effects of reduced soil moisture, loss of vegetation and increased wind energy. The reappearance of shifting dunes in this area will make all kinds of land use more difficult.

In many parts of the world, dry periods are normally associated with high frequencies of wind erosion and dust storms, and this natural effect has been exacerbated in some cases by human disturbances to vegetation and soil surfaces (Goudie and Middleton, 2006). Many cases of such synergy between climatic change effects and pre-existing human impacts can be predicted and Table 11.7 gives a number of examples. Such synergistic effects may also work to ameliorate environmental problems, however. An assessment of the success of soil conservation measures on the highly erodible loess farmlands of the middle reaches of the Huang Ho River in China found that sediment yields in one of the Huang Ho's tributaries had declined by 74 per cent over the period 1957–89 (Zhao *et al.*, 1992). Just half of this reduction was attributed to improvements in soil and water conservation measures, while the other 50 per cent was a reflection of the shift to a drier climate.

TABLE 11.7 Examples of synergy between climate change and more direct human impacts on geomorphology

Phenomenon	Current human abuse	Potential global warming impact
Groundwater reduction in Great Plains, USA	Overpumping by centre pivot irrigation	Increased moisture deficit
Desiccation of Aral Sea and associated dust storms	Excessive irrigation offtake and inter-basin water transfers	Increased moisture deficit
Permafrost subsidence	Vegetation and soil removal, urban heating, etc.	Warming
Quaternary dune reactivation	Intensive grazing and agricultural activities	Further vegetation depletion
Coastal retreat	Sediment starvation by dam construction and coastal engineering structures	Sea-level rise and shifts in storm tracks
Coral reef stress	Pollution, siltation, mining, overexploitation	Overheating, more hurricanes, fast sea-level rise
Coastal flooding	Groundwater and hydrocarbon mining	Sea-level rise and more frequent storms

Source: after Goudie (1993b).

Synergies between climate change and other human effects are also likely to occur in many other areas of the physical environment. Higher temperatures mean that ground-level ozone forms faster and high atmospheric concentrations of ozone persist for longer. Global warming is thus likely to accelerate the photochemical reaction rates among chemical pollutants in the atmosphere, increasing pollution in urban areas.

The implications of a warmer world for marine environments are numerous. A basic chemical change that will have far-reaching knock-on effects is the acidification of the oceans, which is occurring because some of the CO_2 emitted to

the most heavily polluted areas during the 1930s, while rates in present-day Britain for plain carbon steels range from 20 to 100 mm/year (Lloyd and Butlin, 1992). Sulphur corrosion was implicated in the collapse of a steel highway bridge between West Virginia and Ohio in the USA in 1967, a disaster that killed 46 people (Gerhard and Haynie, 1974).

Limestone, marble, and dolomitic and calcareous sandstones are vulnerable to SO_2 pollution since in the presence of moisture, dry deposition of SO_2 reacts with calcium carbonate to form gypsum, which is soluble and easily washed off the stone surface. Alternatively, layers of gypsum can blister and flake off when subjected to temperature variations. Soluble sulphates of chloride and other salts can also crystallize and expand inside stonework, causing cracking and crumbling of the stone surface. Such processes have caused particularly noticeable damage to statues in many urban and industrial areas (Fig. 12.7) and some of the world's most important architectural monuments have been adversely affected, including the Parthenon in Athens and the Taj Mahal in Agra. Limestone monuments outside towns or cities have also been damaged, such as the El Tajin archaeological zone in Veracruz, Mexico (Bravo *et al.*, 2006). The results of one study, in which weathering rates were measured on more than 8000 century-old marble tombstones across North America, suggest that SO_2 pollution was probably responsible for more deterioration than other weathering processes (Meierding, 1993). Upper stone faces in heavily polluted localities with mean SO_2 concentrations of 350 g/m^3 receded at a mean rate >3 mm/100 years due to granular disintegration induced by the growth of gypsum crystals between calcite grains.

Figure 12.7 Acid rain damage to stonework in Oxford, England.

Although modern glass is little affected by SO_2, medieval glass, which contains less silica and higher levels of potassium and calcium, can be weakened by hygroscopic sulphates, which remove ions of potassium, calcium and sodium. Paper is affected by pollutants of SO_2 and NO_2 because these are absorbed, making the paper brittle, and fabrics such as cotton and linen respond to SO_2 in a similar way. Damage to materials such as nylon and rubber have also been attributed to SO_2 as well as low-level ozone.

COMBATING THE EFFECTS OF ACID RAIN

Working on the premise that prevention is better than cure, the most obvious method for combating the effects of acid rain is to reduce the emissions of sulphur and nitrogen oxides from polluting sources. There are numerous pathways that can be taken towards achieving this aim. Reducing emissions from power stations can be approached in a number of ways. Energy conservation is the simplest and arguably the most sensible method of reducing emissions from the burning of fossil fuel, while increasing the use of renewable energy sources also

Figure 12.8 Solar-powered water heaters on rooftops in Athens help to reduce acid rain precursors from the burning of fossil fuels in a city where acid rain threatens human health and numerous ancient monuments.

helps (Fig. 12.8), although such alternatives also come with an environmental price (see Chapter 18). Alternatively, there are many existing technologies available that can reduce acid rain pollutant emissions from power stations and other industrial sources. These include:

- fuel desulphurization, which removes sulphur from coal before burning
- fluidized bed technology, which reduces the SO_2 emissions during combustion
- flue gas desulphurization, which involves removing sulphur gases before they are released into the air.

Similar approaches can also be taken to reduce emissions of NOx from power stations, while catalytic converters and lean-burn engines have been applied to NOx emissions from motor vehicle engines (see Chapter 16). Some of these technocentric approaches can simply transform one type of environmental problem into another, however. Flue gas desulphurization involves using a scrubber to remove SO_2, but the resulting by-products are often disposed of in landfill sites. More sustainable uses of the by-products are being developed, such as that described on page 389 for rehabilitating areas covered by minespoil.

Political aspects of emissions reduction

Many of these actions are costly in economic terms, however, and the uncertainties that have surrounded some of the suggested effects of acid rain have been the reason for some governments' unwillingness to initiate expensive acid rain reduction programmes.

Britain has been a case in point here. The Scandinavian countries were successful in persuading the UN Economic Commission for Europe to set up a Convention on Long-Range Transboundary Air Pollution (CLRTAP), which was formally signed by 35 states in 1979. Its members include all European countries, the USA and Canada. However, when the Convention's protocol on sulphur emissions reduction was adopted in 1985 – the 30% Club, so-called because the members agreed that their sulphur emissions in 1993 would be at least 30 per cent less than their 1980 levels – Britain, among others, refused to join. The case is an interesting one for the light it shines upon the interactions between politics and science.

In the early 1980s Britain became increasingly isolated politically in its reticence to take the issue of transboundary transportation of acid rain pollutants seriously enough to take preventative action. Initially, an influential ally was found in the former West Germany, but domestic pressure turned the Germans in favour of sulphur reductions following widespread fears over the deteriorating health of German forests: so-called *Waldsterben*. While other European countries, particularly those convinced that their ecology was being adversely affected by pollution from their neighbours, were clamouring for concerted action, Britain's response was to call for more research (Dudley, 1986). The British government's logic was contrary to the precautionary principle but was based on the fact that action to reduce emissions would cost a great deal of money, and therefore they had to be convinced that the money was being spent correctly. Evidence that was convincing enough for some countries was not convincing enough for others. Other countries that refused to join the 30% Club, such as Spain and Poland, also did so primarily for economic reasons. In 1986, however, Britain did concede the need to reduce SO_2 emissions and began to introduce flue gas desulphurization equipment to a number of large British power stations.

Irrespective of the political tensions engendered by the 30% Club, its approach had inadequacies, both absolutely and relatively. In absolute terms, many believed that reductions needed to be much greater to make any significant improvements, while it was also recognized that reductions needed to be more specifically targeted at the large emitters and at the worst-affected environments. Hence, the critical load idea was adopted for the new sulphur emission protocol, signed in Oslo in 1994, to replace the 30% Club. The Oslo Protocol marked a significant milestone in international pollution control since it was the first time that different targets were set for each country. The targets take the form of maximum permissible emissions per target year which are based upon the ability of the environment to withstand pollution. Great Britain committed to an 80 per cent reduction in emissions by the year 2010 from the baseline year of 1980. Germany's commitment is 87 per cent, that of Poland 66 per cent and Russia 40 per cent. The benefits of these reductions are already being felt. While 30 per cent of Norwegian territory received amounts of sulphur that exceeded the critical load in 1985, calculations based on the sulphur protocol indicate that the proportion of the national territory where critical loads will be exceeded will be reduced to about 16 per cent by the year 2010 (Table 12.6).

The goals of the Oslo Protocol have been reinforced and extended since 1999 by the Gothenburg Protocol which aims to mitigate a broader range of pollution issues related to acidification, eutrophication and ground-level ozone. Negotiations in Gothenburg were conducted on the basis of scientific assessments of pollution effects and abatement options, including the economic costs of controlling emissions of the various pollutants.

Year	Area where critical load exceeded (% national land area)
1985	30
1990	25
2010	16

Source: Norwegian Institute for Water Research.

TABLE 12.6 Excess deposits of sulphur in Norway

Some of the largest emitters of sulphur and nitrogen are shown in Table 12.7. This table illustrates the success of several industrialized countries in reducing sulphur dioxide emissions over the period 1980–2000. Decreases have been achieved in many cases through pollution control strategies, energy conservation and fuel switching. Even greater reductions have been achieved in other countries, such as Sweden, where sulphur dioxide emissions have been cut from 491 000 tonnes in 1980 to 52 000 tonnes in 2000, an 88 per cent reduction, by a combination of regulatory measures and the introduction in 1988 of a 'sulphur tax' levied on combustion plants. By 2004 it had fallen further to 47 000 tonnes.

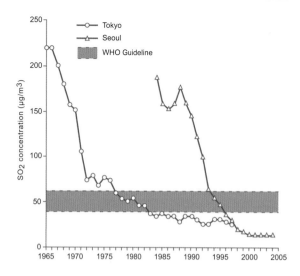

Figure 12.9 Decline of mean annual sulphur dioxide concentrations at Tokyo and Seoul city centres (extended after Dhakal, 2004).

The effect on atmospheric concentrations in many cities in the more developed countries is illustrated by the trends shown for Tokyo and Seoul in Figure 12.9. Worrying trends are illustrated for most of Asia, however, where emissions have more than doubled over the 20-year period.

Recent trends for nitrogen oxides in North America are less encouraging, with little change over the period, but significant decreases have been achieved in much of Europe. China and India increased emissions by half over the decade 1980–90, and although similar data for 1990–2000 are not available, this trend is likely to have continued. Motor vehicles are a major source of nitrogen oxides and larger emissions probably reflect increases in national fleets.

Environmental recovery

Even given the actual and planned reduction in acid rain emissions, the response of affected environments is not necessarily known or guaranteed. There is some evidence for fairly rapid recovery following emissions control, such as that reported for lake fauna downwind of the Sudbury metal smelters in Canada after a 50 per cent reduction in sulphur emissions (Gunn and Keller, 1990), but not all organisms may respond immediately. In many instances there is likely to be a time lag between emissions reduction and a detectable reduction in environmental effects, the so-called memory effect as far as building stone weathering is concerned (Cooke, 1989). Nonetheless, 20 years of micro-erosion meter meas-

TABLE 12.7 Changes in national emissions of sulphur dioxide and nitrogen oxides in selected countries, 1980–2000

Country	Annual emissions (thousand tonnes)			Change 1980–2000 (%)
	1980	1990	2000	
SULPHUR DIOXIDE				
China and centrally planned Asia	7800	13000	18000	131
South and South East Asia	4000	6400	9400	135
USA	23500	21481	16483	–30
Canada	4643	3236	2534	–45
Poland	4100	3210	1511	–63
UK	4880	3754	1165	–76
NITROGEN OXIDES*				
USA	22121	21927	21713	–2
Canada	1959	2104	2058	5
UK	2580	2756	1512	–41
Poland	1229	1280	838	–32

*Note: Emissions for nitrogen oxides are given as nitrogen dioxide equivalents.
Source: UNECE/EMEP emission database at http://webdab.emep.int/accessed August 2002 for all except Asian data from Smith *et al.* (2001).

overextracted groundwater from beneath nearly 20m ha, or one-third of all agricultural land (FAO, 1994). Overpumping of groundwater in coastal locations may result in the contamination of freshwater aquifers by seawater intrusion, as Mistry (1989) describes in the Saurashtra Peninsula in Gujarat, India.

Land subsidence is also commonly associated with irrigated areas where groundwater has been extracted excessively. The resultant problems, which include the flooding of sunken land and damage to infrastructure, can be substantial. Some of the largest land-subsidence rates recorded are in the San Joaquin Valley, California, one of the most intensively farmed agricultural areas in the world. Total subsidence reached 9 m in some areas of the valley by 1970 after nearly half a century of groundwater extraction. Rates of land subsidence tended to decline in the later decades of the twentieth century following the importation of surface water to the valley in the late 1960s. Hence the average rate of surface lowering at benchmark S661 in the Los Banos-Kettleman City area of the valley slowed to 46 mm/yr over the period 1971–95, having averaged 325 mm/yr between 1943 and 1971. The total cumulative land subsidence at this point over the entire 52-year period 1943–95 was 10.2 m (Basagaoglu *et al.*, 1999). About half of the San Joaquin Valley's 1.5 million ha of land under irrigation has experienced subsidence (Zektser 2000).

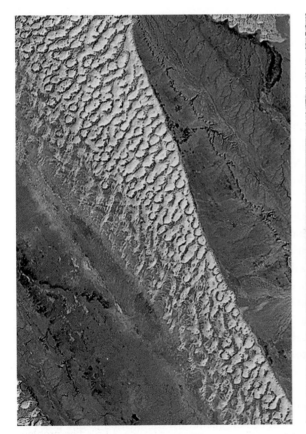 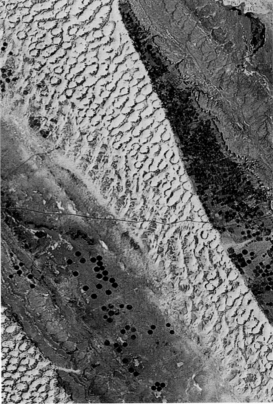

Figure 13.6 The dramatic increase in use of centre-pivot systems to irrigate wheat with water from the Saudi Arabian Minjur aquifer can be seen by comparing these two satellite images of the Tebrak area taken in 1972 and 1986. Bare desert areas in 1972 either side of the sand dune belt running from top left to bottom right are dotted with about 40 distinctive round irrigated areas to the left of the dunes in 1986 and many more to the right. The 1986 image also shows a new highway crossing the dunes just below centre.

An increased incidence of water-associated diseases is another problem often associated with the introduction or extension of irrigation schemes. Amin (1977) reports that the prevalence of schistosomiasis in Sudan's Gezira Project rose from 5 per cent in 1945 to 60 per cent in 1973 (see also page 172). Other detrimental health effects can stem from the excessive use of pesticides on irrigation schemes, as exemplified by central Asian cotton plantations (see below), an example that also illustrates the scale of potential off-site environmental effects on the Aral Sea (see page 156).

AGRICULTURAL PESTS

Losing a portion of a field's crop to pests has been a problem for farmers since people first started cultivating soils. Worldwide, an estimated 67 000 different pest species attack agricultural crops and about 35 per cent of crop production is lost to them each year. Insects cause an estimated 13 per cent of the loss, plant pathogens 12 per cent, and weeds 10 per cent (Pimental, 1991). Hence pests represent a serious problem for farmers and for human society in general.

Pesticides

The use of synthetic chemical sprays to control agricultural pests and diseases dates back to the 1860s when they were used to control Colorado beetle, which damaged potato crops in the USA, and vine mildew in France. Pesticides (which include insecticides, herbicides and fungicides) entered general use in many of the world's agricultural areas along with synthetic fertilizers in the 1950s, following the discovery of DDT in Switzerland in 1939 and 2,4-D in the USA during the Second World War. This development has been a response to an age-old problem but also an attempt to limit the escalation of the pest problems that came about as a result of changing cultivation practices, such as shortened fallow periods, narrow rotation and the replacement of mixed cropping by large-scale monocultures of genetically uniform varieties.

Worldwide, annual sales of pesticides grew from around US$7 billion in the early 1970s to US$25 billion in 1990 (Tolba and El-Kholy, 1992). Most are used in the industrialized countries, but while consumption in these countries has levelled off in recent years, sales to developing countries continue to grow. Most pesticides are used in agriculture, with about 10 per cent used in public health campaigns such as the fight against mosquitoes, which transmit malaria.

One unfortunate aspect of the increasing use of pesticides is the development of resistance to the chemicals. While most individuals of a pest population die on exposure to a pesticide, a few individuals survive by virtue of their genetic make-up and pass on this resistance to future generations. Increasing resistance is often countered by stronger doses of chemicals or more frequent applications, at increasing cost to the farmer, which also speeds up the trend towards resistance, so encouraging the development of new chemicals. Elimination of one pest can also result in the rapid growth of secondary pest populations, however. Widespread applications of DDT in Egypt, for example, to control the American bollworm in cotton plantations, caused a species of whitefly, which

measurements on real fields have concentrated on these important forms, with field workers repeatedly visiting an area to measure rills and gullies, an exercise that can be supplemented by aerial photography.

Measurement of suspended sediment loads in rivers is another commonly used approach, which gives a rough estimate of current erosion on slopes and fields in the catchment area. Not all eroded soil reaches the river, however, and there have been many attempts to estimate 'sediment delivery ratios'. The technique is further hampered by the fact that a proportion of a river's sediment load is eroded from the river's own banks.

A technique used to estimate both erosion and deposition measures the radionuclide caesium-137 present in a soil profile, which can be compared to amounts in nearby undisturbed profiles. The caesium-137, most of which has been released by atmospheric nuclear weapons testing in the 1950s and 1960s, was deposited globally (plus some in Europe and western Asia by the 1986 Chernobyl disaster) and adsorbed by clay minerals in the soil. Once adsorbed, chemical or biological removal of caesium-137 from soil particles is insignificant and it is assumed that only physical processes moving soil particles are involved in caesium-137 transport. Hence caesium-137 has been used as a tracer to provide average rates of soil movement over the medium term (30–50 years) and patterns of erosion and deposition at particular sites by water and, to a lesser extent, by wind.

Field measurements and experiments have also provided data from which general relationships between the factors affecting soil erosion have been derived, and these relationships have been incorporated into models used to predict erosion. The most widely used is the Universal Soil Loss Equation (USLE), developed in the USA to predict soil loss by runoff from US fields east of the Rocky Mountains under particular crops and management systems. The USLE is calculated as:

$$E = R \times K \times L \times S \times C \times P$$

where E is mean annual soil loss, R is a measure of rainfall erosivity, K is a measure of soil erodibility, L is the slope length, S is the slope steepness, C is an index of crop type, and P is a measure of any conservation practices adopted on the field.

The USLE can be adapted for use outside the temperate plains of North America, although it has often been used inappropriately, without such adaptations (Wischmeier, 1976). An equivalent wind erosion equation has also been developed (Woodruff and Siddoway, 1965), and both of these relatively simple models have been further refined to produce more complex computer-run models such as EPIC (Erosion-Productivity Impact Calculator), one of the few erosion models that can be used to predict erosion by both water and wind. Models have also been used to produce soil erosion hazard maps such as that shown in Figure 14.3 for Lesotho, the country with the highest erosion hazard in southern and central Africa thanks to its steep slopes, high rainfall totals, poor soils and average vegetation covers.

Despite the availability of numerous measurement and prediction techniques, the fact remains that there is virtually no reliable soil erosion data for most of the

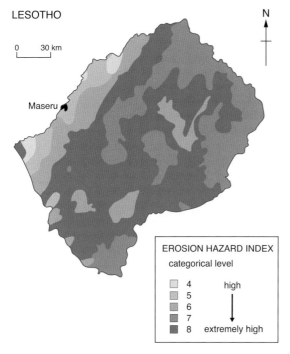

LESOTHO

0   30 km

Maseru

EROSION HAZARD INDEX

categorical level

	4	high
	5	
	6	
	7	
	8	extremely high

Figure 14.3 Erosion hazard map of Lesotho (after Chakela and Stocking, 1988).

world's land surface. An attempt to overcome this deficiency has been made with the Global Assessment of Human-Induced Soil Degradation (GLASOD), which employed more than 250 local soil experts around the world to give their opinion on soil degradation problems to supplement what data are available. The project, carried out by the International Soil Reference and Information Centre in conjunction with the UN Environment Programme, followed a strict methodology by dividing the world's land surface into mapping units corresponding to physiographic zones, and for each unit an assessment was made of water and wind erosion as well as chemical and physical degradation processes. The degree of degradation, its extent and causes were assessed to produce an overall estimate of degradation severity in each unit (Oldeman *et al.*, 1990). Table 14.1 shows the continental areas affected by water and wind erosion.

EFFECTS OF EROSION

The movement of soil and other sediments by erosive forces has a large number of environmental impacts that can affect farmers and many other sectors of society. Many of these effects are consequent upon natural erosion, but are exacerbated in areas where rates are accelerated by human activity. The environmental effects associated with erosion occur due to the three fundamental processes of entrainment, transport and deposition. This three-fold division is used in Table 14.2 to illustrate the hazards posed to human populations by wind erosion, while the following sections are divided into on-site and off-site effects.

TABLE 14.1 GLASOD estimates of land area affected by human-induced soil erosion

| Continent | Area affected in million ha (% total continental area) | |
	Water erosion	Wind erosion
Africa	227.4 (7.7)	186.5 (6.3)
Asia	439.6 (10.3)	222.1 (5.2)
Australasia	82.9 (9.4)	16.4 (1.9)
Europe	114.5 (12.1)	42.2 (4.4)
North America	106.1 (4.8)	39.2 (1.8)
South America	123.2 (7.0)	41.9 (2.4)

Source: Deichmann and Eklundh (1991).

On-site effects

The loss of topsoil changes the physical and chemical nature of an area. Deformation of the terrain due to the uneven displacement of soil can result in rills, gullies, mass movements, hollows, hummocks or dunes. For the farmer, such physical changes can present problems for the use of machinery, and in extreme cases such as gullying, the absolute loss of cultivable land (Fig. 14.4). Deposition of soil may also result in burial of plants and seedlings; loss of soil may expose roots; and sand-blasting by wind-eroded material can both damage plants and break down soil clods, impoverishing soil structure and rendering soil more erodible. Splash erosion can cause compaction and crusting of the soil surface, both of which may hinder germination and the establishment of seedlings, while exposure of hardpans and duricrusts presents a barrier to root penetration.

Erosion has implications for long-term soil productivity through a number of processes. The top layer of the soil profile, the A horizon, is where most biological activity takes place and where most organic material is located. Hence depletion of the A horizon preferentially removes organic material, soil nutrients, including fertilizers and even seeds, and can reduce the capacity of the soil for holding water and nutrients. The subsoil, or B horizons, are much less useful for plant growth.

Some researchers sound a note of caution in directly relating erosion rates to losses in productivity (e.g. Larson *et al.*, 1983), not least because the relationship is highly variable depending upon soil type and crop type, and because crop yields are affected by numerous other factors. These include the amount and timing of rainfall, temperature, pests, diseases and weeds. However, many experiments have shown that as erosion proceeds, crop yields do decline. Figure 14.5 illustrates this for two staple crops in south-west Nigeria for a range of slope angles on the same soil type. Yield declines can be compensated for, of course, by adding fertilizers, assuming the farmer can afford to do so. The additional fertilizer needed to maintain corn yields for an area of the USA is shown in Table 14.3.

Off-site effects

The off-site effects of eroded soil are caused by its transport and deposition. Material carried in strong winds can cause substantial damage to structures such as telegraph poles, fences and larger structures by abrasion. Material transported in dust storms, which can affect very large areas (Fig. 14.6), severely reduces visibility, causing a hazard to transport, and adversely affects radio and satellite communications.

ENTRAINMENT
Soil loss
Nutrient, seed and fertilizer loss
Crop root exposure

TRANSPORT
Sand-blasting of crops
Air pollution
Radio communication problems
Local climatic effects
Transport disruption
Respiratory problems
Disease transmission (human and plants)

DEPOSITION
Nutrient gain (soils, plants and oceans)
Salt deposition and groundwater salinization
Burial of structures
Rainfall acid neutralization
Glacier mass budget alteration
Machinery problems
Reduction of solar power potential
Electrical insulator failure

Source: after Goudie and Middleton (2006).

TABLE 14.2 Some environmental consequences and hazards to human populations caused by wind erosion and dust storms

Change in erosion phase	Additional fertilizer needed (kg/ha)		
	Nitrogen	Phosphate	Potash
Slight to moderate	11	2	7
Moderate to severe	34	1	8

Source: after Rosenberry et al. (1980).

TABLE 14.3 Increase in fertilizer needs for corn as soil erodes in southern Iowa, USA

Figure 14.4 A 15 m deep gully in central Tunisia.

Inhalation of fine particles can aggravate human diseases such as bronchitis and emphysema, and the transport of soil dust contaminated by organisms or toxic chemicals spreads human and plant diseases. An increase in the incidence of meningococcal meningitis in the Sahel zone and Horn of Africa has been associated with airborne desert dust. The annual meningitis epidemics in West Africa, which affect up to 200 000 people between February and May, are closely related in their timing to the Harmattan season when Saharan dust is blown across the region (Sultan *et al.*, 2005). The nutrients attached to soil particles transported by water erosion can cause the eutrophication of water bodies (see Chapters 7 and 8).

The deposition of eroded material can also cause considerable problems for human society. The flood hazard can be increased due to riverbed infilling, and the siltation of reservoirs, harbours and lakes presents hazards to transport and loss of storage capacity in reservoirs. The economic costs thus imposed are often considerable. In Java, the off-site costs due to siltation of irrigation systems and reservoirs and harbour dredging were estimated to be US$58 million in 1987 (Magrath and Arens, 1989). About 25 per cent of the sediment deposited in lakes and reservoirs in the USA is thought to originate from cropland. The resulting damage, which contributes to a 0.22 per cent annual loss in national water storage capacity, has been valued at from US$144 million to US$197 million per year (Crowder, 1987). Deposition of sediment reaching the coastline can adversely affect marine environments used by local populations, including coral reefs and shellfish beds.

Despite the numerous negative aspects of sediment deposition for human society, the positive side of the equation should also be highlighted. Relatively flat, often low-lying areas of deposition provide good, fertile land for agriculture and many other human activities. Flood plains are an obvious example, as are valley bottoms that receive material transported from valley slopes. Wind-deposited dust, or loess, also provides fertile agricultural land – the loess plateau of northern China is the country's most productive wheat-growing area, for example – although it requires careful management because it remains highly erodible. Similarly, evidence is growing that dust deposition may make an important contribution to ecosystem nutrient budgets on land, in lakes and rivers and at sea. Because desert dust can be transported many thousands of kilometres through the atmosphere, these contributions can be far removed from source areas. For example, Saharan dust blown across West Africa in the Harmattan wind is thought to provide key nutrients to the humid tropical rain forests of coastal Ghana, some 2000 km away, but also to the Amazon rain forest at least another 5000 km across the Atlantic Ocean (McTainsh and Strong, 2007).

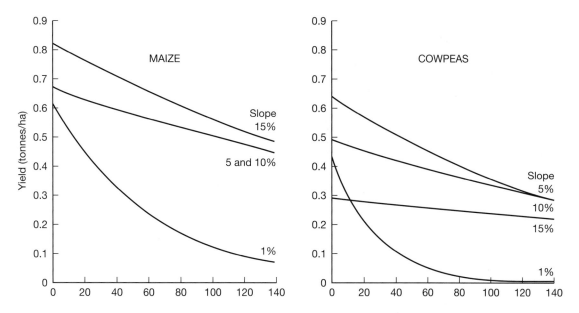

Figure 14.5 Decline in yields of maize and cowpea with cumulative loss of soil in south-west Nigeria (Lal, 1993).

ACCELERATED EROSION

Although some of the adverse effects of soil erosion for human society outlined above may occur due to natural rates, by far the most pressing problems are found in areas where accelerated rates occur. Natural rates vary enormously depending on such factors as climate, vegetation, soils, bedrock and land forms. Information on natural erosion rates, combined with our limited knowledge of the rates of soil formation, are used as yardsticks against which to measure the degree to which human action exacerbates natural processes and the sort of rates that soil conservation measures might aim to achieve (see below). Natural rates of soil formation depend on the weathering of rocks, the deposition of sediment and the accumulation of organic material from plants and animals. They are generally taken to be less than 1 tonne/ha/year, and for many practical purposes acceptable target rates for soil conservation are commonly set between 2.5 and 12.5 tonnes/ha/year, depending on local conditions (Cooke and Doornkamp, 1990). In some countries, however, much lower limits have been established. The Swedish Environmental Protection Board, for example, considers a soil loss of 0.1–0.2 tonnes/ha/year as a recommended limit for preventive measures to be applied on arable land (Alström and Åkerman, 1992).

The two most common effects of human activity that lead to accelerated erosion are modifications to, or removal of, vegetation, and destabilization of natural surfaces. Such actions have a variety of motives: vegetation may be cleared for

Figure 14.6 Dramatic dust storm in Melbourne, Australia, in February 1983. An estimated 50 000 tonnes of topsoil were entrained from Victoria's Mallee region by this storm during a period of severe drought.

Figure 14.7 A landslide blocking a road in the Khasi Hills in north-east India. Very heavy rainfall in this area, where average annual totals approach 12 000 mm in some parts, causes frequent landslides during the monsoon.

agriculture, fuel, fodder or construction; vegetation may be modified by cropping practices or deforestation for timber; land may be disturbed by ploughing, off-road vehicle use, military manoeuvres, construction, mining or trampling by animals. The effects of several of these disturbances on soil erosion by water in central Oahu, Hawaii, are shown in Table 14.4. Other processes of erosion also follow such disturbances: an example of the effects on slope stability and resulting mass movement problems caused by highway construction is given in Table 16.3. Transport routes can cause accelerated landsliding by increasing disturbing forces acting on a slope, both during construction when cuts and excavations remove lateral or underlying support (Fig. 14.7), and through earth stresses caused by passing vehicles. Other human activities that can increase the chance of slope failure do so by decreasing the resistance of materials that make up slopes. This can occur if the water content is increased, as happens when local water tables are artificially increased by reservoir impoundment, for example.

The initial impact of certain activities may be reduced when a new land use is established, however. Many construction activities initially cause marked increases in soil loss, but erosion rates can be reduced to below those recorded under natural conditions when a soil surface is covered by concrete or tarmac. Conversely, soil erosion problems may become displaced by the effects of construction, with water flows from drainage systems causing accelerated soil loss where they enter the natural environment.

Another human impact that may result in temporarily accelerated erosion rates occurs through the use of fire as a management tool. The burning of bush and grasses is a long-established and widely used management technique in the savannas of Africa, used to encourage tender green shoots from perennial grasses for livestock to feed on and to release phosphorus and other nutrients for use by crops. The exposed soil is particularly susceptible to erosion if a new vegetation cover does not become established before an erosive event. Controlled studies on the effects of burning on semi-arid gorse scrubland in south-eastern Spain indicate that when the first significant rains fall on the study plots, the loss of nutrients by water erosion can be an order of magnitude higher in the burned areas compared to the undisturbed control plot (Carreira and Neill, 1995).

There is widespread agreement that the prime causes of accelerated soil erosion are deforestation and agriculture. Deforestation removes the protection

Initial land cover	Disturbance	Increase in erosion rate
Forest	Planting of row crops	× 100–1000
Grass	Planting of row crops	× 120–100
Forest	Building logging road	× 220
Forest	Woodcutting and skidding	× 1.6
Forest	Fire	× 7–1500
Forest	Mining	× 1 000
Forest	Construction	× 2 000
Pasture	Construction	× 200
Row crops	Construction	× 10

Source: El-Swaify *et al*. (1982).

TABLE 14.4 Effects of human activities on erosion rates in Oahu, Hawaii, USA

from raindrop impact offered to soil by the tree canopy, and reduces the high permeability humus cover of forest floors, a permeability that is enhanced by the many macropores produced by tree roots. Cultivation also removes the natural vegetation cover from the soil, which is particularly susceptible to erosion when bare after harvests and during the planting stage. Some crops, such as maize and vines, usually leave large portions of the ground unprotected by vegetation even when the plants mature. Furthermore, mechanical disturbance and compaction of the soil by ploughing and tilling can enhance its erodibility.

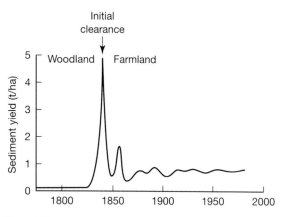

Figure 14.8 Historical reconstruction of sediment yield at Frains Lake, Michigan, USA (Davis, 1976).

An illustration of the dramatic effects on soil loss instigated by deforestation of a tropical forest area is given by experimental work on plots in French Guyana (Fritsch and Sarrailh, 1986). Suspended sediment yields from undisturbed rain forest plots of less than 0.7 tonnes/ha/year increased by up to 50 times after mechanized clear-cutting. When the plots were planted with grasses, erosion rates fell, but were still two to three times higher than under forest cover. A similar pattern of events over a longer period, derived from analysis of sediment and pollen in a lake bed, is shown for an area cleared of woodland in the mid nineteenth century in Michigan, USA (Fig. 14.8). The initial response to clearance was a sharp rise in erosion by 30 to 80 times the rates derived for the pre-settlement period. Fluctuating rates characterized a period of about 30 years as a new steady state was reached under farmland, which is nonetheless some ten times greater than under undisturbed woodland.

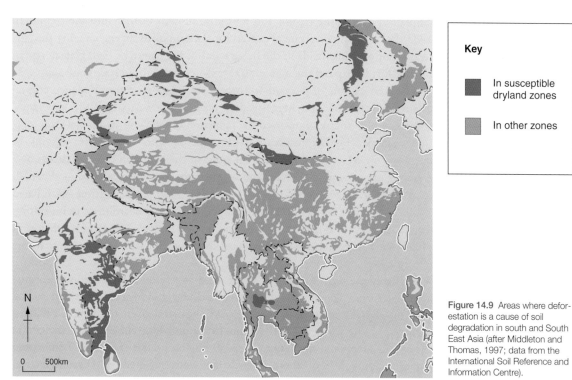

Key

■ In susceptible dryland zones

▨ In other zones

Figure 14.9 Areas where deforestation is a cause of soil degradation in south and South East Asia (after Middleton and Thomas, 1997; data from the International Soil Reference and Information Centre).

These types of effect caused by deforestation are widespread, as Figure 14.9 indicates for most of the countries in south and South East Asia. The map depicts areas where deforestation and the removal of natural vegetation in recent times has resulted in some form of soil degradation (the same classes used for the GLASOD assessment – see above). For the most part, the areas shown on Figure 14.9 are suffering from soil erosion. The driving forces behind deforestation in these areas are diverse. Some analysis of the situations in Viet Nam and the Philippines are given in Chapter 4. In lowland Nepal, locally serious water erosion has resulted from land clearance for subsistence agriculture. A large influx of population from the hills and mountains has felled vast tracts of cool tropical forest on the Terai alluvial plains since the 1960s when malaria was eradicated from the area (Tamang, 1995). Water erosion has also been severe in the Aravalli Hills in eastern India where the rates of vegetation clearance have been among the highest in the country in recent times. The major portion of these hills in Haryana state is village common land, and the situation has become so critical that the state government has begun a village-based plan to combat the erosion problem (Srivastava and Kaul, 1995).

Some of the most significant cases of accelerated erosion by wind have occurred in dry grassland areas used for grain cultivation. In the Maghreb countries of North Africa in the nineteenth century, French settlers brought European agricultural machinery that turned the soil to twice the depth of the traditional hoes, and removed shrubs and weeds, baring the soil to erosive forces. By the early twentieth century, the cropland area of the 'telle' zone had quadrupled, and traditional cultivators had been pushed on to steeper slopes and to the climatic limits of dry cereal crops (Dresch, 1986). The situation has changed little since the independence of Algeria and Tunisia, with the desire to enlarge cropland pushing the tractor and multidisc plough further into the steppe. In 1983 the Algerian government passed legislation positively encouraging the cultivation of marginal lands in the Sahara and in the country's high plateau region in an effort to expand the agricultural resource base, to increase food supply, to combat the exodus of peasants to urban areas and to counterbalance coastal urban development. This homesteading programme was part of the 'new lands' scheme, a plan that also involved the reduction of fallow in traditional crop rotation systems. The extensification of cropland into the desert margins of neighbouring Morocco also proceeded apace in the 1980s, in this case driven by a doubling of prices paid to barley and wheat producers, and relatively good rainfall totals. The average annual area under cereals grew from just over 4.4m ha in 1980–84 to 5.5m ha by 1990 (Swearingen, 1994). In addition to the resulting degradation in these regions as evidenced by the high frequency of wind erosion events, such marginal cropland is almost by definition also severely prone to the effects of drought.

Probably the most infamous case of wind erosion in the western world came after widespread ploughing of the grasslands of the US Great Plains, which created the Dust Bowl of the 1930s (see page 96), but similar environmental mishaps occurred in the former USSR in the 1950s and in a copycat exercise in the Mongolian steppes in the 1960s. Some 40 million hectares of Virgin Lands were put to the plough in northern Kazakhstan, western Siberia and eastern Russia between 1954 and 1960 (Fig. 14.10). Deep ploughing was employed, removing the stubble from the previous year's crop to allow planting earlier in the year, so reducing the chance of losses to early snows at harvest time. Land was also used more intensively, doing away with alternate years when soil was traditionally left fallow under grass. Wind erosion soon began to take its toll (Table 14.5), coming to a head in the early 1960s when drought hit the region.

The introduction, from outside, of agricultural techniques that are inappropriate to local conditions is a widely cited cause of erosion. In many parts of Latin America, management techniques brought by Spanish and Portuguese colonists have been blamed for widespread soil degradation. In Ecuador, for example, farmers have neglected the main principles of pre-colonial agriculture, which were more suited to the mountainous areas and, today, accelerated soil erosion is estimated to affect 50 per cent of the national territory at rates that reach 200–500 tonnes/ha/year in the great basin of Quito (De Noni *et al.*, 1986). In addition to the Spanish conquest, poor agricultural reform and the population explosion at the beginning of the twentieth century are highlighted as significant factors behind the soil erosion situation.

However, evidence from lake sediment cores in central Mexico suggests caution over the ease with which invading Iberians are blamed for unbalancing traditional, supposedly harmonious, systems of soil use. Analysis of the cores indicates that pre-Hispanic agriculture in the Lake Patzcuaro Basin was not as conservationist in practice as was previously thought. Several periods of accelerated erosion have been identified that occurred before the arrival of the Spanish and were of comparative magnitude to those during colonial times. This suggests that the introduction of the plough did not have a greater impact on soil erosion than traditional methods (O'Hara *et al.*, 1993).

Despite questions over where exactly to lay the blame, a long history of accelerated erosion in some regions has meant that a state of system collapse has been reached, as in parts of the Caribbean where erosion has been significant since plantation monoculture was introduced in the early eighteenth century. Large-scale deforestation, the use of fire for land clearance and clean weeding of cropland, which continued after the emancipation of plantation slaves, enhanced rates of degradation. Population increase became a significant factor from the latter years of the nineteenth century, the pressure on resources being exacerbated by the fragmentation of landholdings. Some of the worst-affected areas are on the island of Hispaniola (Haiti and Dominican Republic). In Haiti, large areas of marginal land are thought to be irreversibly degraded and an estimated 6000 ha of land are abandoned to erosion each year (Paskett and Philoctete, 1990).

Figure 14.10 A monument to the expansion of wheat cultivation on the steppes of Kazakhstan, part of the Soviet Union's Virgin Lands programme of the 1950s which has been plagued by accelerated wind erosion.

Station	Mean annual number of dust storm days		Increase
	1936–50	1951–62	
Omsk, steppe	7	16	× 22.3
Isil'-Kul'	8	15	× 21.9
Pokrov-Irtyshsk	4	22	× 25.5
Poltavka	9	12	× 21.3
Cherlak	6	19	× 23.2
Mean	6.8	16.8	× 22.8

Source: Sapozhnikova (1973).

TABLE 14.5 Effect of the Virgin Lands Scheme on the frequency of dust storms in the Omsk region of western Siberia

Another country where accelerated erosion is widely accepted to have reached crisis proportions is Ethiopia. Erosion rates that average 42 tonnes/ha/year on Ethiopian cropland (Table 14.6) reach as high as 300 tonnes/ha/year on some fields in western parts of the highlands where rainfall erosivity is highest. Hurni (1993) suggests that this level of soil loss reduces soil productivity in Ethiopia by 1–2 per cent per year and that at current erosion rates most of the country's cropland soils will be completely lost within 150 years. The crucial factor behind the degradation of Ethiopia's soils and other land resources is the country's large population, and Hurni believes that whatever scenario for soil conservation is proposed, sustainable use of land resources can only be achieved if population growth rates are reduced to zero within 50 years.

TABLE 14.6 Estimated rates of soil loss on slopes in Ethiopia by type of land cover

Land cover/use	Proportion of national land area (%)	Soil loss (t/ha/year)
Cropland	13.1	42
Perennial crops	1.7	8
Grazing and browsing	51.0	5
Totally degraded	3.8	70
Currently uncultivable	18.7	5
Forest	3.6	1
Wood and bushland	8.1	5

Source: after Hurni (1993).

Although serious soil erosion is often associated with the humid tropics and semi-arid areas, it does give cause for concern in more temperate regions. The intensification of agriculture in the UK, for example, has brought erosion problems to the fore, with about 36 per cent of arable land in England and Wales classified as being at moderate to high risk of erosion (Evans, 1990). Sandy and peaty soils in parts of the Vale of York, the Fens, Breckland and the Midlands suffer from deflation during dry periods, but water is the most widespread agent of soil loss. The central reason for the increase in erosion in the past 25 years or so has been a shift in the sowing season, from spring to autumn, for the main cereal crops of wheat and barley. The change has come about because autumn-sown 'winter cereals' produce higher yields, but the shift in sowing season leaves winter cereal fields exposed in the wettest months – October and November – in many parts of the country, since arable fields are at risk from erosion until about 30 per cent of the ground is covered by the growing crop.

Several other aspects of more intensive arable farming have also contributed to the enhanced erosion rates (Boardman, 1990):

- the expansion of arable crops on to steeper slopes made possible by more powerful tractors
- the creation of larger fields by removal of walls, hedges, grass banks and strips has produced longer slopes and larger catchment areas, which generate greater volumes of water on slopes and in valley bottoms
- more powerful machinery is able to work the land even when damp, thus compacting soils along wheel tracks, which tend to channel runoff

McTainsh, G. and Strong, C. 2007 The role of aeolian dust in ecosystems. *Geomorphology* 89: 39–54. A review of the ecological effects of atmospheric soil dust.

Mermuta, A.R. and Eswaran, H. 2001 Some major developments in soil science since the mid-1960s. *Geoderma* 100: 403–26. A wide-ranging overview.

Morgan, R.P.C. 2005 *Soil erosion and conservation*, 3rd edn. Oxford, Blackwell. A very good text detailing the processes of soil erosion, methods of measurement and modelling, and the techniques developed for its control.

Stocking, M.A. 1995 Soil erosion in developing countries: where geomorphologists fear to tread. *Catena* 25: 253–67. A thought-provoking analysis of the supposedly objective science of soil erosion study.

Valentin, C., Poesen, J. and Li, Y. 2005 Gully erosion: impacts, factors and control. *Catena* 63: 132–53. A review of work on this important form of water erosion.

WEBSITES

www.isric.org/ the International Soil Reference and Information Centre contains information on international research programmes on all aspects of soil degradation.

www.swcs.org/ the Soil and Water Conservation Society site includes news, conferences and publications.

www.weru.ksu.edu/ the Wind Erosion Research Unit has much technical information on research programmes as well as a multimedia archive section.

www.wocat.net/ the World Overview of Conservation Technologies and Approaches (WOCAT) provides a forum for the exchange of information on soil and water conservation.

www.soilerosion.net/ The Soil Erosion Site collates reliable information on soil erosion from a wide range of disciplines and sources.

www.ieca.org/ The International Erosion Control Association is the world's oldest and largest association devoted to the problems caused by erosion and sediment.

www.bettersoils.com.au/ information on soil and land care from the Agricultural Bureau of South Australia.

POINTS FOR DISCUSSION

■ Should we be concerned about soil erosion? If so, why?

■ Design a research programme to determine whether the implications of soil erosion are more serious on-site or off-site.

■ Outline the main ways in which people influence erosion rates.

■ There are many techniques to prevent soil erosion, so why are there still areas where soil erosion is a problem?

15 Biodiversity Loss

TOPICS COVERED

Understanding biodiversity, Threats to biodiversity, Threatened species, Threats to flora and fauna, Conservation efforts, Convention on Biological Diversity

Biodiversity, a term that refers to the number, variety and variability of living organisms, has become a much-debated environmental issue in recent times. Although we live on a naturally dynamic planet, where species are prone to extinction and ecosystems are always subject to change, biodiversity has become an issue of major concern because of the unprecedented rate at which human action is causing its loss. The very large and rapid increase in human population over recent centuries has been accompanied by an unprecedented scale of modification and conversion of ecosystems for agriculture and other human activities. At the same time, we have documented increasing numbers of cases where species have been driven to extinction by human activities.

Although the exact definition of biodiversity (or biological biodiversity) is the subject of considerable discussion, it is commonly defined in terms of genes, species and ecosystems, corresponding to three fundamental levels of biological organization. Some authorities also include a separate human element in their definitions: cultural diversity. The Convention on Biological Diversity defines biodiversity as 'the variability among living organisms from all sources including, *inter alia*, terrestrial, marine and other aquatic ecosystems and the ecological complexes of which they are a part; this includes diversity within species, between species and of ecosystems'. Genetic diversity includes the variation between individuals and between populations within a species. Species diversity refers to the different types of animals, plants and other life forms within a region. Ecosystem diversity means the variety of habitats found in an area. Much of this chapter is focused at the species level. Some aspects of genetic and ecosystem diversity are dealt with in more detail elsewhere (see Chapters 4 and 13).

UNDERSTANDING BIODIVERSITY

The 158 states that signed the Convention on Biological Diversity at the UN Conference on Environment and Development in Rio de Janeiro in 1992 agreed that there was a general lack of information on and knowledge of biodiversity, and that there was an urgent need to develop scientific, technical and institutional capacities to provide the basic understanding on which to plan and implement appropriate measures. Although scientists have been systematically counting and classifying other living organisms for at least two centuries, we remain remarkably ignorant of the most basic of information concerning the living things with which we share the Earth. While the numbers of species in some groups of organisms are relatively well known, our knowledge of others is extremely imprecise. The number of bird species, for example, is close to 10 000 (Sibley and Monroe, 1990), but estimates of the number of insect species vary widely (from 2 million to 100 million), with about 1 million having been described (UNEP, 1995). In total, about 1.75 million species have been scientifically described to date, and a reasonable estimate of the total number of species on the planet is 14 million (UNEP, 1995).

The geographical pattern of biodiversity is not even. Most estimates agree that more than half of all species live in the tropical moist forests that cover just 6 per cent of the world's land surface. The factors that influence the distribution of biodiversity are numerous, and probably change in their importance at different scales of both space and time. Table 15.1 is an attempt to summarize some of the most significant environmental variables.

Our knowledge of the world's biomes and individual ecosystems is also unsatisfactory. Indeed, although several systems of classification have been developed, no single measure of ecological community diversity can be uniformly applied to all ecosystems. We are also still trying to understand the ways in which biological diversity affects the functioning of ecosystems. Although genetic diversity is the ultimate basis for evolution and for the adaptation of populations to their environment, it is even less well understood. We know very little about the genetics

TABLE 15.1 A hierarchical framework for processes influencing species diversity

Spatial scale	Dominant environmental variables	Temporal scale
Local: within communities, within habitat patches	Fine-scale biotic and abiotic interactions (e.g. habitat structure, disturbance by fires, storms)	~1–100 years
Landscape: between communities; turnover of species within a landscape	Soils, altitude, peninsula effect	~100–1000 years
Regional: large geographical areas within continents	Radiation budget and water availability, area, latitude	the last 10 000 years (i.e. since end of last glacial)
Continental: differences in species lineages and richness across continents	Aridification events, Quaternary glacial/interglacial cycles, mountain-building episodes (e.g. Tertiary uplift of the Andes)	the last 1–10 million years
Global: differences reflected in the biogeographical realms (e.g. distribution of mammal families between continents)	Continental plate movements, sea-level change	the last 10–100 million years

Source: modified after Willis and Whittaker (2002).

of most living organisms. The few exceptions are for a handful of species identified as having direct importance to certain forms of economic activity, such as
agriculture and human health.

Given the poor state of our knowledge, it is likely that many species that we
have never known about have become extinct. Even among those organisms that
have been described, problems emerge in documenting their disappearance. Just
because no member of a species has been documented for some time does not
necessarily mean that it has become extinct: absence of evidence is not evidence
of absence.

Despite these and other difficulties, estimates of the rate at which species are
becoming extinct, mostly due to human action, indicate that the rate has been
growing exponentially since about the seventeenth century. Many current and
projected estimates of species loss are based upon the rate at which habitats are
being destroyed, modified and fragmented – the most serious threats to species
diversity – coupled with biogeographical assumptions relating to numbers of
species and area of habitat. We should be aware, however, that estimates for habitat loss in tropical forest areas, the most diverse ecosystems, are themselves
subject to wide variations (see page 57). Another, in some ways more effective
strategy, has been to analyse extinction in groups where the size of the species
pool is quite well known. Examples include North American birds, tropical
palms and Australian mammals.

While some earlier projections of global extinction rates suggested that 20–50
per cent of species would be lost by the end of the twentieth century (Myers,
1979; Ehrlich and Ehrlich, 1981), these now seem exaggerated. Reid (1992) estimates a 1–5 per cent loss per century, and figures of 100 000 species lost per year
are frequently quoted (WCMC, 1992). There is general agreement that over the
past few hundred years humans have increased the species extinction rate by as
much as three orders of magnitude (MEA, 2005).

THREATS TO BIODIVERSITY

Ecosystems change and species can become extinct under natural circumstances.
We know that the Earth's climate is dynamic over a variety of timescales, and
plant and animal communities have to adapt to these changes or run the risk of
extinction. Species may also become extinct due to a range of other natural circumstances, such as random catastrophic events, or through competition with
other species, by disease or predation. Indeed, as one biologist puts it: 'Extinction
is a fundamental part of nature – more than 99 per cent of all species that ever
lived are now extinct' (Jablonski, 2004: 589).

Studies of the fossil record, an excellent natural archive of extinctions, show us
that long geological periods when the rate of species extinction was fairly uniform
have apparently been punctuated by catastrophic episodes of mass extinction. In
the last 570 million years of Earth's history five 'mass extinction events' have
occurred, each thought to have removed more than 60 per cent of marine species.
The most severe was during the late Permian period some 245 million years ago,
and the most recent was at the end of the Cretaceous period 65 million years ago
when the dinosaurs and several other families of species were wiped out.

Currently, however, there is widespread fear that another mass extinction event is occurring, one in which the Earth's human population is playing the key role. Although we are not sure of the current rate of species extinction, six fundamental causes of biodiversity loss have been identified (WRI, 1992):

1 the unsustainably high rate of human population growth and natural resource consumption
2 a narrowing spectrum of products from agriculture, forestry and fishing
3 economic systems that fail to value the environment and its resources
4 inequity in the ownership, management and flow of benefits from both the use and the conservation of biological resources
5 deficiencies in knowledge and its application
6 legal and institutional systems that promote unsustainable exploitation.

THREATENED SPECIES

Some species are particularly at risk from the threat of extinction simply because they are only found in a narrow geographical range, or they occupy only one or a few specialized habitats, or they are only found in small populations. Species that occur in only one location are known as endemic. Other factors may also affect the degree of risk faced by certain species. These include:

- low rates of population increase
- large body size (hence requiring a large range, more food and making the species more easily hunted by humans)
- poor dispersal ability
- need for a stable environment
- need to migrate between different habitats
- perceived to be dangerous by humans.

Combinations of some of these characteristics are found in species known as *K*-strategists, and it is these species that are generally more likely to become extinct because they tend to live in stable habitats, delay reproduction to an advanced age and produce only a few, large offspring. By contrast, species that produce many offspring at an earlier age and have the ability to react quickly to changes in their environment, are known as *r*-strategists, and it is their speedier turnover and flexibility that make *r*-strategists less likely to experience extinction.

The wider ecological implications of the loss of a certain species vary between species. Another important aspect of the extinction issue is the fact that certain keystone species may be important in determining the ability of a large number of other species to persist. Hence the loss of a certain keystone species could potentially result in a cascade of extinctions. Such fears have been expressed over tropical insects, many of which have highly specialized feeding requirements.

Species known to be at risk are documented, according to the severity of threat they face and the imminence of their extinction, by the International Union for Conservation of Nature and Natural Resources (IUCN, also known as the World Conservation Union) on so-called Red Lists (Table 15.2). The general term 'threatened' is used to refer to a species of fauna or flora considered to belong to any of the categories shown in Table 15.2.

TABLE 15.2 IUCN Red List categories

Extinct	No reasonable doubt that the last individual has died
Extinct in the wild	Only known to survive in cultivation, in captivity or naturalized well outside past range
Critically endangered	Extremely high risk of extinction in the wild in immediate future
Endangered	High risk of extinction in the wild in near future
Vulnerable	High risk of extinction in the wild in medium-term future
Near threatened	Close to qualifying for Critically endangered, Endangered or Vulnerable
Least concern	Not near threatened
Data deficient	Data insufficient to categorize but listing highlights need for research, perhaps acknowledging the need for classification
Not evaluated	Not assessed against the criteria

THREATS TO FLORA AND FAUNA

Most of the factors currently threatening species of both fauna and flora are induced or influenced by human action. Such actions may be deliberate, as in the case of destruction by hunting, or inadvertent, as in the case of destruction or modification of habitats in order to use the land for other purposes. In practice, many species are at risk from more than one threat and some threats tend to combine: the clearance of forests, for example, makes the hunting of large mammals easier. The threats that a particular species faces may also vary through time. The decline of the New Zealand mistletoe (*Trilepidea adamsii*) began as its habitat was reduced by deforestation, first by the Maoris and at an accelerating rate by British settlers in the late nineteenth century. The population was further reduced by collectors, and the decline of bird populations that were responsible for seed dispersal, due to forest clearance. The final specimens, which disappeared from North Island in 1954, may have been eaten by brush-tailed possums deliberately introduced from Australia during the 1860s to establish a fur trade (Norton, 1991). Although the detailed nature of threats may be complex and variable, some indication of the relative importance of the different threats is given in Figure 15.1, which was compiled for the birds of the world and mammals in Australasia and the Americas.

All of these human-induced reasons for the demise of species have operated in the past. In Britain, for example, the combination of hunting and habitat destruction by deforestation has put paid to many original animal species over the centuries (Table 15.3).

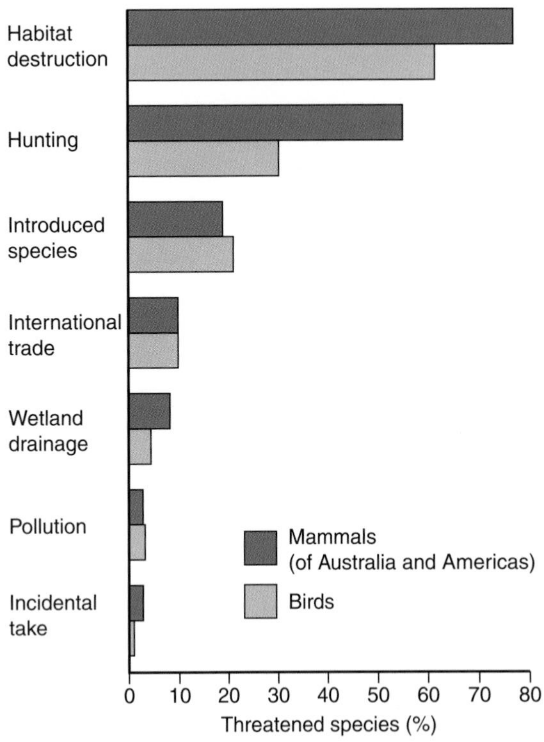

Figure 15.1 Threats to mammals and birds (after WCMC, 1992).

Habitat loss and modification

The destruction of habitats is widely regarded to be the most severe threat to biological diversity, while fragmentation and degradation, which are often precursors of outright destruction, also present significant cause for concern. Habitat loss and degradation was the most pervasive threat to birds, mammals and plants, according to the 2004 IUCN Red List, affecting 86 per cent of all threatened birds, 86 per cent of the threatened mammals assessed and 88 per cent of threatened amphibians (IUCN, 2004).

In many countries, particularly on islands (see below) and where human population densities are high, most of the natural habitat has been destroyed to provide farmland, rangeland and land for settlement and industry. No fewer than 49 out of 61 countries surveyed in the African and Asian tropics are thought to have lost more than 50 per cent of their wildlife habitats (IUCN/UNEP, 1986a; 1986b). In the tropical African countries, 65 per cent of the original wildlife habitat has been lost, with particularly high rates of destruction reported from Gambia (89 per cent), Liberia (87 per cent), Rwanda (87 per cent), Burundi (86 per cent) and Sierra Leone (85 per cent). In the Indomalayan countries the overall loss is 68 per cent, with particularly severe losses reported from Hong Kong (97 per cent), Bangladesh (94 per cent), Sri Lanka (83 per cent), Viet Nam (80 per cent) and India (80 per cent).

The destruction of tropical rain forests, coral reefs, wetlands and mangroves, documented elsewhere in this book, is particularly serious given the high biodiversity of these habitats. Hence the large majority of current human-induced extinctions are occurring in the world's tropical rain forest areas, and insects are the order of species most at risk. Nevertheless, other habitats have suffered equally severe destruction; Table 15.4 shows the percentage of three types lost since pre-agricultural times in selected countries.

Animal	Year
Beaver (*Castor fiber*)	Late 1100s
Wild swine (*Sus scrofa*)	1260
Wolf (*Canis lupus*)	1743
Goshawk (*Accipiter gentilis*)	1850
White-tailed sea eagle (*Haliaetus albicilla*)	1918

Source: from information in Rackham (1986); Peters and Lovejoy (1990).

TABLE 15.3 Dates when the last wild member of selected animal species was killed in Britain

Country	Forests 1980s extent (thousand ha)	% lost	Savanna/ grassland 1980s extent (thousand ha)	% lost	Wetlands/marsh 1980s extent (thousand ha)	% lost
Australia	13 000*	95	75 900	nd	17 000	c.95
Canada	274 000*	48	27 663	nd	127 000	nd
Burundi	117	91	246	80	14	nd
Ethiopia	5570	86	27 469	61	0	0
France	131	c.99	250	nd	1171	nd
Malaysia	18 008	42	0	0	2214	35
Namibia	15 020	52	14 741	59	225	10
Peru	74 270	12	13 900	41	1303	nd
Thailand	13 107	73	0	0	83	96

nd: no data
*Primary forest extent only
Source: after WRI (1994: 320–1, Table 20.3).

TABLE 15.4 Habitat extent (1980s) and loss since pre-agricultural times in selected countries

There are numerous examples of species that have been driven to the edge of extinction because of the loss of their habitat. In the UK, for example, the distribution of the threatened green winged orchid (*Orchis morio*) has been severely reduced by the loss of 40 per cent of unintensified lowland grassland between 1932 and 1992 (DoE, 1992). Internationally, one of the best-known threatened species, the giant panda (*Ailuropoda melanoleuca*), has also suffered from progressive human encroachment into its habitat. Once found throughout much of China's high-altitude regions and beyond, the species is now confined to a few sites near Chengdu (Fig. 15.2). The panda's heavy reliance upon its specialized bamboo diet, which occasionally requires forays into lowland regions during natural bamboo die-offs, puts the normally shy creature in direct conflict with encroaching human populations.

These factors, combined with the extreme difficulties encountered by attempts at captive breeding, look set to add the panda to a long list of species whose ultimate fate can be traced to destruction of their habitat by humans; this is despite huge efforts to conserve the species. A network of panda reserves, designed to protect 60 per cent of the animal's range, has been established in China, but not all of these protected areas have been successful in their prime objective. Research on the 200 000 ha Wolong Nature Reserve has shown that panda habitat is still being destroyed faster inside one of the world's most high-profile protected nature reserves than in adjacent areas that are not protected. Further, the rates of destruction were higher after the reserve was established in 1975 than before (Liu *et al.*, 2001). It appears that the Wolong Nature Reserve has been a victim of its own success. Towns and settlements have thrived in and

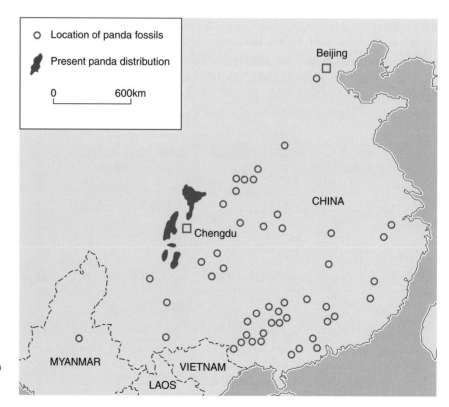

Figure 15.2 Past and present distribution of pandas (reprinted with permission from Roberts, 1988. Copyright, 1988, American Association for the Advancement of Science).

The largest marine protected area is the Great Barrier Reef Marine Park in Australia (345 400 km²), but generally marine habitats are less well protected than those on land. The total protected sea area is only about 0.5 per cent of the surface area of the oceans (Chape *et al.*, 2003).

The types and quality of protection and management in these areas also vary greatly. A lack of political and financial support limits the success of many protected areas. The need to maintain levels of protection is well illustrated by the Operation Tiger reserves set up in several Asian countries in the early 1970s to protect the Asian tiger from local people faced with the loss of their domesticated livestock, and in some cases fellow villagers. Threats from the tiger have been enhanced in many areas due to the loss of its forest habitat to agricultural lands.

While Operation Tiger has long been hailed as a conservation success story, the story's most recent chapter has not been a happy one. Further loss of habitat and continued poaching have resulted in dramatic changes to tiger populations. Tigers now occupy just 7 per cent of their historical range (Dinerstein *et al.*, 2007), an expanse that once stretched from the Caspian Sea to the island of Bali in Indonesia. Even in India, widely considered to be the stronghold for wild tigers, conservationists were shocked to discover in 2005 that intense poaching had eliminated all tigers from supposedly well-protected sanctuaries such as the Sariska Tiger Reserve, and had depleted populations in other tiger reserves such as Bandhavgarh and Rhanthambore (Fig. 15.6).

Conflict between the aims of conservation and those of local people is a key issue in the threatened species debate since without local involvement in both the design and management of protected areas, adequate protection can only be achieved if the park agency has the authority and ability to enforce regulations. This is both undesirable and often unattainable, and this realization represents a major recent shift in practical conservation philosophy.

Even in those areas that receive maximum protection, active conservation management is usually needed because often it is not sufficient simply to cordon off an area and leave it be. Such management is not always an easy task, however. A ban on hunting, for example, is theoretically easy to introduce, and grazing goats, sheep, pigs and even rabbits are relatively easy to control and even eliminate, but a threat from an introduced plant is much more intractable.

Effective management is also dependent upon a sufficient understanding of the ecology of the organ-

Continent/Country	Area protected (thousand hectares)	Area protected (% land area)
WORLD	1 506 435	11.4
ASIA (exc. Middle East)		
Bhutan	1204	30.2
Japan	5221	14.0
Uzbekistan	2050	4.6
EUROPE		
Austria	2348	28.0
Greece	427	3.2
UK	6049	24.8
MIDDLE EAST & N AFRICA		
Algeria	11 864	5.1
Israel	461	22.3
Yemen	0	0
SUB-SAHARAN AFRICA		
Botswana	17 492	30.2
Cameroon	3741	8.0
Mali	4667	3.7
NORTH AMERICA		
Canada	62 875	6.3
USA	149 009	15.8
CENTRAL AMERICA & CARIBBEAN		
Costa Rica	1206	23.5
Cuba	149	1.3
Jamaica	176	15.9
SOUTH AMERICA		
Chile	2689	3.6
Surinam	1846	12.7
Uruguay	66	0.4
OCEANIA		
Australia	74 531	9.7
Fiji	25	1.4
New Zealand	6471	24.3

Source: from UNEP-WCMC (2004).

TABLE 15.7 Protected areas in selected countries

Figure 15.6 Habitat loss and poaching are the major threats to the world's remaining wild populations of tiger (*Panthera tigris*). This one is in Rhanthambore National Park, an Operation Tiger reserve in northern India.

isms in question, which is not always the case. Although the gradual decline in British colonies of the large blue butterfly (*Maculinea arion*), a dry grassland species, was largely due to the fact that 50 of its former 91 sites were ploughed or otherwise fundamentally changed in the period 1800–1970 (Fig. 15.7a), its eventual extinction from Britain in 1979 was due to ignorance. Conservationists were aware of the large blue's highly specialized life cycle: eggs are laid on *Thymus praecox*, on which the larvae feed briefly before being adopted and raised by *Myrmica* species of ant. But the disappearance of the large blue from another 41 sites, including four nature reserves where *Thymus* and *Myrmica* remained abundant, proved enigmatic. The realization that only one species of *Myrmica* ant could act as host, and that regular heavy grazing was necessary to maintain appropriate soil surface temperatures came too late to save the large blue.

A similar pattern of events occurred with the heath fritillary (*Mellicta athalia*), a species that has declined as its woodland clearing habitat has disappeared and because specially designated nature reserves were not adequately managed (Fig. 15.7b). The heath fritillary is still one of the rarest butterflies in Britain, but a clearer understanding of the make-up of its narrow niche may yet save it from extinction (Thomas, 1991). Likewise, the lessons learned over the loss of the large blue have been put to good use in recent attempts to reintroduce a similar subspecies from Sweden.

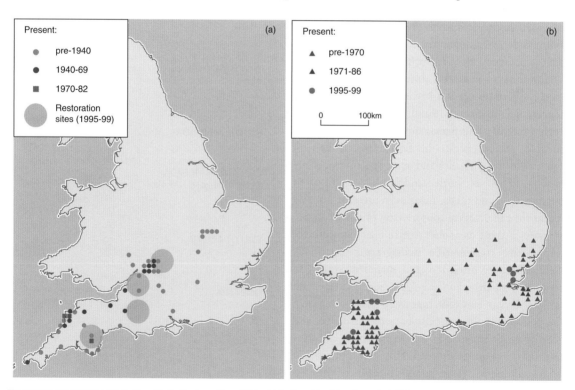

Figure 15.7 Decline in the distribution of butterflies in southern Britain: (a) the large blue (*Maculinea arion*); (b) the heath fritillary (*Mellicta athalia*) (after Heath *et al.*, 1984; Asher *et al.*, 2001).

Following a re-establishment trial on the edge of Dartmoor in 1983, it has since been reintroduced or has spread to seven other sites in the Cotswolds in Gloucestershire, and the Polden Hills and Mendip Hills in Somerset (Asher *et al.*, 2001).

Bans on hunting and trade

Legislative bans on threatening activities have been widely implemented to safeguard certain species. One example is the ban on the catching and selling of coelacanths introduced in the Indian Ocean island state of the Comoros as part of a conservation plan to protect the small population of this fish, first found in 1938, which previously had been thought to have become extinct 65 million years ago (Fricke and Hissman, 1990).

However, a ban on hunting and trade is, in practice, like any legislation, only as effective as the ability of states to uphold it. If enforcement is weak, and incentives are large enough, poachers will continue to operate in spite of the law. The seemingly intractable problem of African elephant poaching during the 1980s inspired drastic conservation measures, with some countries implementing shoot-on-sight policies to deal with poachers in protected areas. But the placement of the African elephant on Appendix I of the Convention on International Trade in Endangered Species (CITES) in 1989 has dramatically reduced the world price of ivory, resulting in a downturn in poaching of the African elephant. Nonetheless, the listing on Appendix I was not welcomed by all conservationists. In the southern African countries of Botswana, Malawi, Namibia, South Africa and Zimbabwe, well-managed elephant herds are large and expanding, to the extent where they have to be culled to offset the risk of degradation in their ranges. The ban meant that ivory from the culled animals could not be sold to maximum profit. As a result, a decision was taken in 1997 to allow the resumption of some limited trade in African elephant ivory.

Problems still occur with trade bans, and the case of the Old World fruit bats (or flying foxes) is an interesting one in this respect. The flying foxes constitute a single family (*Pteropodidae*) with 41 genera and 161 species, which play an important ecological role among Pacific islands as pollinators and seed dispensers for hundreds of plant species, many of which have important economic and subsistence value to humans (Fujita and Tuttle, 1991). One of the central threats to the fruit bats is from hunters. Indigenous people on Guam have eaten them for at least 2500 years, but Guam's bat population was decimated in the years after the Second World War with the proliferation of firearms used in hunting. Many other south Pacific islands' fruit bat populations have subsequently suffered declines as exporters have supplied the Guam market. Listing on CITES Appendix I has had some success in curbing the threat to some of the species, but problems have arisen because of the lack of wildlife inspectors to uphold the law and the fact that several other islands in the region are, like Guam, effectively part of the USA, and therefore the trade is considered domestic rather than international (Sheeline, 1993).

Some conservationists argue that bans can only be a short-term measure to protect certain species. Long-lasting protection can only be envisaged if the people who demand certain products can be persuaded against them. Concerted publicity

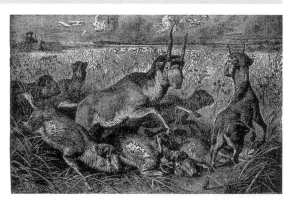

Figure 15.8 Saiga antelopes (*Saiga tatarica*) fleeing a hunter in Siberia. This engraving was made in the late 1800s when the saiga was widely hunted for its meat, hide and horn. Having recovered from the brink of extinction thanks to a hunting ban introduced in the 1920s, the saiga became threatened again by a resumption in illegal trade in the 1990s.

campaigns by animal rights groups have had considerable effect in this respect in certain European countries where ornamental furs are concerned. The fact that if a market for products persists, the threat it represents to species does not disappear can be illustrated by the case of the saiga antelope, which inhabits the dry steppe grasslands and semi-arid deserts of central Asia. Hunting of the saiga during the nineteenth century in Russia (Fig. 15.8) pushed the species to the brink of extinction before being outlawed in the 1920s. Subsequently, controlled cropping allowed the saiga to recolonize most of its original range, but deterioration in law enforcement since the collapse of the Soviet Union in the early 1990s has resulted in an upsurge in the illegal trade in saiga horn destined for medicinal markets, particularly in China. The result has been both a catastophic fall in numbers and a severe distortion in the saiga population's sex ratio because only the males have horns. In consequence, there are serious fears of a reproductive collapse.

Off-site conservation practices

While the conservation of species is best achieved by their maintenance in the wild, through protected area programmes and legislative measures, other practices may be necessary for species whose populations are too small to be viable in the wild or are not located in protected areas. Maintenance of species in artificial conditions under human supervision is a strategy known as off-site, or *ex situ*, conservation. The off-site approach includes game farms, zoos, aquaria and captive breeding programmes for animals – although in reality few of these are actively involved in the conservation of endangered species – while plants are maintained in botanical gardens, arboreta and seed banks.

In practice, off-site techniques complement on-site approaches in a number of ways, such as by providing individuals for research, the results of which can be fed back into management techniques in the wild. Perhaps the ideal way in which the maintenance of captive individuals of species can help in the biodiversity issue is by providing individuals that can be reintroduced into the wild.

Such programmes are expensive, logistically demanding, and require long-term management and monitoring to assure and assess their success. Plant reintroductions are generally viewed as a high-risk strategy with uncertain indications of their long-term success (WCMC, 1992). Reintroduction of animals is also a difficult task, but one notable success has been the reintroduction of the Arabian oryx (*Oryx leucoryx*) to Oman, a species that is thought to have become extinct in the wild in 1972. Individuals kept in captivity in the Middle East and elsewhere were released to the wild in Oman in batches throughout the 1980s and now seem to be established. An equivalent reintroduction programme has also been established in neighbouring Saudi Arabia. A similar programme was initiated

protection threshold defined by the EU Ozone Directive, computed as a mean over eight hours. The moving eight-hour average of ozone concentration at Liosia exceeded 110 μg/m^3 on 140 days in 1988 (EEA, 1997).

Many observers believe that most of the environmental issues that make transport unsustainable can only be properly addressed by focusing on ways in which behaviour can be changed, to reduce the demand for the activity that produces the problem in the first place (Whitelegg, 1993). As the Athens example shows, such changes can be very difficult to make, but moderation of the environmental impacts of transport will come about ultimately from government, through regulation, legislation, and other ways in which transport modes are encouraged and discouraged. Some suggestions as to the types of approaches that can be taken at different levels of government to ameliorate the problems are suggested in Table 16.8.

Government level	Policies
Local	Improve land-use planning and traffic management
Central	Change pricing and tax policies to assist development of alternative fuels, to improve transport efficiency, to encourage shifts to 'greener' modes of travel, and to reduce unnecessary travel
European	Impose 'environmentally optimal' community-wide policies involving fuel and vehicle tax harmonization, vehicle speed limits and heavy vehicle weights

Source: after Transnet (1990).

TABLE 16.8 Suggested complementary policy solutions to transport problems for different levels of government in Europe

FURTHER READING

Amatayakul, W. and Ramnäs, O. 2001 Life cycle assessment of a catalytic converter for passenger cars. *Journal of Cleaner Production* 9: 395–403. Lifecycle assessment demonstrates how the catalytic converter displaces environmental impacts rather than reduces them.

Banister, D. 2005 *Unsustainable transport: city transport in the new century*. London, Routledge. This book addresses the links between transport and sustainable urban development, advocating changes to technology, institutional structures and social behaviour.

Carpenter, T.G. 1994 *The environmental impact of railways*. Chichester, Wiley. This book details impacts on people, such as noise and pollution, and resources.

Chapman, L. 2007 Transport and climate change: a review. *Journal of Transport Geography* 15: 354–67. A comprehensive overview of both the technical and policy issues.

Galil, B.S. 2007 Loss or gain? Invasive aliens and biodiversity in the Mediterranean Sea. *Marine Pollution Bulletin* 55: 314–22. Assessment of the impact of alien species in the Mediterranean.

Goldemberg, J. 2006 The ethanol program in Brazil. *Environmental Research Letters* 1 014008 (5pp). The history of this programme and how it could be replicated in other countries. (Open access journal: www.iop.org/EJ/abstract/-link=5887848/1748-9326/1/1/014008)

Henderson, S., Dawson, T.P. and Whittaker, R.J. 2006 Progress in invasive plants research. *Progress in Physical Geography* 30: 25–46. An authoritative overview of research into biological invasions.

LaDochy, S. 2005 The disappearance of dense fog in Los Angeles: another urban impact? *Physical Geography* 26: 177–91. Decreasing fog incidence at LA airports is partly attributed to the city's improved air quality.

Lovins, A.B. and Cramer, D.R. 2004 Hypercars, hydrogen, and the automotive transition. *International Journal of Vehicle Design* 35: 50–85. A review of how changes in the design and manufacture of cars can dramatically reduce the energy needed to move them.

Spellerberg, I.F. 1998 Ecological effects of roads and traffic: a literature review. *Global Ecology and Biogeography* 7: 317–33. A good summary of studies on impacts and methods for mitigation.

WEBSITES

www.cities21.com/ the International Council for Local Environmental Initiatives site has information on programmes for sustainable urban transport.

www.dot.gov/ the US Department of Transportation covers issues related to all forms of transport.

www.geocities.com/sustrannet/ the SUSTRAN network promotes and popularizes people-centred, equitable and sustainable transport with a focus on Asia and the Pacific.

invasions.bio.utk.edu/ the Institute for Biological Invasions site contains a wide range of information.

www.aqmd.gov/ southern California's Air Quality Management Plan site has news, pollution data and information on transport programmes.

greenercars.com/ a guide to 'green' cars and trucks.

www.issg.org/ the Invasive Species Specialist Group site contains a wealth of information on problems, management solutions, and so on.

www.sma.df.gob.mx/simat/ atmospheric quality in Mexico City.

POINTS FOR DISCUSSION

- Is it possible to prevent biological invasions? Would it be desirable?
- Is air pollution just an unfortunate side effect of our need to move?
- If you were asked to propose measures to make transport more sustainable in your area, what would you suggest?
- Assess the ways in which transport is related to other environmental issues covered in this book.

17 Waste Management

TOPICS COVERED

Types of waste, Disposal of waste, Reuse, recovery, recycling and prevention

KEY WORDS

landfill, prior informed consent, polluter-pays principle, Superfund programme, Basel Convention, end-of-life vehicle (ELV), life-cycle assessment (LCA), cleaner production, closed-loop processing cycle

Wastes are produced by all living things – excreted by an organism or thrown away by society because they are no longer useful and if kept may be detrimental. But the make-up of waste means that once discarded by one body its constituents may become useful to another. In the natural world, a waste produced by an animal, for example, is just one stage in the continual cycle of matter and energy that characterizes the workings of the planet: an animal that urinates is disposing of waste products its body does not need, but the water and nutrients can become resources for other organisms. Similarly, sewage from a town can be used by bacteria that break it down in a river, for example, or an old shirt discarded by one person might be worn by another, often poorer, individual. The term 'waste' is therefore a label determined by ecology, economics and/or culture.

Much of the waste produced by human society consists of natural material and energy, although we have also created products not found in the natural world, such as CFCs and plastics, which can become wastes. The issues surrounding wastes stem from problems of disposal. People's use of resources, and hence production of wastes, has accelerated in the period since the Industrial Revolution, and this fact, combined with the growing number of people on the planet, has created increasing volumes of waste that need to be disposed of. This disposal requires careful management since too much waste disposed of in a certain place at a particular time can contaminate or pollute the environment, creating a hazard to the health, safety or welfare of living things. Examples of waste products and their impacts on the environment are found throughout this book. They include wastes produced by agriculture (Chapter 13), energy production (Chapter 18) and mining (Chapter 19), and pollution of the atmosphere (Chapters 11, 12 and 16), aquatic environments (Chapters 6, 7 and 8) and urban environments (Chapter 10).

TYPES OF WASTE

Waste can take many different forms: solid, liquid, gas, or energy in the form of heat or noise. The problems associated with its disposal can stem from a range of other properties, including its chemical make-up, whether it is organic or inorganic, the length of time taken for it to be broken down into less hazardous constituents, and its reactivity with other substances – so-called synergy. The sources of waste are also diverse, stemming from virtually every human activity, including:

- mining and construction
- fuel combustion
- industrial processes
- domestic and institutional activities
- agriculture
- military activities.

Collection of data on waste has had a relatively low priority in many countries, and the methods for their compilation vary widely. Statistics that are available are often given as weights, but the large differences between quantity and quality mean that these figures can only give a general indication of the nature of the waste disposal problem. The waste arisings for the UK, which totalled about 400 million tonnes annually in the early 1990s, are shown by source in Figure 17.1. The general absence of annually updated data makes the recognition of trends difficult.

Since some wastes are inherently more dangerous than others, categories such as 'special', 'controlled' and 'hazardous' are often identified and such wastes dealt with in a more careful manner. In the UK, where the disposal of different types of waste is regulated by different laws, so-called special wastes, for example, are those deemed dangerous to life and are subject to regulations designed to track their movement from production to safe disposal, or from 'cradle to grave'. Although there is no universal agreement over what constitutes hazardous wastes, they include substances that are toxic to humans, plants or animals, are flammable, corrosive or explosive, or have high chemical reactivity. Such hazardous substances include acids and alkalis, heavy metals, oils, solvents, pesticides, PCBs (polychlorinated biphenyls) and various hospital wastes.

DISPOSAL OF WASTE

All wastes are disposed of into the environment, but some enter the environment in a more controlled manner than others (Fig. 17.2). Some wastes are emitted directly from the source without treatment, others are collected and sometimes treated before disposal. Wastes produced from the combustion of

Figure 17.1 Waste arisings by sector in the UK (after DoE, 1992).

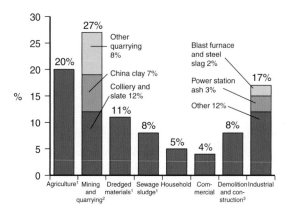

Global Casino 4th Ed 17.01 Key

While people may recognize that such facilities are necessary, the 'not in my backyard' syndrome is a powerful force in determining where such facilities are located. In practice, many such locally undesirable land uses, or LULUs, are sited in poor and minority communities. While at first this pattern may appear to reflect discrimination in siting procedures, research in the USA suggests that the situation may not always be so clear-cut. In some examples, LULUs appear to change community dynamics by driving down property values, resulting in a higher proportion of African Americans and the poor around such sites, so that the dynamics of the housing market are more to blame than any discrimination in the choice of LULU site (Been, 1994).

Strong public feelings have often been foremost in pushing for more stringent emission standards for incinerators. In many European countries, these standards are now stricter than those applied to other energy sources, and some observers fear that the use of incinerators may be discouraged as a consequence. In practice, the total environmental impact of incinerators should be assessed and compared to similar measures for both alternative energy production and alternative waste treatment facilities (Nilsson, 1991).

Part of this total environmental impact stems from the need to dispose of the ash generated by incineration, a final waste product that is usually buried in landfill sites. Pressure on available space for landfills, combined with the pollution dangers of heavy metals and dioxins remaining in the ash, have prompted research into the possible reuse of incinerator ash. One form of treatment developed in Japan is to convert incinerated waste ash into melted slag, which is then artificially crystallized to form stones (Nishida *et al.*, 2001). Crystallization gives the stones a hardness equal to natural stones, decomposes most of the dioxins in the process, and successfully contains hazardous heavy metals. The stones can then be used in civil engineering works as aggregates and building materials.

The construction industry is also one of the main users of the ashes produced in Swedish combustion plants, incorporating it into the construction of roads and surfaces in landfills, but also as ballast or filler in concrete. However, since non-coal ashes in Sweden tend to be rich in calcium, they are also used in forestry to balance the pH of acidic soils, and have been shown to improve growth rates of spruce trees (Ribbing, 2007).

International movement of hazardous waste

As controls on the disposal of hazardous wastes have tightened in developed countries, there has been movement of both operations and wastes themselves to areas where legislation is less stringent or poorly enforced. During the 1980s it became increasingly apparent that such trade in hazardous wastes was on the increase, both between industrialized and less-developed countries, and also between western and eastern Europe (Yakowitz, 1993). International concern over this trend led ultimately to the Basel Convention on the Control of Transboundary Movements of Hazardous Wastes and their Disposal, which came into force in 1992. The convention is based on a series of guiding principles originally adopted by the OECD countries, three of which are particularly important (OECD, 1991a):

1 The principle of non-discrimination – OECD members will apply the same controls on transfrontier movements of hazardous wastes involving non-member states as those applied to movements between member states.
2 The principle of prior informed consent – movements of waste will not be allowed without the consent of the appropriate authorities in the importing country.
3 The principle of adequacy of disposal facilities – movements of waste will only be permitted when wastes are directed to adequate disposal facilities in the importing country.

The Basel Convention also bans exports to countries that have not signed and ratified the treaty, and incorporates requirements to control the generation of hazardous wastes and obligations to manage them within the country of origin unless there is no capacity to do so (Hilz and Radka, 1991). However, following continuing concerns that the Basel Convention was not strong enough, a number of the signatory countries agreed in 1994 to add an amendment that actually bans altogether the export of hazardous wastes from OECD to non-OECD countries. This amendment, which has become known as the Basel Ban, had not entered into force by early 2008, but is for the most part effective since it is considered morally binding by the signatories.

REUSE, RECOVERY, RECYCLING AND PREVENTION

Although landfill and incineration are currently the most frequently used methods of waste disposal, they are generally considered to be low down on the list of possible techniques devised from an environmental impact perspective, as the EU's hierarchy of treatment techniques for solid wastes indicates (Table 17.2). Reusing a product, as opposed to discarding it, obviously makes environmental sense, and the advantages of waste recovery and recycling have also long been recognized. As for reuse, these advantages include a reduction of resource consumption, and a curb to the cost and inadequacies of disposal. In practice, waste products are reused when it is economically viable to do so and viability is assessed for a variety of motives. The history of industrial development is punctuated with examples of waste products being reappraised and turned into valuable resources. In the early nineteenth century, for example, Britain's fledgling chemical industry on Merseyside was using the Leblanc soda process to produce alkalis by treating salt with sulphuric acid, producing highly corrosive hydrogen chloride as a waste product. Realization that this pollutant was a lost resource, combined with fears of legal action from local landowners over the effects on surrounding vegetation, spurred industrialists to convert the hydrogen chloride to chlorine, which was used to make bleaching powder (Elkington and Burke, 1987). Another example from the nineteenth century concerns a resource that, today, most people take for granted. In the 1870s, when Nicolaus Otto found that a mix of flammable gas and air could be spark-ignited within the cylinder of a piston machine to generate movement, the flammable gas used was obtained from gasification of a waste product that came from the petroleum refinery process that produced paraffin for lamps. The waste product was called petrol (Svidén, 1993).

The perception shift that underlies these and many other examples highlights the fact that something that is considered a waste today can become a resource tomorrow. As Dijkema *et al.* (2000) put it, a substance or object is qualified as waste when it is not used to its full potential. This type of thinking can be summarized in a formula adopted by the multinational Minnesota Mining and Manufacturing (3M), a company distinguished by its commitment to a constant succession of innovative products:

pollutants (waste materials) + knowledge (technology) = potential resources

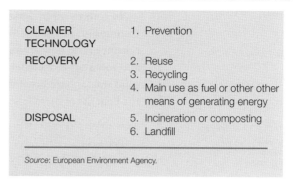

CLEANER TECHNOLOGY	1. Prevention
RECOVERY	2. Reuse
	3. Recycling
	4. Main use as fuel or other other means of generating energy
DISPOSAL	5. Incineration or composting
	6. Landfill

Source: European Environment Agency.

TABLE 17.2 Priorities for waste treatment in the EU

Reuse, recovery and recycling

There is a relationship between affluence and waste. In general terms, richer societies, and richer members of society, produce more waste than their less affluent counterparts. Indeed, realization of the economic value of certain wastes promotes reuse, recovery and recycling. In many developing countries, informal scavenging of municipal wastes from city dumps is widely practised and the materials recovered are put to a variety of uses (Fig. 17.6). It provides employment to individuals who otherwise would have none, particularly important in those countries where social security systems are inadequate or non-existent. These people are usually among the poorest sectors of society and often form discrete social groups or belong to minorities. Examples include the Zabbaleen in Egypt; Mexico's Pepenadores, Catroneros and Buscabotes; Basuriegos, Cartoneros, Traperos and Chatarreros in Colombia; Chamberos in Ecuador; and Cirujas in Argentina. One estimate suggests that in Asian and Latin American cities up to 2 per cent of the population earns a livelihood by scavenging, recovering materials to sell for reuse or recycling, as well as a range of items for their own consumption (Wilson *et al.*, 2006).

Studies of this informal sector have also highlighted the important role of such scavenged resources as inputs to small-scale manufacturing industries. In the Tanzanian capital of Dar es Salaam, these industries provide consumer goods that are much cheaper than if they were made from imported raw materials. Low-cost buckets, charcoal stoves and lamps are all made from scavenged metals from city dumps and sold to people who live in squatter settlements in the city (Yhdego, 1991).

Figure 17.6 A novel reuse for soft drinks cans in Namibia.

In today's more developed countries such informal waste recovery was also common more than 100 years ago, but more formalized recovery and recycling schemes have now sprung up. These schemes are also most advanced for metals and some other materials such as paper and glass, and collection points for such solid wastes have become a familiar sight in many cities in recent years. Some of the benefits of these schemes in environmental terms are shown in Table 17.3.

TABLE 17.3 Environmental benefits of substituting secondary materials for virgin resources

Environmental benefits	Aluminium	Steel	Paper	Glass
Reduction (%) of				
energy use	90–97	47–74	23–74	4–32
air pollution	95	85	74	20
water pollution	97	76	35	—
mining wastes	—	97	—	80
water use	—	40	58	50

Source: Bartone (1990).

Among the critical factors affecting the quantities of material that are recycled are the capacity of the recycling plant and equipment, and the size of the market for recycled materials. In some cases, these factors have been influenced by legislation. In extreme cases, some types of packaging are banned altogether. In Denmark, for example, beer and soft drinks were simply not allowed to be sold in cans for many years (although the ban was repealed and replaced with a deposit and return system in 2002). More commonly used measures include laws designating a certain level of use of recycled materials and the imposition of a tax on products that do not incorporate a certain amount of recycled material. The Canadian city of Toronto, for example, has a local law which states that daily newspapers must contain at least 50 per cent recycled fibre or the publishers will not be allowed to have vending boxes on the city's streets. Taxes on waste products are in line with the 'polluter-pays' principle and can encourage both the reduction of waste and the increase of recycling rates. Taxation has been suggested as a possible solution to the widespread problem of packaging waste, a priority waste problem in Europe and elsewhere. Imposition of a tax on packaging effectively incorporates the full social cost of a product into the retail price by including the cost of disposal of its wrapping (Pearce and Turner, 1992). The EU Packaging Directive imposed an obligation on industry to recover or recycle at least half of all its packaging by 2001.

Another EU directive has been introduced to tackle the complex disposal issues associated with old motor vehicles. Under the directive, car manufacturers have become responsible for disposing of so-called end-of-life vehicles (ELVs) in the European Union, with a target of a 95 per cent recovery/reuse rate by 2015. The manufacturers are responsible for all or a significant part of the costs of takeback, reuse and recycling of vehicle components, while the national governments are obliged to provide authorized treatment facilities for the ELVs (Smink, 2007).

Denmark was one of the first countries to introduce a comprehensive waste taxation scheme to promote reuse and recycling as part of a waste management policy developed in the mid 1980s (Andersen, 1998). The policy was in response to the country's serious waste disposal problem: per-capita generation of waste was among the highest in Europe; Denmark was running out of landfill space; and there was widespread public concern about air pollution from incinerators. The tax is levied on most of the household and industrial waste delivered to Danish landfills and incinerators, designed to reduce the overall quantity of waste, to ease the burden on the country's limited landfills and to lower dioxin emissions from incineration. It has also been an integral part of Denmark's various national waste management plans, the first of which was introduced in 1989 with the aim of achieving a 54 per cent recycling rate for all waste by 1996. No taxes are levied on waste that is reused or recycled.

The Danish waste-reduction policy, in which the taxation system has played an important role, has registered considerable success. In the ten years from 1987 to 1996, Denmark achieved a reduction of 26 per cent in the quantity of waste delivered to landfills and incinerators, and reached an overall recycling rate of 61 per cent. By 2004, the national recycling rate reached 64 per cent, with 12 per cent of waste disposed of in landfill and the remaining 24 per cent going to incineration.

Taxes on waste are used to increase the economic incentives to recycle, but such intervention is not always necessary. In economic terms, the large energy savings gained from recycling of most metals make the practice worthwhile anyway. In the case of aluminium, the conversion of alumina to aluminium by electrolysis – the Hall–Héroult process – accounts for 80 per cent of the energy used in the entire production process, a stage that is bypassed when aluminium is recycled (Fig. 17.7). These and other benefits have encouraged the increasing use of recycling in those industries that use metals.

Manipulation of the retail price of a consumer product is an economic instrument that has long been used to encourage reuse of certain articles. The charging of a returnable deposit on glass bottles is a good example, providing an economic incentive to return the bottle for reuse. It is a practice that is still widely used in many developing countries, but one that has declined in some more developed economies as returnable glass bottles have largely been replaced with throwaway plastic ones. In some countries, such as Germany and Switzerland, legislation has been passed to encourage moves back to the refilling of drinks containers, but in some other countries similar measures could significantly increase the price to

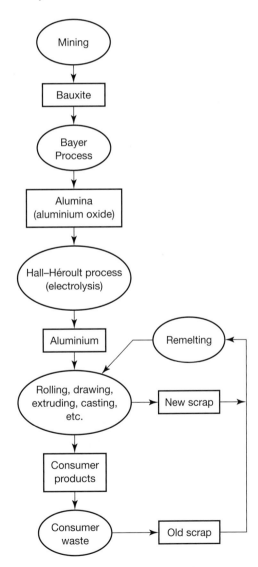

Figure 17.7 Stages in the production of aluminium goods.

the consumer, a politically sensitive step to take. In the USA, for example, reusable bottles were common when bottling plants were small and widely distributed throughout the country, but recent decades have seen a centralization of bottling facilities, in part as a response to the lower transport costs imposed by lighter plastic bottles. Hence, an increased emphasis on returnable glass bottles would entail considerably higher transport costs. Such economic factors have been partly responsible for the increasing use of the recycling option, which has become widespread practice in many developed countries in recent years. For the OECD countries, the average recovery rate for glass rose from 22 per cent in 1980 to 32 per cent in the late 1980s (OECD, 1991a), and in a number of European countries recycled material makes up more than 75 per cent of all glass used (Fig. 17.8).

An industrial process that has a long history of waste product recycling is the steel industry. Steel slags from the Basic-Bessemer or Thomas process have been used as a phosphate fertilizer since 1880. The hardness and structural stability of blast furnace and steel slags have also enabled their use as aggregates for road construction and as armourstones in hydraulic engineering works, to stabilize and refill riverbeds and banks scoured by erosion (Motz and Geiseler, 2001). These uses help to relieve the pressure on natural aggregates like gravel, sand and processed rocks, the excavation of which leaves scars on the landscape. Steel converter slag has also been used more recently to treat wastewater. The process utilizes the slag's iron oxide, or magnetite component, which can adsorb nickel, a heavy metal, from wastewater (Ortiz *et al.*, 2001).

Wastewater is commonly reused or recycled in many countries, and is widely recognized as a significant, growing and reliable water source that is particularly important in drylands where water is a scarce resource. Indeed, as Bakir (2001) points out, wastewater production is the only potential water source that will increase as the population grows and the demand on fresh water increases. The use of treated or untreated wastewater in landscaping and agriculture is common in many countries of the Middle East and North Africa, including the United Arab Emirates, Oman, Bahrain, Egypt, Yemen, Syria and Tunisia. Water resources management strategies in several countries, such as Jordan, sensibly consider wastewater as a part of the water budget.

In many cases domestic wastewater is diverted to cropland for irrigation. The water itself is a valuable resource and sewage is typically high in key plant nutrients (phosphorus and nitrogen). In Mexico, wastewater from almost all cities that have a sewerage system is used in this way to irrigate about 150 000 ha of crops nationally. The largest such zone is in the Mezquital Valley where wastewater and storm runoff channelled out of Mexico City considerably increases yields (Table 17.4). However, these increased yields come at an environmental price, since none of Mexico City's wastewater receives any conventional sewage treatment before it is used in this way. One characteristic of sewage is its high

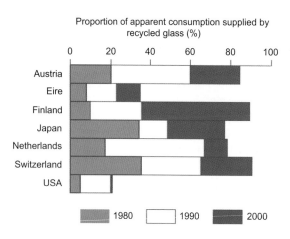

Figure 17.8 Glass recycling in selected countries (from data in OECD, 2005)

heavy metal content, a function of sewage systems mixing industrial and household wastes, and long-term applications of wastewater in the Mezquital Valley have led to an accumulation of heavy metals in soils and their uptake into the crops themselves. There is also evidence of an increase in parasitic infections among agricultural workers and their families due to their exposure to raw sewage (Siebe and Cifuentes, 1995). In some cases, infectious diseases can be transmitted from sewage-irrigated crops to the general public. An outbreak of cholera in Jerusalem in 1970 was thought to be caused by consumption of vegetables irrigated with wastewater. The risks of this kind of disease transmission can be limited by simple measures, however. Irrigation with wastewater during planting is less hazardous than during the growing cycle, and certain crops (e.g. fruit and vegetables) are more likely to carry disease than others.

Crop	Wastewater irrigation	Fluvial irrigation	Rain-fed agriculture
Maize	4.8	2.9–4.0	0.37
Bean	1.4	0.28–1.2	0.18
Barley	3.1	2.0	1.4

Source: after Siebe and Cifuentes (1995).

TABLE 17.4 Crop yields (t/ha) with different agricultural practices in the Mezquital Valley, central Mexico

In countries where sewage is treated, the sludge that remains after treatment is also reused as a fertilizer due to its high nutrient content. About half the sewage sludge produced in the UK, and one-third of that in France and Germany, is reused in this way, but in these and other countries, further use is limited by the high heavy metal content. Hence sewage sludge not used as fertilizer is disposed of by ocean dumping, dumping in landfill and municipal garbage dumps, or by incineration. Indeed, continued concern over the pollution content of sewage sludge, combined with a rising demand for organic and quality-assured food products, prompted Switzerland to end its use as a fertilizer in 2005.

As population and industrialization continue to increase, however, and the treatment of water and sewage becomes more widely used in order to reduce the pollution impacts from untreated sewage outlets, so more sludge will need to be disposed of. Switzerland has incinerated all of its sewage sludge since 2005, but a more innovative approach to this increasing dilemma of disposal can turn a problem into a benefit by realizing the value of the heavy metals themselves. One estimate of the potential yield of some of the high-value metals in sewage sludge suggests that global production of palladium from sewage sludge could be of the same order of magnitude as that from mining production (Table 17.5). The future disposal of sewage sludge should concentrate on the control of pollutants at source and the extraction of metals (Lottermoser and Morteani, 1993), an approach that would yield numerous benefits, including:

- more widespread use of sludge as a fertilizer
- revenue from metals extracted
- conservation of geological metal resources
- saving on expensive waste repository space
- prevention of environmental impacts on terrestrial and marine ecosystems.

Metal	Current production (t/year)	Production from sewage sludge (t/year)
Gold	1600	100
Platinum	100	8
Palladium	100	80

Source: after Lottermoser and Morteani (1993).

Waste prevention: cleaner production

There is no doubt that the best way to manage waste is to prevent it at source wherever this is possible. The argument that prevention is better than cure is put by UNEP's Industry and Environment Programme Activity Centre:

> When end-of-pipe pollution controls are added to industrial systems, less immediate damage occurs. But these solutions come at increasing monetary costs to both society and industry and have not always proven to be optimal from an environmental aspect. End-of-pipe controls are also reactive and selective. Cleaner production, on the other hand, is a comprehensive, preventative approach to environmental protection.
>
> (UNEP IE/PAC, 1993: 1)

Cleaner production is achieved by examining all phases of a product's life cycle from raw material extraction to its ultimate disposal – so-called life-cycle assessment or LCA – and reducing the wastefulness of any particular phase. LCA involves identifying and quantifying the environmental loads involved in each stage of a product's life cycle (e.g. the energy and raw materials consumed, the emissions and wastes generated) and assessing the options available for reducing these impacts (Fig. 17.9). Incorporating LCA into cleaner production means that the entire process can encompass such aims as:

- conservation of energy and raw materials
- reduction in the use of toxic or environmentally harmful substances
- reduction of the quantity and toxicity of wastes and pollutant discharges
- extension of product durability.

Cleaner production embodies both the ideas of environmental sustainability and economic efficiency. In practice it involves improving the productivity of energy and material use to reduce consumption of resources and cut pollution per unit output. A range of industrial examples of such cleaner production, is shown in Table 17.6. They range from low-tech changes in production like the example of a textile factory in India, to more capitally intensive modifications, to large-scale production facilities such as cement and automobile manufacture, and new product development. Nevertheless, for all the examples shown, the payback time for the capital expenditure incurred is three years or less, indicating the immediate economic feasibility of such actions.

Hydropower

Hydropower is the only renewable resource used on a large scale today for electricity generation. At the turn of the current century, one-third of the countries in the world relied on hydropower for more than half their electricity supply, and large dams generate about 19 per cent of electricity overall (World Commission on Dams, 2000). The main constraints on further development are the social and environmental impacts associated with dams, which are outlined in Chapter 9, although many of these problems can be mitigated by improved planning with the inclusion of public participation at an early stage. It should also be noted that reservoirs used for hydroelectricity generation are likely to emit significant quantities of atmospheric pollutants (see page 175).

Although much uncertainty surrounds the estimates of potential hydroelectric power that could be generated, there is agreement that, to date, only a relatively small proportion of this resource has been developed, and the greatest potential lies in the developing world and the countries of the former USSR. The potential for small-scale hydroschemes, designed to serve local needs, is thought to be particularly great (Moreira and Poole, 1993).

Wind energy

The wind's energy has been used by sailing ships and windmills to power human activities for thousands of years, and wind pumps are still a common feature of rural landscapes today, particularly in dry regions where they are used to pump groundwater to the surface (Fig. 18.3). Modern wind turbines for electricity generation are a comparatively recent phenomenon, which some suggest have the potential to supply as much as 20 per cent of global electricity demand (Grubb and Meyer, 1993).

Much of the pioneering work on the large-scale generation of wind-derived electricity has been carried out in California where developments were encouraged by favourable tax policies. California now produces just over 1 per cent of its electricity from wind farms, much of it coming from the 7500 turbines at Altamount Pass. Denmark has also put a great deal of effort into developing its wind power potential, encouraged by investment incentives and enthusiastic public support. The achievements have been considerable: turbines in the Danish countryside and offshore generated nearly 19 per cent of its electricity consumption in 2004, up from 4 per cent ten years before. Denmark considers that the amount of renewable energy in the national electricity supply could reach 80 per cent by 2025 (DEA, 2005) and a

Figure 18.3 Wind power is widely used in rural areas, particularly to pump groundwater to the surface in regions where surface water is in short supply, as shown here on the Mediterranean island of Malta.

large part of this will come from offshore wind farms in the North Sea and the Baltic Sea (EEA, 2001). Following establishment of the world's first offshore wind farm at Vindeby in 1991, Denmark has rapidly developed its offshore generating capacity in the twenty-first century (Table 18.2). The turbines at the new Horns Rev II farm in the North Sea and at Rødsand II in the Baltic will be four times as big as previous models, with blades 60 m in diameter on 55-metre towers. Long-term development of the technology means that Danish offshore wind power has become as cheap to produce as building new coal-fired power stations, and comparable in cost to gas-fired stations, without the disadvantage of CO_2 emissions.

TABLE 18.2 Danish offshore wind farms

Name	Start-up year	Total capacity (MW)
Vindeby, Falster	1991	5
Tunø Knob, Odder	1995	5
Middelgrunden, Copenhagen	2001	40
Horns Rev I	2002	160
Samsø	2003	23
Rønland, Harboøre	2003	17
Frederikshavn	2003	8
Nysted/Rødsand I	2003	165
Horns Rev II	2009?	200
Rødsand II	?	200

Source: after DEA (2005).

There are several environmental impacts associated with wind farms. Noise was a serious concern surrounding earlier generations of turbines, but modern designs make little sound above the rush of the wind. Problems with bird kills persist, however, for some larger species such as eagles, and interference with TV reception and sensitive electronics is also experienced around turbines with steel blades. The land requirement of large wind farms has been another issue of concern, although land between individual machines can still be used for other activities such as farming and ranching. Land values at Altamount Pass, for example, have increased markedly following installation of the wind farms, as royalties have generated extra income for ranchers while ranching has continued. Perhaps the most serious objection to wind power in many areas is on aesthetic grounds, since some people frown upon the idea of landscapes covered in windmills. In the UK, for example, more than 50 well-known literary figures wrote to *The Times Literary Supplement* in 1994 to protest at plans to increase the number of wind turbines on the moors above Haworth because of the area's associations with the novels of the Brontë sisters.

Many of these drawbacks associated with wind farms may be avoided by constructing the turbines offshore, an approach that has great potential along much of the western European coastline. In an assessment of the potential impacts on the marine environment, Petersen and Malm (2006) point out that effects during the construction phase should be negligible if appropriate care is taken to avoid areas containing rare habitats or species. Similarly, disturbances associated with windmill operation – noise, vibrations and electromagnetic fields – are considered to be of

Gill, A.B. 2005 Offshore renewable energy: ecological implications of generating electricity in the coastal zone. *Journal of Applied Ecology* 42: 605–15. A comprehensive assessment of possible positive and negative impacts along coastlines.

Kaygusuz, K. 2002 Sustainable development of hydropower and biomass energy in Turkey. *Energy Conversion and Management* 43: 1099–120. An assessment of present and future use of two renewable energy sources.

Löfstedt, R. 1998 Sweden's biomass controversy: a case study of communicating policy issues. *Environment* 40(4): 16–20, 42–5. The debate over biomass in a country committed to phasing out nuclear power.

Parker, P., Rowlands, I.H. and Scott, D. 2003 Innovations to reduce residential energy use and carbon emissions: an integrated approach. *The Canadian Geographer* 47: 169–84. Research from a community in Canada on limiting energy use in the home.

Patterson, W. 2007 *Keeping the lights on: towards sustainable electricity*. London, Earthscan. A readable account arguing that electricity is about infrastructure and should be perceived as a commodity.

Pimentel, D., Pleasant, A., Barron, J., Gaudioso, J., Pollock, N., Chae, E., Kim, Y., Lassiter, A., Schiavoni, C., Jackson, A., Lee, M. and Eaton, A. 2004 US energy conservation and efficiency: benefits and costs. *Environment, Development and Sustainability* 6: 279–305. This paper argues that the US economy could save about a third of its current energy consumption through conservation and efficiency measures.

Sims, R.E.H., Hastings, A., Schlamadinger, B., Taylor, G. and Smith, P. 2006 Energy crops: current status and future prospects. *Global Change Biology* 12: 2054–76. A comprehensive review of energy crops.

Smith, J. 2005 *Chernobyl: catastrophe and consequences*. Berlin, Springer-Praxis. A comprehensive assessment of the Chernobyl accident, its long-term environmental consequences and solutions to the problems found.

WEBSITES

www.worldenergy.org/wec-geis/ the World Energy Council site contains information, data and reports on all aspects of energy.

www.caddet.org/ specializes in the collection and dissemination of information on new energy-saving technologies.

www.eere.energy.gov/ the US Department of Energy's Energy Efficiency and Renewable Energy Network has much information and many links to related sites.

www.iaea.org/ the International Atomic Energy Agency site covers many aspects of atomic energy, including up-to-date data and reports.

www.reeep.org/ The Renewable Energy and Energy Efficiency Partnership is a global public-private partnership involved in clean energy policy and finance.

www.renewableenergy.com/ a comprehensive site with news and links covering all forms of renewables.

www.pembina.org/ a Canadian body dedicated to the advancement of sustainable energy

POINTS FOR DISCUSSION

■ How would an increase in our reliance on renewable energy sources, as against fossil fuels, contribute to solving other environmental issues?

■ Human society's unsustainable use of fossil fuels is the root cause of virtually all other environmental issues. How far do you agree?

■ Should governments do more to encourage the development of renewable energy sources or should they leave it to the power companies?

■ Review the arguments for and against the banning of nuclear power.

19 Mining

TOPICS COVERED

Global economic aspects of mineral production, Environmental impacts of mining, Rehabilitation and reduction of mining damage, The true costs of mining

KEY WORDS

tailings, subsidence, crownhole, acid mine drainage, bioleach, full-cost pricing

We only need to look at the names used to describe key periods in the early development of societies – the Stone Age, the Bronze Age and the Iron Age – to realize the long importance of mining as a human activity. People have been using minerals from the Earth's crust since *Homo habilis* first began to fashion stone tools 2.5 million years ago. Today, we are more dependent than ever before upon the extraction of minerals from the Earth. Virtually every material thing in modern society is either a direct mineral product or the result of processing with the aid of mineral derivatives such as steel, energy or fertilizers.

The naturally occurring elements and compounds mined are usually classified into four groups:

1 metals (e.g. aluminium, copper, iron)
2 industrial minerals (e.g. lime, soda ash)
3 construction materials (e.g. sand, gravel)
4 energy minerals (e.g. coal, uranium, oil, natural gas).

In terms of volume extracted, construction materials are by far the largest product of the world's mining industry. They are found and extracted in every country. An estimated 11 billion tonnes of stone, and 9 billion tonnes of sand and gravel were taken from the ground in 1991. About 125 000 tonnes of crushed rock, for example, is used to build 1 km of motorway. Metallic minerals are mined in smaller quantities. World production of iron ore in 2005 was 1.5 billion tonnes, bauxite 176 million tonnes, and phosphate 154 million tonnes (British Geological Survey, 2007).

GLOBAL ECONOMIC ASPECTS OF MINERAL PRODUCTION

The location of mineral concentrations in the Earth's crust is a fact of nature, but there are a host of human and natural factors that determine if and when a mineral is recognized as a resource, classified as a reserve, and eventually exploited. Such factors include global and local economic and political influences, as well as the local availability of basic requirements for mining such as energy and water. While the use of minerals dates from before the time of *Homo sapiens*, it was the

Industrial Revolution that sparked their large-scale exploitation. Between 1750 and 1900, global mineral use increased ten-fold as the population doubled and, since 1900, use has increased more than thirteen-fold (Bosson and Varon, 1977).

The rapid increase in society's use of minerals has periodically sparked concern over their imminent depletion, a sentiment expressed strongly in the 1970s by the Club of Rome (Meadows *et al.*, 1972). Although the amount of minerals in the lithosphere is finite, improvements in technology and changing price/cost relationships, as well as shifting perceptions of the political risks of operating in particular countries, mean that estimates of reserves are constantly being re-evaluated. The dynamics of changing resources are illustrated at the level of one mine by the Palabora copper mine in South Africa, which at its start-up as an open-pit operation in 1966 was estimated to contain an ore deposit with 1.8 million tonnes of copper, giving the mine an operational life of 24 years. By 1991, however, the estimate had changed to 4.7 million tonnes, with a life of 35 years (Table 19.1). Improved technology and economic changes help to explain the increase in reserves, lowering the cut-off grade of exploitable ore. The estimated lifetime of the mine has since been extended still further, to 55 years from start-up, by the decision to develop an underground mine at Palabora. A further 2.3 million tonnes of contained copper were estimated to be economically accessible from the mine at the beginning of 1998 (Schickler, personal communication, 1998).

TABLE 19.1 Estimates of reserves at Palabora copper mine, South Africa

	Defined at start-up in 1966	Full potential as seen in 1991
Reserves before mining:		
Tonnage (million tonnes)	259	854
Grade (% copper)	0.69	0.55
Contained copper (million tonnes)	1.79	4.67
Cut-off grade (% copper)	0.3	0.15
Mine life from start-up (years)	24	35

Source: Crowson (1992).

Another important factor is the simple fact that large areas of the world's land surface have not been mapped in detail for their minerals, let alone explored, particularly where underlying as opposed to surface geology is concerned. New ores are regularly discovered and new mines opened, such as the large copper mine at Neves Corvo in southern Portugal, which began operations in 1989 and produced more than 100 000 tonnes of contained copper in 1997. These factors combine to balance the fears of those who suggest that the end is nigh for global mineral exploitation. In the words of one mining industry official: 'it is highly improbable that society will run out of minerals over the long term' (Crowson, 1992: iv). Indeed, the recycling of metals already taken from the lithosphere reduces some of the need for exploiting virgin resources, and Crowson suggests that these materials should be regarded as a renewable resource since most metals can be recycled indefinitely.

On the national scale, most countries have adequate reserves of minerals used in the construction industry and these materials (with the exception of cement) are seldom traded internationally. The use of other minerals, particularly metals, is very heavily concentrated in the rich countries, however, and their movement is an important component of international trade. Many developing countries rely heavily upon mineral exports as sources of foreign exchange, with at least 17 countries deriving around 40 per cent or more of their export income from non-fuel mineral exports in the 1990s (Table 19.2). The sources of minerals for major industrial nations vary. Some industrialized countries have considerable domestic reserves of certain minerals: Australia mined 34 per cent of global bauxite production in 2005, for example, while for other minerals less developed countries are important sources. Generally, industrialized countries import their minerals from proximate areas of the developing world: from Latin America to the USA, Africa to western Europe, and Asia and Oceania to Japan. Most such ores are shipped from their country of origin with minimal processing, since trade barriers often act to prevent developing-country producers from adding value to their raw materials.

TABLE 19.2 Economic importance of mining, as 'relevance'* of mining for exports in per cent, in selected countries, 1990–99

Country	Main minerals	Relevance of mining for exports (%)
Guinea	Bauxite/alumina	85
Congo, D R	Copper, diamonds	80
Zambia	Copper	75
Niger	Uranium	71
Botswana	Diamonds, copper, nickel	70
Namibia	Diamonds, uranium, copper	55
Jamaica	Bauxite/alumina	51
Sierra Leone	Bauxite/alumina	50
Suriname	Bauxite/alumina	48
Chile	Copper	47
Mauritania	Iron ore	46
Papua New Guinea	Copper, gold	45
Peru	Gold, copper	44
Mongolia	Copper, molybdenum	43
Central African Republic	Diamonds	42
Ukraine	Iron ore, manganese	40
Mali	Gold	40

* 'Relevance' reflects both the share of minerals and metals in exports and the share of mining and quarrying in GDP.
Source: IFC (2002).

In 1990, the European Community, Japan and the USA accounted for 60 per cent of the world consumption of aluminium and refined copper, 58 per cent of refined lead, 55 per cent of tin and 50 per cent of zinc. However, since the Second World War, mineral use in the wealthier nations has not been growing as fast as in developing countries. Between 1950 and 1990, for example, the percentage of global aluminium used by developing countries rose from 2 per cent to 19 per cent, for zinc the percentage rose from 3 per cent to 25 per cent over the same period, and for steel the rise was from 5 per cent to 25 per cent (Wellner and Kürsten, 1992). This increase is largely accounted for by emerging industrial nations such as Brazil, China, India, Mexico and the 'Asian tigers' of the Pacific Rim.

The slowdown in demand in richer countries is explained by several factors. Industrial economies grew more slowly after the oil crisis of the mid 1970s, and structural change in these economies, with less emphasis on heavy industry, and moves towards services and high technology, has meant a slowdown in demand for physical materials. The growth of demand for virgin metals has also declined, with more emphasis on recycling and the introduction of new materials such as plastics and ceramics.

ENVIRONMENTAL IMPACTS OF MINING

Concern at the environmental impacts of mining is by no means a recent phenomenon. Georgius Agricola (1556), author of the world's first mining textbook, could have been writing today as he outlined the strongest arguments of mining's detractors in sixteenth-century Germany:

> [T]he woods and groves are cut down, for there is need of an endless amount of wood for timbers, machines and the smelting of metals. And when the woods and groves are felled, then are exterminated the beasts and birds, very many of which furnish a pleasant and agreeable food for man. Further, when the ores are washed, the water which has been used poisons the brooks and streams, and either destroys the fish or drives them away.
>
> (Agricola, 1556: 8)

Little appears to have changed in the more than 400 years since Agricola. In recent times, environmentalists have often quoted this passage as evidence of the long-standing environmental impact of mining. Interestingly, the quote is often used out of context, since Agricola in fact dismissed these anti-mining sentiments on the grounds that the environmental cost was far outweighed by the benefits to society:

> If we remove metals from the service of man, all methods of protecting and sustaining health and more carefully preserving the course of life are done away with. If there were no metals, men would pass a horrible and wretched existence in the midst of wild beasts; they would return to the acorns and fruits and berries of the forest.
>
> (Agricola, 1556: 14)

There can be no doubting that mining involves an environmental impact, and the destruction of habitats suggested in Agricola's textbook is perhaps the most obvious from among a diverse catalogue of ecological changes that the various types of mining operation can cause (Table 19.3). The question as to whether such impacts should be regarded as worth the benefits derived from the minerals extracted is a complex one, which will be returned to after consideration of the physical problems involved.

Habitat destruction

Vegetation is stripped and soil and rock moved, both for the extraction process itself and the concomitant building of plant, administration and housing facilities, and the history of mining activity has left considerable areas of disrupted habitat. The scale of damage is greatest at so-called opencast or strip mining sites. Several small coral islands in the Pacific Ocean exploited for their phosphate, the

TABLE 19.3 Environmental problems associated with mining

Problem	Type of mining operation			
	Open-pit and quarrying	Opencast (as in coal)	Underground	Dredging (as in tin or gold)
Habitat destruction	X	X	—	X
Dump failure/erosion	X	X	X	—
Subsidence	—	—	X	—
Water pollution	X	X	X	X
Air pollution*	X	X	X	—
Noise	X	X	—	—
Air/blast/ground vibration	X	X	—	—
Visual intrusion	X	X	X	X
Dereliction	X	—	X	X

X: Problem present
—: Problem unlikely
*: Can be associated with smelting, which may not be at the site of ore/mineral extraction
Source: modified after Whitlow (1990).

fossilized remains of centuries of birds' droppings, are among the worst affected. Opencast phosphate mining on the Pacific island state of Nauru involved scraping off the surface soil to enable removal of the phosphate from between the walls and columns of ancient coral. A severely degraded landscape of highly irregular solution-pitted limestone remains over about 80 per cent of the island's 2100 ha area. Many of the indigenous plants and animals that previously inhabited the mined-out areas have either disappeared or are endangered. Indeed, virtually all of these mined areas, except for narrow corridors either side of gravel roads, are now 'totally unusable for habitation, crops, or anything else that might benefit the people of Nauru' (Gowdy and McDaniel, 1999: 334).

Disposal of waste rock and/or 'tailings' – the impurities left after a mineral has been extracted from its ore – usually destroys still larger areas of natural ecosystems. This is an increasing problem, both because of the growth in demand for minerals and because as rich ores are mined out, so lower-grade deposits are worked, producing more waste per unit of mineral produced. While four centuries ago the average grade of copper ore mined was about 8 per cent (Bosson and Varon, 1977), the average grade in the 1990s was 0.91 per cent, which means about 990 million tonnes of waste generated for the 9 million tonnes of copper produced.

Similar product-to-waste ratios are found in the china clay mines of south-western England, where the production of 1 tonne of kaolin produces 1 tonne of mica, 2 tonnes of undecomposed rock ('stent') and 6 tonnes of quartz sand. In Cornwall and Devon, where china clay has been mined since the 1770s, these waste materials are dumped on surrounding land to produce a devastated landscape of heaps, pits and lagoons, with disused land in between, covering an area of 9100 ha (Bradshaw and Chadwick, 1980). On the national scale, such mining waste-lands can cover a significant proportion of the national land area. Punning (1993) reports that excavation of Estonia's 4 billion tonnes of oil shale reserves, the world's largest commercially exploited deposit, plus sand, gravel and peat extraction, has devastated at least 45 000 ha, or 1 per cent, of the national land area. Table 19.4 shows the areas disturbed in the countries of the former Soviet Union.

TABLE 19.4 National areas of land disturbed by mining in the countries of the former Soviet Union

Country	Area of disturbed land, beginning 1989 (thousand hectares)	Years required to reclaim
Russia	1180	11
Ukraine	198	8
Belarus	120	13
Uzbekistan	52	32
Kazakhstan	167	16
Georgia	3	7
Azerbaijan	21	19
Lithuania	32	27
Moldova	3	6
Latvia	44	44
Kyrgyzstan	7	16
Tajikistan	6	15
Armenia	8	82
Turkmenistan	5	7
Estonia	47	78

Source: after Bond and Piepenburg (1990).

To date, however, the largest areas of strip mining in the world are for coal (Fig. 19.1). In the USA, which produces about 60 per cent of its coal by this method, it has affected vast areas of the Appalachian Mountains and large areas of the states of Ohio, West Virginia and Kentucky. On average, surface mining for coal consumes 10–30 ha of land for every million tonnes of coal produced in the USA, but in other parts of the world, local conditions and available technology can result in much higher land consumption-to-production ratios. In southern Russia's Kuznetsk Basin, for example, the figure is about 166 ha per million tonnes (Bond and Piepenburg, 1990).

In areas where smelting takes place near the extraction site, further damage can be caused by cutting trees to fuel smelters. In Copper Basin, Tennessee, USA, an area of 14 500 ha was deforested in the nineteenth century to smelt copper ore in vast open-air pits, and the charcoal requirements for iron ore smelting in the Grande Carajás Project in Pará

Figure 19.1 Opencast coal mining at Gartzweiler, Germany.

state, Brazil, will spur the cutting of an estimated 50 000 ha of tropical forest each year during the mine's expected 250-year life (Fearnside, 1989). Although fuel for smelting was originally proposed to be grown on plantations, in practice much of the charcoal has been made from natural forest.

The environmental impacts of mining are not just limited to terrestrial ecosystems. The mining of coral and sand for road and building materials is a widespread threat to coastlines in many parts of the world (Fig. 19.2) and particularly to island reefs in the Pacific Ocean. Apart from the physical destruction of reefs to provide limestone, and the introduction of toxic substances to the marine environment during the mining process, the dredging of sand causes beach erosion and alters water circulation, leading to sedimentation on reefs (IUCN, 1988; see also page 122).

Marine ecosystems can also be degraded by any form of mining in the coastal zone. A range of effects has been observed on the coral reefs fringing Misima Island in Papua New Guinea following the start of opencast mining for gold in 1989 (Fallon *et al.*, 2002). Increased soil erosion from the mine caused higher sedimentation rates on the reef, causing effects ranging from coral mortality due to smothering to contamination from metals contained in the sediment.

When exploitation of polymetallic (manganese) nodules from the deep-sea bed becomes a commercial proposition, although this is likely to be a long time in the future, it too will bring disturbances to the world's oceans. Impacts will occur at different levels in the water column: at the sediment surface due to collector impact, immediately above the seabed due to the plumes of sediment raised, and at other levels as abraded nodule materials and sediments are discharged (Thiel and Schriever, 1990). The most commercially significant concentrations of nodules are found in the Pacific and Indian oceans.

Figure 19.2 Sand mining from beaches in Oman, in areas where building sand is scarce, is threatening breeding sites of endangered green and hawksbill turtles. Coastal erosion studies indicate that many of these beaches are ancient and slow to generate, hence removal of sand threatens their existence. Some beaches are earmarked for tourist development, another reason for their protection.

Geomorphological impacts

Mining involves the movement of quantities of soil and rock, and thus by definition is a human-induced geomorphological process. The scale of the process has reached the level whereby estimates suggest that as much as a hundred times more material is stripped from the Earth by mining than by all the natural erosion carried out by rivers (Goudie, 2006: 162). The impacts of mining, however, are much more localized than the denudation caused by rivers. The opencast copper mine at Bingham Canyon in Utah, USA, reputed to be the largest human excavation in the world, has involved the removal of more than 3400 million tonnes of material over an area of 7.2 km^2, to a depth of 770 m. Nevertheless, such features can attain significant proportions on the national scale: surficial scars on the landscape of Kuwait, created by the oil-generated construction boom, cover large parts of the national land area, with some individual quarries measuring up to 40 km in length (Fig. 19.3). Reconstruction of the country's urban fabric after the Gulf War of the early 1990s further enlarged these surface features.

New land forms are also created by the deposition of wastes, and these can create new geomorphological hazards, such as landslides and subsidence. The death of 150 people at Aberfan, South Wales, in 1966, when waste piles from the Merthyr Vale coal mine suddenly collapsed, graphically illustrated the dangers of unregulated waste tipping.

Care must be taken with opencast excavations to avoid such problems associated with slope instability, which can occur in both active and abandoned workings. The city centre of Izmir, in Turkey, is peppered with 70 abandoned

Figure 19.3 Distribution of sand and gravel quarries in Kuwait (after Khalaf, 1989).

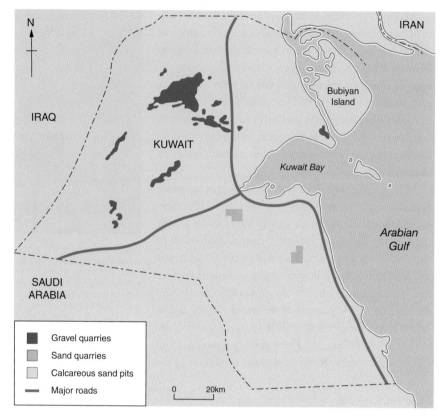

quarries formerly worked for their building stone, most of it good-quality andesite. The quarries were initially located beyond the urban area but are now within the city centre thanks to Izmir's expansion. Most of these old stone quarries were abandoned without taking any precautions against possible slope failures, and sliding and toppling are now common hazards faced by local residents (Koca and Kincal, 2004).

Surface subsidence is caused by underground workings, and is most commonly associated with coal mining where whole seams of material, frequently several metres thick, are removed, resulting in overlying strata collapsing downwards. Two major types of mining subsidence can be identified (Scott and Statham, 1998):

1 *crownholes* – localized crater-like holes that appear at the surface following collapse of strata into a mine
2 *general subsidence* – settlement of the ground surface over a wide area resulting from the collapse of part of the mine.

Damage to mining equipment, buildings, communications and agriculture through the disruption of drainage systems are the most common results. In the USA, for example, subsidence due to underground coal mining affects 800 000 ha in 30 states (Gray and Bruhn, 1984). The problem is also common in Polish Silesia and in the Ruhr Valley cities of Germany. Subsidence into old gold mine workings meant that an entire street of houses had to be moved in the town of Malartic in Quebec, Canada (McCall, 1998).

Collapse also occurs when water is pumped out of mine workings, lowering local water tables, which results in the drying out and shrinkage of materials such as clays, and through the reduction in underground fluid pressure that results from oil and natural-gas extraction. Blunden (1985) notes that marine inundation is a danger caused by subsidence from oil and gas extraction in areas near sea level and quotes examples from oil fields on the shore of Venezuela's Lake Maracaibo, coastal locations in Japan and the Po Delta in Italy. A particularly dramatic example occurred in the Wilmington oilfield in southern California where abstraction between 1928 and 1971 caused 9.3 m of subsidence at Long Beach, Los Angeles (Table 19.5).

Location	Area affected (km^2)	Maximum subsidence (m)	Period	Rate (mm/year)
Inglewood, USA	–	2.9	1917–63	63
Maracaibo, Venezuela	450	5.03	1929–90	82
Wilmington, USA	78	9.3	1928–71	216

Source: after Cooke and Doornkamp (1990); Goudie (2006).

TABLE 19.5 Examples of ground subsidence due to oil and gas abstraction

Pollution

Pollution from mineral extraction, transportation and processing can also present serious environmental problems, affecting soil, water and air quality. Examples of pollution emanating from the transport of oil are given elsewhere (see Chapters 6 and 7), while here the emphasis is on mine workings and smelting.

Down and Stocks (1977) note four major water pollution problems associated with mining, all of which can cause serious damage to aquatic life and, on occasion, to human health:

1 heavy metal pollution
2 acid mine drainage
3 eutrophication
4 deoxygenation.

Many tailings contain metal ores and other contaminants, formerly locked up in solid rock, which can be leached into soils and waterways, and blown into the surrounding atmosphere. Metals are also released into the environment during smelting. Contamination by heavy metals released by these activities has been very extensive from the earliest times. The concentration of copper found in Greenland ice layers began to exceed the natural background concentration about 2500 years ago due to smelting emissions during Roman and medieval times, particularly in Europe and China. Similarly, the lead content of Greenland ice was about four times the background concentration during the period 2500 BP to 1700 BP (Nriagu, 1996). Deposits of such metals in other parts of the environment may continue to act as significant secondary sources of contamination for hundreds of years after mining has ceased. Historic lead and zinc mining in the English Pennines has left a legacy of metals in alluvial deposits that are released under flood conditions, significantly affecting water quality in this part of northern England (Macklin *et al.*, 1997).

Some of the highest heavy metal concentrations are derived from uranium tailings and pumped water from iron mines, but one of the most notorious examples of deleterious effects on human health came from a lead–zinc mine in Toyama prefecture, Japan. Cadmium-polluted water from the mine, which was used in rice paddy fields, led to an outbreak of 'itai-itai' disease, a cadmium-induced bone disorder. About 100 deaths were reported from the disease among long-term residents of the area between 1947 and 1967 (Nriagu, 1981).

Even small flows of polluted water can harm both the flora and fauna of aquatic ecosystems, but damage can be greatly intensified by large accidental discharges. One such incident, the 1998 Aznalcóllar mining accident in south-west Spain, severely affected one of the most important bird breeding and over-wintering sites in western Europe, the Coto Doñana. A breach in the Aznalcóllar tailing pond released 5 million m^3 of acid waste into the Agrio River, the main tributary of the Guadiamar River which flows into the Doñana nature reserve. The waste, from the processing of pyrite ore, entered ecologically sensitive areas of the park, including breeding areas for internationally endangered bird species, causing sustained decreases in pH from 8.5 to 4.5 and resulting in massive contamination of the ecosystem by metals, including arsenic, lead and zinc. The acid conditions facilitated the solubilization of these metals, leading to water concentrations that were lethal for aquatic wildlife (Solà *et al.*, 2004). The accident caused considerable fish and invertebrate kills and has had severe consequences for the protected bird species dependent on the impacted habitats and adjacent areas.

Acid mine drainage is responsible for water pollution problems in major coal-mining and metal-mining areas around the world. It was originally thought to be associated only with coal mining, but any deposit containing sulphide, and particularly pyrite, can be a source, and it is produced from the working of many other minerals. Reactions with air and water produce sulphuric acid, and pH values of polluted waterways may be as low as 2 or 3. Acid mine drainage is not just a problem of operational workings, but may continue as a pollution source for some years after mine closure (Robb, 1994). Surface tailings can also produce acid effluents; Hägerstrand and Lohm (1990) report that acid produced from sulphides in tailings around the Falun copper mine in central Sweden, which has been worked for 1000 years, have seriously damaged several lakes in the region and are still producing sulphuric acid. A large survey of freshwater bodies in acid-sensitive areas of the USA concluded that 3 per cent of lakes sampled and 26 per cent of streams had been acidified by acid mine drainage (Baker *et al.*, 1991).

When tailings dry out, dust blow can also cause localized pollution. Fine material blown from the quartzite dumps that surround Johannesburg, a city that grew up on the gold-mining activity in South Africa's Witwatersrand, used to stop work at food-processing factories and cause traffic chaos due to decreased visibility on windy days before the dumps were stabilized with vegetation (Bradshaw and Chadwick, 1980).

The processing of minerals can also release dangerous compounds into surrounding environments. In Brazil, where about 500 000 mostly small-scale prospectors were involved in gold mining in the late 1990s, the use of mercury as an amalgamate to separate fine gold particles from other minerals in riverbed sediments contaminates waterways in 'gold-rush' zones. Miners released an estimated 100 tonnes of mercury – an extremely toxic metal that accumulates in the food chain, and can cause birth defects and neurological problems – into the basin of the Madeira River, a tributary of the Amazon, each year. Fish eaten by the local population were found to contain mercury at concentrations up to five times the Brazilian safety limit (Malm *et al.*, 1990). Similar accumulations of mercury after use by artisanal gold miners have been reported from many other parts of South America, including Bolivia, Colombia, Peru and Venezuela. Its use in the 1950s and 1960s at the Discovery mine in the Canadian Northwest Territories means that nearby Giauque Lake is still designated a contaminated site by Environment Canada (Meech *et al.*, 1998). Globally, gold mining is thought to be responsible for about 10 per cent of all anthropogenic emissions of mercury (Lacerda, 1997).

Sulphur dioxide (SO_2) released from the open-air smelting of nickel ore at Sudbury, Ontario, Canada, in the early years of the twentieth century, destroyed vegetation over a 10 000 ha area. Construction of a closed plant with a 387.5 m stack in 1972 turned a local problem into a regional one, affecting lakes up to 60 km downwind, some with a pH of 5.5 or less. Nickel emissions from the stack have also been high. Nickel concentrations are naturally low in lake waters, with a global mean of 10 g/l. Some lakes in the Sudbury area have been found with nickel concentrations of 300 g/l. The combination of acid rain and heavy metal pollution has rendered many of the lakes in the area biologically dead (Blunden, 1985).

Very long-lasting ecological effects of SO_2 emissions have also been reported from the Falun copper mine in Sweden where the first step in copper extraction was to roast the ore in the open air to reduce its high sulphur content. This process oxidized the sulphide, emitting sulphur to the air as SO_2. These emissions, which date from at least the thirteenth century, reached a maximum during the 1600s (Fig. 19.4) when Falun produced two-thirds of the world's copper supply. Deposition of SO_2 in the area around Falun exceeded the critical load in this region for centuries and acidification of local soils is still apparent, although it is limited to the most heavily polluted area 12 km to the north-west and to the south-east of the mine. Lakes in the Falun area also became more acidic dating from the seventeenth century, although the pH decrease has been moderate. However, despite 300 years of lowered emissions since the 1600s (the mine was closed in 1993), none of the acidified lakes in Falun shows pH recovery due to a large store of sulphate in the soil, although land use change in the last 100 years is also likely to have had some effect (Ek *et al.*, 2001).

Elevated concentrations of pollutants can become hazardous to human health, if they enter the food chain, long after their release by mining activities. High accumulations of harmful elements have been measured in wild-growing mushrooms – very popular among the inhabitants of many central and east European countries – in numerous areas of contem-

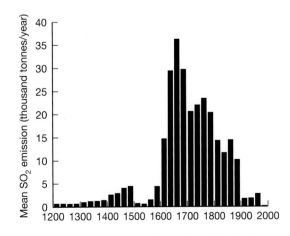

Figure 19.4 Estimated annual emissions of sulphur dioxide as 25-year means from the Falun mine, Sweden, 1200–2000 (Ek *et al.*, 2001).

porary and historical mining and smelting. Harmful levels of cadmium and lead, for example, were determined in wild mushrooms near a historical silver-mining area in South Bohemia, Czech Republic, by Svoboda *et al.* (2006), despite the fact that the mining and processing of silver ores took place mainly during the second half of the sixteenth century. The elevated cadmium and lead concentrations detected by these authors led them to recommend that restrictions should be introduced on the consumption of mushrooms picked in the area.

Miscellaneous impacts

The attraction of mining operations as sources of employment may have deleterious effects on other labour-intensive areas of the economy such as agriculture. Lewis and Berry (1988) cite Zambia's Copper Belt as an example, and Barrow (1991) suggests that Brazil's Pelada gold mine has had a similar effect. Itinerant miners venturing into little-explored terrain also carry with them new diseases and problems associated with alcohol, bringing often disastrous consequences for local populations. Gold prospectors in Amazonia, so-called *garimpeiros*, have spread virulent strains of malaria into the reserves occupied by the Yanomani indians in northern Amazonas. Local tribes with little resistance to the new strains of parasites have suffered severe outbreaks of malaria (Smith *et al.*, 1991), and met with previously unknown diseases such as measles.

The relationship between gold mining and malaria in Brazil is a complex one (Confalonieri, 1998) and the disease is rife among the miners themselves as well as local indigenous populations. The temporary shelters in mining camps provide little or no protection against mosquitoes, whose numbers typically increase when miners destroy riverbanks, widening riverbeds to become swamplike habitats ideal for mosquito breeding. Costly treatment for malaria is beyond the means of many *garimpeiros* and those who can afford to buy antimalarial drugs often stop taking the course when the fever subsides but before they are entirely cured. One result is the emergence of drug-resistant strains of the disease. Exposure among miners to mercury (see above) may also be playing a part in the high incidence of malaria, since mercury exposure is suspected to damage the immune system, perhaps increasing susceptibility to the disease. Malaria incidence in Brazil has risen steadily in recent decades, in line with the Amazonian gold rushes, from about 50 000 cases in 1970 to more than 0.5 million in the mid 1990s. The large majority of these cases are in the Amazon Basin, and indigenous populations have been severely hit. In the state of Roraima, where *garimpeiros* invaded the homeland of 10 000 Yanomani indians in 1987, malaria was responsible for 25 per cent of Yanomani deaths in the period 1991–95.

There are also cases where mining operations have had serious political ramifications. A classic example in this respect can be cited from the Panguna copper mine on the island of Bougainville in Papua New Guinea, where discontent over the distribution of mining revenues was a factor in precipitating a revolt out of a long-simmering dispute between the islanders and the PNG government. Discontent over the unequal distribution of the income derived from mining was not helped by the fact that 130 000 tonnes of metal-contaminated tailings were dumped into the Kawerong and Jaba rivers every day, severely depleting biological activity in the waters. The resulting conflict led to guerrillas taking over the island and the subsequent closure of the mine in 1989.

REHABILITATION AND REDUCTION OF MINING DAMAGE

Many techniques are available for the amelioration, curtailment or restoration of damage caused by mining and its associated activities (e.g. Down and Stocks, 1977; Bradshaw and Chadwick, 1980; Blunden, 1985), and there is little doubt that for a variety of reasons the mining industry in general has recently adopted a more benevolent approach to its environmental impact than in times past. Site surveys prior to mining, retention and replacement of topsoil after excavation, and careful reseeding with original species can be employed to return environments to something close to their original states.

For mining operations located near a coast, disposal of tailings underwater can be an attractive alternative to land-based impoundment. Under the right conditions, it can also be less costly and less environmentally damaging. A good example occurred at Island copper mine off Vancouver Island in western Canada, where more than 400 million tonnes of tailing solids generated over the course of the mine's 25 years of operation were deposited deep on the ocean floor with little environmental impact. The mine's environmental monitoring programme, which continued after closure in 1995, showed that by the year 2000 water quality and plankton biodiversity were indistinguishable from that in control areas (Ellis, 2003). Pipeline transport technology now makes it feasible and cost-effective to implement such underwater tailing placement for a mine up to 200 km from the shoreline.

Waste dumps and tailings on land can be stabilized with vegetation both to ameliorate their visual impact and to reduce the risks of slope failure (Fig. 19.5), or flattened and properly drained as in the case of the waste tips at Aberfan. Acidic minespoil often requires the application of alkaline material before a vegetation cover can be successfully established, and one method of so doing currently being developed uses waste by-products from dry-flue gas desulphurization scrubbers fitted to industrial chimneys to remove sulphur gases (Stehouwer *et al.*, 1995). The scrubbers use lime, limestone or dolomite sorbents to react with SO_2, forming anhydrite. The resulting by-products – a mixture of coal ash, anhydrite and residual sorbent – often have pH levels of 12 or greater due to the residual sorbent. The use of this material to help neutralize acidic mining wastes before rehabilitation is a good illustration of how the reappraisal of waste products can create new resources (see page 345). Disposal of scrubber waste has previously been in landfill sites, but the efforts being made in many countries to reduce acid-rain emissions means that the volume of these by-products will rise substan-

Figure 19.5 An area of rehabilitated waste rock dumps at Bingham Canyon copper mine, Utah, USA.

tially in coming years. Using them on acidic minespoil is therefore a much more sustainable method that helps to resolve two different environmental issues.

The full range of options available to deal with the problems of acid mine drainage is reviewed by Johnson and Hallberg (2005). Source control methods (Table 19.6) are designed to prevent or minimize the generation of acidic waters by excluding either, or both, oxygen and water, which are needed for acid mine drainage to form. This can be achieved by flooding and sealing abandoned deep mines. Alternatively, mine tailings can be stored underwater or sealed on the ground surface in some way, usually with a layer of clay, which can then be covered in topsoil and planted with vegetation. Other ways of neutralizing the acid include the application of some form of surface coating to isolate the relevant chemicals, or the application of biocides to kill the lithotrophic (rock-eating) bacteria that play a pivotal role in generating acid mine drainage.

Preventing the formation of acid mine drainage is not always practical, however, and a number of strategies to minimize the impact of the polluting water on streams and rivers is also available. These techniques are often divided into 'active' and 'passive' processes. The former generally means the continuous application of alkaline materials (e.g. lime, calcium carbonate, magnesium oxide) to neutralize the acidic waters, while the latter refers to the use of natural or constructed wetland ecosystems that have the same effect. The passive approaches have the advantage of requiring relatively little maintenance, and few recurrent costs, when compared to active approaches, although they may be expensive to set up in the first place.

Mining wastes themselves are used for a variety of purposes in many countries, particularly in road construction and for landfill (Table 19.7), but transportation costs to areas of high demand often limit their use. Of the 27 million tonnes of china clay waste produced each year in Devon and Cornwall, in southwestern England, about 1.5 million tonnes are used by local industries, but only a small proportion of the 12 million tonnes of china clay sands that have potential for use as aggregates are used, because local demand is low (DoE, 1992).

Many of the efforts made to reduce pollution originating in mining wastes have also stemmed from the realization that the pollutants are themselves economically valuable. A 40 per cent reduction in SO_2 emissions from the Sudbury nickel smelter, for example, was achieved in the late 1960s when the gas was converted into sulphuric acid. Similarly, the use of new biotechnologies for recovering wasted resources, such as microbes to 'bioleach' metals from tailings, have also been developed in response to the lower grades of accessible ores and lower operating costs. Microbial mining of copper sulphide ores has been practised on an industrial scale since the late 1950s and, since then, bioleaching has also become common at uranium and gold mines. Another development in mining biotechnology is the use of bacterial cells to detoxify waste cyanide solution from gold-mining operations (Agate, 1996). The recycling of minerals, particularly metals, also helps to reduce environmental impacts, of course (see Chapter 17).

Flooding/sealing of underground workings
Underwater storage of tailings
Land-based storage in sealed waste heaps
Total solidification of tailings
Blending of acid-generating and acid-consuming mineral wastes
Microencapsulation (coatings)
Application of biocides

Source: after Johnson and Hallberg (2005).

TABLE 19.6 Source control methods used to prevent or minimize the generation of acid mine drainage waters

destruction of vegetation ever undertaken in warfare. About 100 million litres of herbicides (including the infamous 'Agent Orange', nicknamed according to the coloured identification band painted on the storage barrels) were sprayed over thousands of square kilometres of the country between 1961 and 1971 in an effort to deprive North Vietnamese forces of the cover provided by dense jungle (Stellman *et al.*, 2003). Most spraying was targeted on forest but cropland was also sprayed as a tactic for decreasing enemy food supplies, and although missions were only conducted during light winds to avoid non-target contamination, drifting sprays actually caused damage over much wider areas (Orians and Pfeiffer, 1970). An example of repeated wind-drift spray damage to rubber trees on the 9 km² Plantation de Dautieng is shown in Figure 20.3.

About half of Viet Nam's mangrove forests were completely destroyed by aerial spraying, an area that has been slow to recover. Revegetation of the sprayed mangroves was essentially complete by the mid 1980s, but not always with the same commercially preferred species. Dioxins in the defoliants used were also toxic to other forms of life. The effects on animals are not well documented but a few studies and much anecdotal evidence suggest decreased abundance of many species, and herbicide-related illness in domestic livestock (Westing, 1984). It is thought that at least 3000 hamlets were sprayed directly with defoliant, affecting between 2 million and 4 million people (Stellman *et al.*, 2003). There is no doubt that the dioxins linked to Agent Orange and other defoliants entered the food chain in Viet Nam. Elevated dioxin levels are still clearly detectable in soils, livestock, fish and people decades after Agent Orange was last used in the country (Schecter *et al.*, 2003).

In total, an estimated 22 000 km² of farmland and forest was destroyed in Viet Nam, mainly in the south, by tactical spraying, intensive bombing and mechanical clearance of forest. A further 1170 km² of forest was destroyed by cratering from 13 million tonnes of bombs, and another 40 000 km² by bombardment (Collins *et al.*, 1991). The conflict left an estimated 26 million bomb and shell craters across 170 000 ha of Indochina, most in South Viet Nam, representing displacement of 2.6 billion m³ of earth (Westing and Pfeiffer, 1972).

The military experience of defoliant chemical use in Viet Nam was subsequently repeated on a smaller scale in El Salvador during the 1980s, where government forces, with US backing, laid waste areas held by or sympathetic to anti-government guerrillas. The term 'ecocide' has been coined for such widespread destruction (Weinberg, 1991).

February 1965

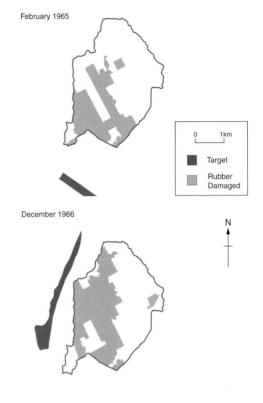

December 1966

May 1967

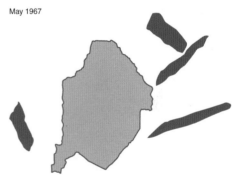

Figure 20.3 Damage to rubber trees on the Plantation de Dautieng by wind drift of aerially sprayed defoliants during the Viet Nam War (reprinted with permission from Orians and Pfeiffer, 1970. © 1970, American Association for the Advancement of Science).

Another military method involving large-scale devastation to the natural environment, sometimes with that very aim in mind, is the destruction of various forms of infrastructure. Agricultural infrastructure is an obvious target. Afghanistan's irrigation systems were the subject of systematic destruction during the Afghan-Soviet war, leaving up to one-third of all irrigation systems damaged (Formoli, 1995). Dams have also been common targets in this respect. Allied bombing of the Möhne, Eder and Sorpe dams in the Ruhr valley of Germany during the Second World War, for example, aimed to cripple the German economic heartland. Water released from the damaged Möhne and Eder dams killed 1300 people, left 120 000 homeless and ruined 3000 ha of arable land as well as numerous factories and power plants. But the most devastating example of deliberate dam breaching occurred during the Second Sino-Japanese War of 1937–45 when the Chinese dynamited the Huayuankow dike on the Huang Ho River near Chengchow to stop the advance of Japanese forces. The mission was successful in this respect and several thousand Japanese troops were drowned, but the flow of water also ravaged major areas downstream: several million hectares of farmland were inundated, as well as 11 cities and more than 4000 villages. At least several hundred thousand Chinese drowned and several million were left homeless (Bergström, 1990).

Oilfields have also been the target of deliberate damage. Retreating Austrian forces systematically destroyed facilities on Romanian oilfields in 1916–17, as did Iraqi forces before being driven out of Kuwait in 1991. In the latter example, an estimated 7–8 million barrels of oil were discharged, more than twice the size of the world's previously largest spillage caused by a blowout in the Ixtoc-1 well in the Bay of Campeche off the Mexican coast in 1979. The resulting oil slick contaminated large areas of Kuwait and a 460 km stretch of the northern coast of Saudi Arabia. An estimated 30 000 seabirds died in the immediate aftermath of the spills (Readman *et al.*, 1992), but the long-term effects on the Gulf's ecology are remarkably few. Just three and a half years later, there were no visible signs of immediate or delayed effects on coral reefs in Saudi waters (Vogt, 1995) and rapid recovery has been recorded in most other parts of the marine ecosystem. This finding is consistent with observations made during the Al-Nowruz oil well spill during the Iran–Iraq war, which suggests that the Gulf's ecology has high resilience to oil pollution (Saenger, 1994).

Fires started in 613 Kuwaiti oil wells caused the burning of 4–8 million barrels a day, and resulted in massive clouds of smoke and gaseous emissions, although fears of effects on the climate were unfounded. Other disturbances to the desert surfaces of Kuwait were caused by the large-scale movements of military vehicles and the building of an earth embankment along the border with Saudi Arabia (Fig. 20.4). Experience of similar surface destabilization during the desert campaigns of North Africa in 1941 and 1942 saw wind erosion dramatically increase

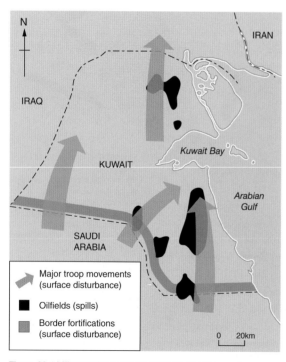

Figure 20.4 Military action in Kuwait 1990–91 and its impacts on surface terrain (after Middleton, 1991).

during the height of the fighting, but deflation subside back to pre-war levels within a few years of the end of the campaign (Oliver, 1945). Large military vehicles also have more long-lasting effects in desert areas, compacting soil, crushing and shearing vegetation, and altering the vertical and horizontal structure of plant communities. Compositional changes to soil and vegetation from a single tank pass during military manoeuvres in the Mojave Desert were found still to be evident 40 years after training had ceased (Prose, 1985).

There are many other environmentally damaging consequences of warfare. In Croatia, for example, Richardson (1993) documented the numerous dangers caused by damage to industrial and municipal plants in the war that followed the break-up of Yugoslavia in the early 1990s. One of the most dangerous and possibly long-lasting hazards was caused by the release of PCBs from damaged transformers in many Croatian towns, including 50 in Dubrovnik alone. Contamination of soils, rivers and groundwater was expected. PCBs bioaccumulate up the food chain, they are highly toxic to fish, and there is some evidence linking them to the occurrence of certain cancers in humans.

Numerous impacts on wildlife have also been documented. Some mammal species have been brought close to and beyond extinction due to the direct and indirect effects of war. The last semi-wild Père David's deer was killed by foreign troops during the Boxer Rebellion in China in 1898–1900, although the species still survives in captivity. Similarly, the European bison was pushed close to extinction during the First World War by hunting to supply troops with food; it recovered in numbers during the interwar years but its numbers were again decimated in the Second World War. Many Pacific island endemic bird taxa were also lost or pushed towards extinction by warfare and its associated disturbances during the Second World War. On the twin islands of Midway, for example, extinctions of the Laysan finch and the Laysan rail occurred (Fisher and Baldwin, 1946). In central Africa, war has several times in recent years threatened the survival of the 600 mountain gorillas in the Virunga volcanoes, which straddle the borders of Rwanda, Zaire and Uganda.

Conversely, however, some species of wild animals can benefit during wartime because of decreased exploitation. Westing (1980) notes the cases of various North Atlantic fisheries during the Second World War and a number of fur-bearing mammals in northern and north-eastern Europe, such as the polar bear, red fox and wolf. During the Viet Nam War, tigers increased in abundance in some areas thanks to the ready availability of food provided by corpses.

Disruption and destruction does not necessarily cease with the end of hostilities. On average, 10 per cent of all munitions used in any war fail to explode, and remain to threaten humans, livestock and wildlife; they also impede post-war reconstruction and rehabilitation efforts in agriculture, forestry, fishing, mining and other related activities (Fig. 20.5). Landmines are a particular problem; they are present on a huge scale in some countries (Table 20.3) and can take many years to clear. In Poland, more than 84 million items of

Figure 20.5 An area in Afghanistan closed off to human use due to landmines.

Country	Number of landmines (million)
Afghanistan	9–10
Angola	9–15
Iraq	5–10
Kuwait	5
Cambodia	4–7
Western Sahara	1–2
Mozambique	1–2
Somalia	1
Bosnia and Herzegovina	1
Croatia	1

Source: Ruel (1993); UN Unit for the Coordination of Humanitarian Assistance.

TABLE 20.3 Estimated number of landmines in the worst-affected countries and territories, early 1990s

explosive ordnance from the Second World War (including more than 14 million mines) had been disposed of by the early 1980s, with 350 000 being located and destroyed every year (Westing, 1984).

Nuclear war

There is little direct information on the possible environmental effects of a nuclear war, but some insight can be gained from the detonation of the only two nuclear devices used in warfare to date, in Japan at the end of the Second World War (Table 20.4), although these were relatively small devices by today's standards. The most important cause of death and physical destruction was the combined effects of blast and thermal energy. The fireball created by the blasts was intense enough to vaporize humans at the epicentre and burn human skin up to 4 km away. Ionizing radiation comprised about 15 per cent of the explosive yield of the bombs, and among its effects was radiation sickness among many survivors of the blast.

TABLE 20.4 Destruction caused by the first atom bombs dropped in wartime

	Hiroshima	Nagasaki
Date of detonation	6 August 1945	9 August 1945
Type	Uranium 235	Plutonium
Height of explosion (m)	580	503
Yield (kiloton TNT)	12.5	22
Total area demolished (km^2)	13	6.7
Proportion of buildings completely destroyed (%)	67.9	25.3
Proportion of buildings partially destroyed (%)	24.0	10.8
Number of people killed (by 31 December 1945)	90 000–120 000	70 000

Source: Ohkita (1984).

There is a limited amount of information on the ecological effects of nuclear explosions, which has been gleaned from observations made after above-ground tests. Severe damage to vegetation caused by detonations decreases more or less geometrically with distance from the blast epicentre. After explosions, plants re-invade damaged areas at a rate of succession that would be expected after a severe disturbance, as Shields and Wells (1962) documented for a Nevada Desert test site after numerous above-ground detonations.

Considerable research has been undertaken into the possible global effects of a major nuclear exchange, much of it focusing on the potential climatic effects. Although results vary with different scenarios, simulations using general circulation models (GCMs) have raised the spectre of a 'nuclear winter' in which the aftermath of a nuclear war would be characterized by darkened skies over large parts of the Earth due to smoke and dust injected into the atmosphere. Such effects could con-

military purposes and to secure access to large groundwater reserves; and if the Gulf region had not been such a key supplier of oil supplies to the West it seems unlikely that western troops would have intervened to such an extent over the Iraqi invasion of Kuwait in 1990–91. Indeed, of the 50 or so armed conflicts fought in mid 1994, about 20 were considered (by Westing, 1994) to be environmentally induced in some way.

Some observers suggest that environmental change, particularly in the form of degradation and dwindling renewable resources, is set to become an increasingly potent cause of conflict as world population is likely to exceed 9 billion within the next 50 years and global economic output may increase five-fold (Homer-Dixon *et al.*, 1993). The degradation and loss of

Figure 20.8 This defunct tank near the border between Ethiopia and Eritrea is a relic of Ethiopia's civil war, which ended in 1991. Eritrea's independence in 1993, an outcome of this conflict, meant that Ethiopia became landlocked. This loss of access to the sea was a significant factor in the war between Ethiopia and Eritrea in 1998–2000.

productive land, fisheries, forests and species diversity, the depletion and scarcity of water resources, and pressures brought about by stratospheric ozone loss and potentially significant climatic change may precipitate civil or international strife. In decades to come, five general types of violent conflict produced by environmental scarcity are envisaged by Homer-Dixon (1999), whose list of potential flashpoints expands in spatial scale from local to possibly global:

1 disputes arising directly from local environmental degradation (e.g. due to factory emissions, logging or dam construction)
2 ethnic clashes arising from population migration and deepened social cleavages caused by environmental scarcity
3 civil strife (e.g. insurgency, banditry and *coups d'état*) caused by environmental scarcity that affects economic productivity and hence people's livelihoods, the behaviour of elite groups and the ability of states to meet these changing demands
4 interstate war induced by environmental scarcity (e.g. water)
5 North–South conflicts (developed vs developing worlds) over migration of, adaptation to, and compensation for global environmental problems such as threats to biodiversity, global warming, ozone depletion and decreases in fish stocks.

Such root causes of conflict have been identified from past eras. Pennell (1994), for example, has suggested that environmental degradation and economic isolation, and consequent impoverishment, made piracy an attractive option for inhabitants of the Guelaya Peninsula in north-western Morocco in the mid nineteenth century. A key aspect of such scenarios is the role played by certain groups that are faced with dwindling finite resources. Such groups may be within a certain country or they may be identifiable on the global scale as countries with unequal access to resources. A proposed chain of factors in this equation, which leads to violence, is suggested in Figure 20.9.

Some researchers have highlighted examples of such events in more recent history. Bennett (1991) presents a number of studies of African conflicts in this vein, while in Central America, Durham (1979) considers that the root causes of the

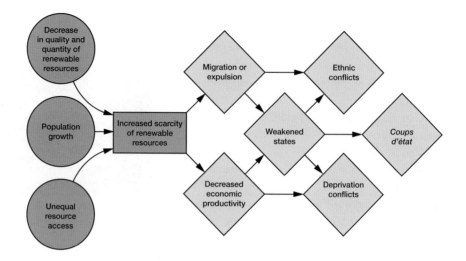

Figure 20.9 Some sources and consequences of renewable resource scarcity (Homer-Dixon *et al.*, 1993).

1969 'Soccer War' between El Salvador pand Honduras ran much deeper than the national rivalry over the outcome of a football match that ignited the conflict. He traces the origins of a war in which several thousand people were killed in a few days to changes in agriculture and land distribution in El Salvador that began in the mid nineteenth century, forcing poor farmers to concentrate in the uplands. Despite their efforts to conserve the land's resources, growing human pressure in a country with annual population growth rates of 3.5 per cent reduced land availability, and resulted in deforestation and soil erosion on the steep hillsides. Many farmers consequently moved to Honduras and it was their eventual expulsion that precipitated the war. In the years following the Soccer War, this competition for land was not addressed and *campesino* support for leftist guerrillas provided a powerful contribution to the country's subsequent ten-year civil war.

The importance of population pressure and unequal access to resources has also been emphasized in other domestic settings. In one analysis of the terrible genocidal violence that occurred during 1994 in Rwanda, one of the most densely populated countries in Africa, the intense pressure on land resources has been stressed (André and Platteau, 1998). These authors do not suggest that the acute competition for land was a direct cause of Rwanda's 1994 genocide, in which more than 0.5 million people, most of them from the Tutsi ethnic group, were killed. However, they do suggest that Rwanda's progressively increasing scarcity of land, one of the most basic resources in an essentially agricultural nation (Fig. 20.10), 'goes a long way towards explaining why the violence spread so quickly and devastatingly throughout the countryside' (André and Platteau, 1998: 38). At its simplest level, this perspective sees the Rwandan genocide as the result of a Malthusian crisis in which the human population had become too large for the country's available resources.

Other research has even suggested that countries whose wealth is largely dependent on the export of primary commodities (including both agricultural produce and mineral resources) are particularly prone to political instability and civil violence (Collier and Hoeffler, 2000). This theory points to numerous civil

Figure 20.10 Intensive agricultural land use in north-west Rwanda. The scarcity of land in this very densely populated country probably played some part in the ethnic tensions that led to genocide in 1994.

wars that are at least in part a fight for control of certain primary commodities and/or in which trade in natural resources is a significant source of finance for particular armed groups (recent examples include diamonds in Sierra Leone, drugs in Colombia, and timber in Cambodia). The authors refer to their explanation as a 'simple greed model'.

To end this section on a more positive note, the conservation value of the Korean demilitarized zone mentioned earlier in this chapter has been put forward as a possible mechanism to help build trust and understanding between rival powers. Kim (1997) suggests that joint maintenance of the ready-made nature reserve, already completely protected and clearly delimited thanks to its origin as a buffer zone, can foster mutual respect between North and South Korea, while helping to preserve the peninsula's biodiversity.

FURTHER READING

Amery, H.A. 2002 Water wars in the Middle East: a looming threat. *The Geographical Journal* 168: 313–23. A good overview of the region's hydropolitical issues as a potential cause of conflict.

Giordano, M.F., Giordano, M.A. and Wolf, A.T. 2005 International resource conflict and mitigation. *Journal of Peace Research* 42: 47–65. A paper that emphasizes the need for institutional measures to deal with international conflicts over natural resources.

Goodhand, J. 2003 Enduring disorder and persistent poverty: a review of the linkages between war and chronic poverty. *World Development* 31: 629–46. An analysis of the relationship between violent conflict and poverty.

Kahl, C.H. 2006 *States, scarcity, and civil strife in the developing world*. Princeton, Princeton University Press. An examination of how demographic and environmental stresses can result in violent conflict.

Le Billon, P. 2001 The political ecology of war: natural resources and armed conflicts. *Political Geography* 20: 561–84. An interesting, in-depth analysis of the links between warfare and resources.

Rubenson, S. 1991 Environmental stress and conflict in Ethiopian history: looking for correlations. *Ambio* 20: 179–82. This paper presents a case study of environmental stress and degradation in Ethiopia, and their links to social and political conflict.

Thomas, W. 1995 *Scorched earth: The military's assault on the environment*. Philadelphia, New Society Publishers. A catalogue of the military's environmental impacts.

Warner, F. (ed.) 2000 *Nuclear test explosions: environmental and human impacts*. SCOPE Report 59, Chichester, Wiley. A series of papers on the medical and environmental effects of nuclear testing.

Wiley, K.B. and Rhodes, S.L. 1998 The transformation of the Rocky Mountain arsenal. *Environment* 40(5): 4–11, 28–35. Case study of how a severely contaminated military waste dump has become a nature reserve.

Zhang, D.D., Jim, C.Y., Lin, G.C.-S., He, Y.-Q., Wang, J.J. and Lee, H.F. 2006 Climatic change, wars and dynastic cycles in China over the last millennium. *Climatic Change* 76: 459–77. An investigation of how palaeotemperature changes are linked to agricultural carrying capacity, population size and armed conflicts between states, regions and tribes in China.

WEBSITES

www.gci.ch/ one of Green Cross International's major programmes is concerned with the environmental impact of warfare.

www.library.utoronto.ca/pcs/state.htm site for the Environmental Scarcities, State Capacity and Civil Violence project, with case studies on water in China, cropland in India and Indonesian forests.

www.sipri.org/ the Stockholm International Peace Research Institute site contains information on military capabilities and expenditure.

www.opcw.org/ home page of the Chemical Weapons Convention.

www.icbl.org/ the International Campaign to Ban Landmines site.

www.pmrma.army.mil/ US army site covering the contamination and remediation of Rocky Mountain Arsenal.

POINTS FOR DISCUSSION

- Does the human cost of warfare mean that the environmental cost is unimportant?
- Do you think that conflicts over natural resources are set to become more frequent in coming decades?
- Should atomic weapons be banned and is it realistic to do so?
- Can national armies be managed sustainably and should different rules apply during conflicts?

21 Natural Hazards

Natural hazards such as earthquakes, floods, tropical cyclones and disease epidemics are normal functions of the natural environment. They do, therefore, affect all living organisms but they are usually only referred to as disasters or catastrophes when they impact human society to cause social disruption, material damage and loss of life. As such, natural hazards should be defined and studied both in terms of the physical processes involved and the human factors affecting the vulnerability of certain groups of people to disasters.

Although some places are more hazardous than others, all locations are at risk – there is always the chance of a disaster – from some natural hazard or other. All places also have some natural advantages, however, and the presence or absence of human activities in any location is the result of weighing up the risks relative to the advantages. In many locations, the physical phenomenon responsible for a hazard also offers some of the advantages: a river, for example, will flood, which may be hazardous, but it is also a source of water and its flood plain is a location with flat land and fertile soils. Hence the hazard should be seen as an occasionally disadvantageous aspect of a phenomenon that is beneficial to human activity over a different timescale. This is illustrated in Figure 21.1, where the shaded zone represents an acceptable variability of a physical element: variations in its

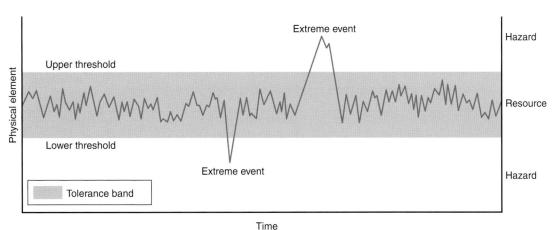

Figure 21.1 A physical element is perceived as a resource by society when its variations in magnitude are within certain limits, but is perceived as a hazard when they exceed certain thresholds (after Hewitt and Burton, 1971).

magnitude that society has adapted to and considers a resource. When this variability exceeds a certain threshold, however, the same physical element becomes a hazard for a period of time. In the case of the river, this could mean either a flood or a water shortage. Ironically, beyond the timescale of the hazardous event occurring, the very same hazard may contribute to the resource element of the location: when a flood happens, it presents a hazard to the occupants of the flood plain, but the flood plain is only there because the river floods occasionally.

To complicate matters, however, not all people who choose to live in a particular area enjoy the same degree of choice – a flexibility that may be dictated by the economic means at their disposal, among other things. To complicate matters further, there is a wide range of ways in which people respond to hazards and, again, the rich often have more options in this respect than poorer members of society. The study of natural hazards is very much a geographical subject, therefore, since it includes analysis of both the physical and the human environment.

HAZARD CLASSIFICATIONS

Natural hazards can be classified in many different ways. Physical geographical approaches may divide them according to their geological, hydrological, atmospheric and biological origins, as shown in Figure 21.2. They can also be classified spatially, as certain hazards only occur in certain regions: avalanches occur in

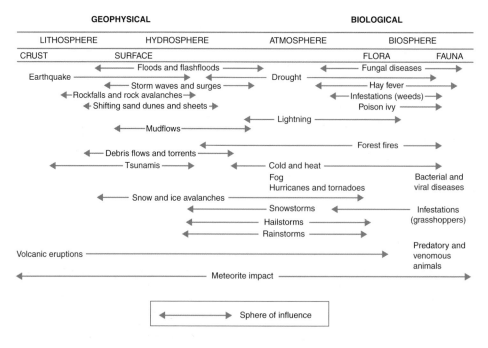

Figure 21.2 Types of natural hazard, by sphere of occurrence, medium and materials (after Gardner, 1993).

snowy, mountainous areas, for example, and most volcanic eruptions and earth-quakes occur at tectonic plate margins. Another approach divides hazards into rapid-onset, intensive events (short, sharp shocks such as tornadoes) and slow-onset, pervasive events, which often affect larger areas over longer periods of time (such as droughts). Table 21.1 is an attempt to classify hazards in this way, and gives some indication of the frequency and predictability of events in time.

Although these classifications provide a useful summary of hazard types, many disasters involve composite hazards. Hence, an earthquake may cause a tsunami wave at sea, landslides or avalanches on slopes, building damage and fires in urban areas, and flooding due to the failure of dams, as well as ground shaking and displacement along faults. Similarly, many natural disasters cause disruption to public hygiene and consequently result in heightened risks of disease transmission.

Other approaches to defining and classifying disasters focus on such factors as the areal extent or the scale of damage: Burton *et al.* (1978), for example, postulate that a 'disaster' must cause more than US$1 million in damage, or the death or injury of more than a hundred people. Such an absolute approach has disadvantages, however, since a certain level of damage will have a different impact on society depending upon the strength of that society to cope with the disaster, a recognition used to assess disaster-proneness at the national level (see below). There is a case for defining a disaster at any scale, from the personal to the regional, national and global, but in practice it is generally fair to say that very

Disaster	Frequency or type of occurrence	Duration of impact	Length of forewarning (if any)
Lightning	Random	Instant	Seconds–hours
Avalanche	Seasonal/diurnal; random	Seconds–minutes	Seconds–hours
Earthquake	Log-normal	Seconds–minutes	Minutes–years
Tornado	Seasonal	Seconds–hours	Minutes
Landslide	Seasonal/irregular	Seconds–decades	Seconds–years
Intense rainstorm	Seasonal/diurnal	Minutes	Seconds–hours
Hail	Seasonal/diurnal	Minutes	Minutes–hours
Tsunami	Log-normal	Minutes–hours	Minutes–hours
Flood	Seasonal; log-normal	Minutes–days	Minutes–days
Subsidence	Sudden or progressive	Minutes–decades	Seconds–years
Windstorm	Seasonal/exponential	Hours	Hours
Frost or ice storm	Seasonal/diurnal	Hours	Hours
Hurricane	Seasonal/irregular	Hours	Hours
Snowstorm	Seasonal	Hours	Hours
Environmental fire	Seasonal; random	Hours–days	Seconds–days
Insect infestation	Seasonal; random	Hours–days	Seconds–days
Fog	Seasonal/diurnal	Hours–days	Minutes–hours
Volcanic eruption	Irregular	Hours–years	Minutes–weeks
Coastal erosion	Seasonal/irregular; exponential	Hours–years	Hours–decades
Soil erosion	Progressive (threshold may be crossed)	Hours–millennia	Hours–decades
Drought	Seasonal/irregular	Days–years	Days–weeks
Crop blight	Seasonal/irregular	Weeks–months	Days–months
Expansive soil	Seasonal/irregular	Months–years	Months–years

Source: after Alexander (1993).

TABLE 21.1 Natural disasters classified according to frequency of occurrence, duration of impact and length of forewarning

poor societies commonly suffer the highest numbers of casualties, while very rich societies suffer the highest property damage. In a survey of natural disasters from 1977 to 1997, Alexander (1997) found that about 90 per cent of disaster-related deaths occurred in developing countries while some 82 per cent of economic losses were suffered by developed countries.

Another difficulty arises in distinguishing between purely 'natural' events and human-induced events. This chapter is not concerned with such obviously human-induced hazards and catastrophes as industrial accidents or pesticide poisonings. However, in one sense, all 'natural' disasters can be thought of as human-induced since it is the presence of people that defines whether or not an event creates a disaster. Many of the natural physical processes that cause disasters can also be triggered or made worse by human action: while a volcanic eruption is a purely natural process, for example, the failure of a slope, producing a landslide, can be induced by many human activities, such as road-cutting, construction or deforestation. The composite nature of many disasters also blurs the distinction: the major cause of death due to an earthquake is usually crushing beneath buildings, so is the disaster natural or human-induced? Some researchers believe that the difficulty of making this distinction has made the division pointless, and prefer to talk of 'environmental' hazards that refer to a spectrum with purely natural events at one end and distinctly human-induced events at the other (e.g. Smith, 2001). The phrase 'na-tech' (natural-technological) is also used.

RESPONSE TO HAZARDS

Responses can be made by individuals, particular groups or the whole society, and they are related to the information available on past events and the probability of recurrence, the perception of that information, and the awareness of particular opportunities. One form of response might be to change the land use in a particular area or to move an activity to another location. Other responses can be categorized into those that aim to reduce losses and those that accept losses. The range of possible adjustments in these categories that can be made in response to the hazard from volcanic lava flows is indicated in Table 21.2. In practice, the most effective responses often involve a combination of measures.

Some approaches take action to reduce the risk of impact by preventing or modifying events. Since there is no known way of altering the eruptive mechanism, modifying the event itself is not an option for lava flows, but other hazard events can be prevented or modified. Floods, for example, can be prevented over a long period by impounding water behind a dam, and frosts can be prevented by installing a heating system in an orchard. Other approaches aim to modify the loss potential through prediction, either in time (so issuing hazard warnings to enable evacuation) or in space (by producing hazard-zone maps that can be used to regulate land use in hazard-prone areas). These examples illustrate the ways in which responses can operate over a variety of timescales, from the long-term view of building a dam or regulating land use, to the immediate efforts involved in evacuating a threatened area. Most of these responses are more generally characteristic of the more developed countries, which have sufficient economic resources, infrastructure and trained personnel to organize and carry out such actions.

Figure 21.5 A public information board in Dominica, a typical small-island developing state, indicating the range of hazards faced by the island's inhabitants.

EXAMPLES OF NATURAL DISASTERS

The following sections take a closer look at a number of major natural causes of disaster. The selection is based on an analysis of the causes of deaths from all types of disasters over the period 1900–90 compiled by the US Office of Foreign Disaster Assistance (Blaikie *et al.*, 1994). Civil strife and famine were by far the largest causes of death, accounting for nearly 88 per cent of all casualties. Although natural events such as drought and flooding are often implicated as triggers for the onset of famine (see Chapter 5), the most significant direct natural causes of death were earthquakes, volcanoes, cyclones, epidemics and floods.

Earthquakes

Each year, around 1 million earth tremors are recorded over the Earth's surface, but the vast majority of these are so small that they are not felt by people. The handful of major earthquakes that occur each year can cause widespread damage, however, causing some of the world's most devastating natural disasters. China has suffered some of the worst fatalities in major earthquakes: the 1556 event in Shensi caused more than 800 000 deaths, and the Tangshan earthquake of 1976 resulted in up to 250 000 fatalities.

Most earthquakes are caused by abrupt tectonic stress release around the margins of the Earth's lithospheric plates, although they also occur at weak spots near the centre of plates. While the locations of plate boundaries and most associated faults are well known, the precise timing and location of individual earthquakes are virtually impossible to predict in any reliable way. A combination of seismic monitoring and observations of natural phenomena, including animal behaviour, were used in the only successful prediction of a large-scale earthquake, which devastated the Chinese city of Haicheng in Liaoning Province in February 1976. An evacuation of Haicheng and two other cities was ordered 48 hours before the main earthquake, almost certainly saving many thousands of lives (Adams, 1975).

The main environmental hazard created by seismic earth movements is ground shaking, which is related to the magnitude of the shock and normally assessed on the Richter scale, a complex logarithmic scale that measures the vibrational energy of a shock. In April 1906 an earthquake along the San Andreas fault in California, USA, caused slippage by up to 6 m along 300 km of the fault, and the transient waves unleashed by the slip devastated large parts of San Francisco. Local site conditions have an important effect on ground motion, with greater structural damage usually found in areas underlain by unconsolidated material as opposed to rock. Particularly severe damage was caused during the earthquake of 1985 in the central parts of Mexico City, which is built on a dried lake-bed. Similarly, a relatively modest-magnitude earthquake, registering 5.4 on the Richter scale, in San Salvador in 1986, caused unusually large destruction since most of the city is built on volcanic ash up to 25 m thick.

Another serious earthquake hazard associated with soft, water-saturated sediments is soil liquefaction, in which intense shaking causes sediments to lose strength temporarily and behave as a fluid. Loss of bearing strength can cause buildings to subside and soils can flow on slopes of greater than 3 degrees. Mudflows, landslides, and rock and snow avalanches triggered by ground vibrations often play a major role in earthquake disasters, particularly in mountainous areas. In a study of major earthquakes in Japan, landslides were found to cause more than half of all earthquake-related deaths (Kobayashi, 1981).

Tectonic displacement of the seabed is the main cause of large sea waves, or tsunamis, which can travel thousands of kilometres at velocities greater than 900 km/h and cause great damage when they hit coastlines. Tsunamis are most common in the Pacific where one of the largest and most damaging waves, measuring 24 m in height, drowned 26 000 people in Sanriku, Japan in 1896. The Indian Ocean tsunami of December 2004 caused even greater loss of life – an estimated 300 000 people dead or missing – making it one of the most devastating natural disasters in modern history. A megathrust earthquake off the coast of northern Sumatra was one of the largest ever recorded, registering 9.3 on the Richter scale, and triggered waves up to 30 m high that spread out across the ocean at the speed of a jet aircraft (Lay *et al.*, 2005). The tsunami directly affected about 2 million people. Most of the fatalities and the most intense and widespread destruction occurred in the province of Aceh, Sumatra, the coast nearest to the epicentre, only about 10 minutes away in terms of tsunami propagation time. The next most heavily impacted area was the coast of Thailand, followed by India and Sri Lanka, but damage and casualties were also reported from much further afield, including Bangladesh, Seychelles and Somalia (Table 21.4). The total economic impact of this international disaster was in the billions of US dollars.

Some attempts have been made to regulate the intensity of earthquakes on land by injecting pressurized water along faults to stimulate many small tremors and thus reduce the probability of major movements, but the technique still runs the risk of itself inducing a major earthquake. Hence, responses to the hazards associated with earthquakes focus on reducing risk and coping with the losses.

Country (region)	Human toll approx.	Land/infrastructure damage	Marine environment damage
Indonesia (Aceh, Sumatra)	165,000 dead 115,000 missing 410,000 displaced	Coastal and low-lying infrastructure destroyed (e.g. roads, towns, aquaculture/farming). Groundwater salinized	Seagrass beds (20% loss) Coral reefs (30%) Mangroves, rivers and wetlands damaged
Thailand (Phangnga, Phuket, Krabi, Trang, Satun, Ranong provinces)	5000 dead 3000 missing 8500 injured	Coastal and low-lying infrastructure destroyed in Phuket (e.g. roads, buildings). Fishing fleets lost. 1500 ha agricultural land salinized	Seagrass beds (5% impacted) Coral reefs (13%) Mangroves (0.2%)
Sri Lanka (west and south coast)	35,000 dead	>150,000 houses and 2/3 of fishing boats destroyed. Coastal damage high in coral-mining areas. Extensive solid waste transport. Groundwater salinized. Coastal roads/railway destroyed	Damage to coral reefs and mangroves
Maldives (all islands)	13,000 displaced	Damage on 69 of 199 inhabited islands. Groundwater salinized. Coastal/beach erosion high. Fisheries infrastructure damage.	None found
Seychelles (La Digue, Praslin, Mahe islands)	2 dead	Infrastructure damage at low-lying points. Some groundwater salinization and solid waste movement	Carbonate-substrate reefs highly impacted, granitic reefs intact. Mangroves slightly eroded. Some seagrasses smothered
Yemen (Socotra island, Al Mahra governorate)	No deaths or injuries reported	Localized beach erosion and some groundwater/well salinization. Major damage to fisheries infrastructure	No assessment
Somalia (Puntland)	300 dead 4,500 displaced	Fishing boats destroyed. Waste (some hazardous) impacts	No assessment

Source: after UNEP (2005).

TABLE 21.4 Damage to some of the regions worst hit by the tsunami of 26 December 2004

Since the failure of structures is a major cause of injury during seismic shaking, much effort has gone into building location and design. Earthquake-hazard zoning maps have been produced for many countries and some of the approaches used for building in particularly hazardous sites are shown in Figure 21.6. Building codes are effective only if enforced, however, and several recent examples of major damage and loss of life in urban areas have occurred in cities where such codes have not been followed (see page 203).

Even in places where strict building codes are adequately enforced, major damage and loss of life can still occur because more vulnerable older buildings have not been upgraded. The earthquake that hit south-central Japan in January 1995 resulted in the total destruction of 56 000 buildings and severe damage to another 110 000 in the small city of Kobe, causing more than 6000 deaths. Most of these buildings were constructed before the introduction of new Japanese earthquake code standards in 1981, while damage to post-1981 structures was minimal. Although the cost of upgrading all older buildings in a large Japanese city to these new standards would be enormous (perhaps US$50–100 billion), the lesson of Kobe suggests that such a scheme would still make financial sense. The total direct economic loss from the Kobe disaster has been estimated conservatively at US$130 billion, making it the most costly natural disaster in human history and the most devastating to hit a developed country. Additional direct and indirect losses from the disruption to business and loss of productivity is likely to raise the overall cost to more than US$200 billion (Chandler, 1997). The technology to upgrade older buildings is available, but to date the political will to implement such a programme has been lacking.

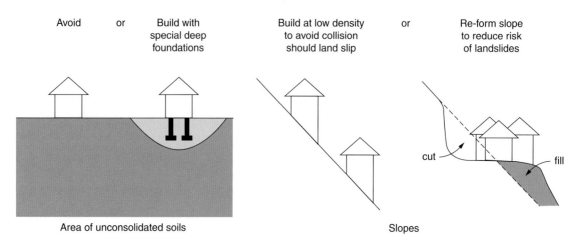

Figure 21.6 Some approaches to building on sites at high risk of disturbance during earthquakes (after Smith, 2001).

Volcanic eruptions

Volcanic eruptions have killed around 250 000 people in the last 400 years due to a range of associated hazards, which include falls of rock and ash, the force of lateral blasts, emission of poisonous gases, debris avalanches, lava flows, mudflows known as 'lahars', and 'pyroclastic flows' made up of suspended rock froth and gases (Chester, 1993), and their environmental effects can extend over very great distances (Table 21.5). Active volcanoes may also present more persistent hazards to human health through long-term exposure to carbon dioxide, radon and other pollutants (Baxter, 2000). Only about 500 volcanoes are thought to have actually erupted in historical time, although the traditional categories of 'active', 'dormant' and 'extinct' are not infrequently found wanting when supposedly inactive volcanoes erupt, sometimes causing widespread destruction (e.g. Mount Pinatubo, the Philippines, 1991). Like earthquakes, the distribution and activity of volcanoes is controlled by global tectonics.

Solid particles ejected from a volcano during an eruption, generally known as tephra, can cause a variety of hazards many hundreds of kilometres from the volcano. Smaller particles may be inhaled, with consequent respiratory problems such as asthma and

Distance from volcano	Hazard
Up to 10 km	Lava flows Pyroclastic flows and surges Earthquakes Ground subsidence and cracking Jökulhlaups
Up to 100 km	Atmospheric blast Lahars Debris avalanches
Up to 1000 km	Tephra fall Gases
Up to 10 000 km Planet-wide	Tsunami Climatic effects

TABLE 21.5 Hazards associated with volcanic eruptions

linked to the fact that far greater numbers of people in developing countries suffer from malnutrition, inadequate water supply and sanitation, poor hygiene practices and overcrowded living conditions. Indeed, the global trend towards urbanization, with many of the fastest urban growth rates being recorded in the poorer countries of the world, has been cited as a major factor in the increased frequency of many infectious diseases (Olshansky *et al.*, 1997).

An infectious disease is caused by a host being invaded by a parasite or other pathogen, which might be a bacterium, virus or worm. The pathogen carries out part of its life cycle inside the host and the disease is often a by-product of these activities. Many pathogens also need a vector, an 'accomplice', to help them spread from host to host, a role often played by an insect. Many of the major diseases of the developing world are associated with water, an association in which three typical situations can be distinguished (Table 21.7), although some diseases may fall under more than one category. Although any disease represents a natural hazard to individuals and groups of people, the emphasis here will be on epidemics, relatively sudden outbreaks of a disease in a certain area. Two diseases associated with water will be examined: cholera and malaria.

TABLE 21.7 Classification of diseases associated with water

Role of water	Comments and examples
Waterborne	Diseases arise from presence in water of human or animal faeces or urine infected with disease pathogens, which are transmitted when water is used for drinking or food preparation (e.g. diarrhoea, dysentery, cholera, typhoid, guinea worm)
Water hygiene	Diseases result from inadequate use of water to maintain personal cleanliness (e.g. waterborne diseases above as well as infestation with lice or mites)
Water habitat	Diseases for which water provides the habitat for vectors. The pathogen may enter the human body from the water directly (e.g. bilharzia is transmitted when a fluke leaves a snail vector and penetrates human skin as people wash or swim), or indirectly via a fly (e.g. trypanosomiasis – sleeping sickness) or mosquito (e.g. malaria)

Source: after GEMS (1988).

Cholera is caused by a bacterium known as Vibrio, which can survive outside the human gut in such environments as water, moist foodstuffs, human faeces and soiled hands, all of which can act as media for its transmission. The disease originated in south Asia, notably in the Ganges–Brahmaputra Delta, and appears to spread and recede geographically in cycles. It first reached Europe in the nineteenth century, causing six major pandemics, and realization of the key transmission role played by dirty water was a central force behind the public health movement in many European countries in the nineteenth century. These measures have helped to all but eradicate cholera from most developed countries, but a seventh pandemic spread from Indonesia in the early 1960s, reaching Africa and southern Europe within ten years. Its rapid spread through Africa caused many deaths after a period of about 75 years when the disease was a relatively minor ailment (Stock, 1976). The pandemic reached South America at Lima,

Peru, in January 1991 where it is thought to have been brought from Asia in a ship's ballast water. The warming of coastal and inshore waters by an El Niño/Southern Oscillation event at the time may have stimulated the growth of a plankton harbouring the cholera bacterium (Reid, 1995). The bacterium contaminated fish and shellfish, which were consumed by the local human population, and the spread of the disease was facilitated when it entered Lima's drinking-water supply via inadequately treated wastewater. From its landfall in Peru, where over 1700 cases per day were reported during the first four months, the disease spread throughout much of South America within a year (WHO, 1992). The outbreak of a more recent epidemic in Bangladesh at the end of 1992, involving a new, hardier strain of the cholera Vibrio first identified in a coastal algal bloom, has raised fears of an eighth pandemic (Levins *et al.*, 1994). Although it may not be possible to prevent totally the emergence of new cholera strains and the cyclic spread of the disease, there is no doubt that the introduction of basic sanitary measures, the provision of safe drinking water and the promotion of less crowded living conditions in developing countries would do a great deal towards limiting the spread of this often fatal disease. It is the lack of these basic provisions that makes cholera a common killer in refugee camps in many tropical areas.

Unlike cholera, the transmission of malaria requires a vector. The disease is caused by a one-cell parasite called plasmodium that is transmitted from one person to another through the bite of a female Anopheles mosquito, which needs blood to nurture her eggs. Transmission of this plasmodium parasite occurs naturally within certain climatic limits: the 15 °C July and January isotherms, which are roughly coincident with extremes of latitude at 64° N and 32° S. Hence malaria is a disease that occurs under natural circumstances across most of the world's land surface. In recent times, however, its geographical distribution has been radically changed by significant successes in malaria eradication.

If we go back roughly 100 years, to the early 1900s, malaria-affected areas stretched as far north as southern Canada, Norway, Sweden, Finland and Russia. In England, the disease was known as 'marsh ague' or 'marsh fever', and it was a common cause of death among many inhabitants in and around wetlands in the nineteenth century (Dobson, 1980). Malaria was still common in parts of Europe, such as the Rhine Delta and low-lying parts of Mediterranean countries until after the Second World War, but western Europe was declared free of the disease in 1975.

Efforts to control malaria have resulted in significant successes and its eradication in numerous areas. In 1900, 140 countries reported cases of the disease, but by 2002 that number had fallen to 88 (Hay *et al.*, 2004). In terms of the proportion of the global population at risk from the disease, this reduction in its range equates to a decrease from 77 per cent of the world's population at risk in 1900, to 48 per cent in 2002.

The first attempts to combat malaria were based on the association between the disease and stagnant waters and swamps, recognized by the ancient Greeks and Romans as early as 2600 BP. This awareness led to operations to drain wetland areas with the aim of improving the health of the nearby population. These schemes also had the additional benefit of making more land available for agricultural use, thus increasing food production.

The role of a vector – the mosquito, which breeds in standing water – was realized in the late nineteenth century, enabling more concerted efforts at environmental management. A major triumph in controlling mosquitoes was recorded in the area of the Panama Canal during the early twentieth century. Initial attempts to construct the canal by the French in the late 1800s had failed partly due to the large numbers of workers who died from malaria and yellow fever, another mosquito-borne disease. When the canal was finally completed by the Americans in 1914, it was thanks in no small part to the control of these diseases through mosquito eradication. Swamp areas were drained and any remaining standing or slow-moving bodies of water were covered with a combination of oil and insecticide. The towns of Panama City and Colón were provided with piped running water to do away with the need for the domestic water containers that served as perfect breeding sites for the mosquito, and roads were paved to further eradicate puddles (Fig. 21.8).

The first half of the twentieth century saw many similar examples of environmental management in other parts of the world, based on drainage and infrastructural improvements, designed to reduce the occurrence of malaria. This approach was complemented in the 1950s by concerted campaigns using DDT and other powerful insecticides. DDT kills mosquitoes and was thus widely used to interrupt transmission of the disease. In 1955, the World Health Organization (WHO) adopted its Global Eradication Campaign emphasizing chemical control of mosquitoes by spraying DDT in homes. These strategies helped to eradicate malaria from most temperate and many subtropical areas, and the disease was all but wiped out in Europe and North America (although in more recent times, increasing international travel to the tropics has resulted in cases among some temperate-zone residents).

Malaria, however, is still endemic in most parts of the developing world and, despite numerous attempts at global eradication since the 1950s, has reached epidemic proportions in a number of countries in association with high population densities, poor sanitation, environmental degradation and civil unrest. Accurate assessment of the malaria burden is difficult because most deaths from the disease occur

Figure 21.8 Urban infrastructure here in Casco Viejo, the old town area of Panama City, was significantly improved as part of a successful strategy to combat malaria while constructing the Panama Canal during the early twentieth century. This involved paving the streets and putting the town's sewerage system and water supplies underground.

at home, the clinical features of malaria are very similar to those of many other infectious diseases and good-quality microscopy is available in just a few centres. However, worldwide, malaria is thought to account for at least a million deaths annually, most in young children, among about 500 million clinical cases. Its main impact is in sub-Saharan Africa where at least 90 per cent of deaths from malaria occur (Greenwood and Mutabingwa, 2002). Resistance of the pathogen to drugs and resistance of mosquitoes to insecticides, as well as the rudimentary level of health services in many areas, have combined to increase the malaria problem in sub-Saharan Africa over the past three decades. Much research into antimalarial drugs was conducted in the USA during the Viet Nam War, but since then, less effort has been focused on a disease that is just one of many that continue to plague the inhabitants of the poorer parts of the world.

Another influence on the geographical pattern of malaria incidence is global warming, since even subtle changes in temperature can have significant effects on the distribution of mosquitoes. Models of global climate change suggest that the current level of cases per year could increase significantly by 2100 (Stone, 1995). The greatest changes in transmission potential occur in areas of seasonal malaria and around the margins of existing transmission, such as highland areas. Such an expansion of the malarial zone has been evident in Rwanda in recent years where substantial increases in temperature since the early 1960s peaked in the late 1980s, and malaria became established in areas where it had previously been rare or absent. The incidence of the disease in high-altitude zones rose by 500 per cent, and most of this increase has been a function of higher temperatures and higher rainfall (Loevinsohn, 1994). Elsewhere in the highlands of East Africa, however, recent increases in the incidence of malaria have too hastily been attributed to global warming (Hay *et al.*, 2002). The rise in antimalarial drug resistance, population migrations, and the breakdown of health services and vector-control operations have all contributed to the resurgence of malaria in East African areas where no significant climate change has been detected.

Floods

Floods are one of the most common natural hazards and are experienced in every country. They occur when land not normally covered by water becomes inundated, and they can be classified into coastal floods, most of which are associated with storm surges (see above and Chapter 7), and river channel floods. Atmospheric phenomena are usually the primary cause of river flooding. Heavy rainfall is most commonly responsible, but melting snow and the temporary damming of rivers by floating ice can be important seasonally. The likelihood of these factors leading to a flood is affected by many different characteristics of the drainage basin, such as topography, drainage density and vegetation cover, and human influence often plays a role – especially by modifying land use (including the effects of urbanization) and through conscious attempts to modify the flood hazard.

Techniques for predicting floods are well developed. Most floods have a seasonal element in their occurrence and they are often forecasted using meteorological observations, with the lag time to peak flow of a particular river in response to a rainfall event being calculated using a flood hydrograph. Return periods for particular flood magnitudes can be calculated for engineering purposes, although long periods of historical data are required, which are by no means available for all river basins, and developments can alter a river's flood characteristics. Flood-hazard maps are commonly utilized for land-use zoning.

Many of the human responses to the flood hazard shown in Table 21.8 (see also Table 8.3) have been put into practice on the Mississippi River in the USA, one of the world's largest and most intensively managed rivers. Channel straight-

assist in preventing fluvial flooding from upriver by stopping seawater from enhancing already unusually high river levels. The designers of the Thames Barrier envisaged that the number of closures would increase to around ten per year on average in the first two decades of the twenty-first century because of predicted sea-level rise due to both ground subsidence in south-east England and the effects of global warming. The barrier was designed to protect London from flooding until at least the year 2030.

FURTHER READING

Berkes, F. 2007 Understanding uncertainty and reducing vulnerability: lessons from resilience thinking. *Natural Hazards* 41: 283–95. A theoretical paper focusing on how society can cope with hazards.

Bonacci, O., Ljubenkov, I. and Roje-Bonacci, T. 2006 Karst flash floods: an example from the Dinaric karst (Croatia). *Natural Hazards and Earth System Sciences* 6: 195–203. Analysis of a particularly dangerous type of flooding. (Open access journal: www.nat-hazards-earth-syst-sci.net/6/195/2006/)

Chester, D.K., Degg, M., Duncan, A.M. and Guest, J.E. 2001 The increasing exposure of cities to the effects of volcanic eruptions: a global survey. *Environmental Hazards* 2: 89–103. A risk assessment of volcanic hazards in major cities.

Hansell, A.L., Horwell, C.J. and Oppenheimer, C. 2006 The health hazards of volcanoes and geothermal areas. *Occupational and Environmental Medicine* 63: 149–56. An excellent overview of the wide range of health impacts associated with volcanic activity.

Pelling, M. and Uitto, J.I. 2001 Small island developing states: natural disaster vulnerability and global change. *Environmental Hazards* 3: 49–62. An analysis of natural hazard risks and development pressures faced by SIDS.

McGuire, B., Mason, I. and Kilburn, C. 2002 *Natural hazards and environmental change*. London, Arnold. With a focus on rapid-onset geophysical events this book highlights the links between environmental change and natural hazards.

Messerli, B. and Hofer, T. 2006 *Floods in Bangladesh: history, dynamics and rethinking the role of the Himalayas*. Tokyo, United Nations University Press. A thorough assessment of a country characterized by flooding.

Nott, J. 2006 *Extreme events: a physical reconstruction and risk assessment*. Cambridge, Cambridge University Press. Assessments of the many methods used to reconstruct the variability of hazards from long-term natural archives.

Smith, K. and Petley, D. N. 2008 *Environmental hazards: assessing risk and reducing disaster*, 5th edn. London, Routledge. All major rapid-onset events of both the natural and human environments – including seismic, mass movement, atmospheric, hydrological and technological hazards – are covered in this book, which emphasizes the physical aspects of hazards and their management.

Wisner, B., Blaikie, P., Cannon, T. and Davis, I. 2003 *At risk: natural hazards, people's vulnerability and disasters*, 2nd edn. London, Routledge. This book emphasizes the importance of the human factors behind hazards that become disasters, looking at the social, political and economic causes of people's vulnerability to natural events.

WEBSITES

geohazards.cr.usgs.gov/ site run by the US Geological Survey, covers landslides, earthquakes and volcanoes with an emphasis on the USA.

www.eri.u-tokyo.ac.jp/ the Earthquake Research Institute at the University of Tokyo.

www.solar.ifa.hawaii.edu/Tropical/ tropical storms worldwide, current and past.

www.ffwc.gov.bd/ the Bangladesh Flood Forecasting and Warning Centre has data satellite imagery and management information.

www.swissre.com/ includes annual reports on hazards and catastrophes compiled by the insurance industry.

www.cidi.org/ the Centre for International Disaster Information has situation reports on numerous natural disasters.

www.unisdr.org/ the International Strategy for Disaster Reduction aims to help all societies to become resilient to the effects of natural and technological hazards and disasters.

www.em-dat.net/ designed for humanitarian agencies, the Emergency Events Database, EM-DAT, contains data on the occurrence and effects of over 12 800 mass disasters across the world since 1900.

POINTS FOR DISCUSSION

- Can natural hazards ever be construed as good for human society?
- Since the precise timing and location of earthquakes are virtually impossible to predict, why do people live in zones that are renowned for their earthquake activity?
- Are some countries naturally more hazardous than others?
- If floods are the most common natural hazard, why are we not better at coping with them?

22 Conclusions

KEY WORDS

systemic and cumulative change, multi-pollutant/ multi-effect approach, command-and-control approach, debt-for-nature swap

Environmental issues are not new phenomena. People have always interacted with the natural world and these interactions have always thrown up challenges to human societies. Mistakes have been made and solutions often found to problems encountered or created. However, as human society has become more complex, as our numbers have increased, so the range and scale of environmental issues have multiplied. Although there are still many sizeable portions of the Earth that show little obvious evidence of human impact (e.g. many hyper-arid deserts, the deep oceans, parts of the polar regions and some of the tropical rain forests), there is nowhere that is not affected to some extent by changes in the chemical make-up of the atmosphere and associated changes in climate and pollution levels (Fig. 22.1). Likewise, the nature of relatively unaffected parts of the planet also has an impact on those regions that are directly used by human populations, through their effects on global climate and biogeochemical cycles.

Figure 22.1 This landscape in northern Greenland shows little obvious sign of human impact, although the Inuit population has hunted wildlife here for about 4500 years, albeit at sustainable levels. However, cores taken from Greenland's ice sheet show contamination transported through the atmosphere from Europe began to exceed natural background levels as early as Roman times.

It is the global nature of so many environmental issues that has thrust them to prominence in our minds. Environmental scientists have recognized two types of global environmental change: 'systemic' change through a direct impact on globally functioning systems (e.g. emissions of greenhouse gases that affect global climate) and 'cumulative' changes that attain global significance through their worldwide distribution (e.g. species loss) and/or because of their effects on a large proportion of a global resource (e.g. soil degradation on prime agricultural land). The impacts of both are recognized as being of global proportions, but the appropriate responses to systemic and cumulative change vary. Addressing a systemic global environmental issue like global warming requires a truly global strategy: all countries must take action together to combat the potential dangers. Addressing a cumulative global environmental issue can also benefit from a worldwide approach, through the exchange of data and comparison of strategies, for example. However, many cumulative global environmental issues need to be tackled at the local level because the precise causes of problems are often different in different places.

Several common themes emerge from the preceding chapters on individual issues. Numerous issues have arisen as a direct result of deliberate attempts to manipulate the natural environment to our advantage (e.g. widespread soil erosion on agricultural land, the Aral Sea tragedy, the impacts of big dams). Other issues have arisen as unexpected, indirect repercussions of activities conducted to improve human societies (e.g. contamination by fertilizer residues, global warming, acid rain). The complexities of many environmental issues are also clear. Most are related to some form of environmental change. Sometimes this change is rapid, at other times it is more gradual, but always these changes are occurring in complex systems that involve both people and nature. Cause and effect are not always obvious (e.g. the many factors affecting forest decline), and human activities and natural forces can sometimes combine to give a synergistic effect (see Table 11.7). Effects on the natural environment are also not always immediate or expected, due to the operation of thresholds, feedbacks and time lags. Many environmental issues overlap and interact. Deforestation in the tropics is a major cause of biodiversity loss, and global warming has been seen to have all sorts of potential knock-on effects for many other issues.

A full understanding of many issues is hampered by our imperfect knowledge of the physical environment. There are still many 'blank spaces on the map', both literally and metaphorically (Fig. 22.2), because we remain a long way off knowing all the basic information about this planet and indeed its peoples. The collection and analysis of data, both the measurement and monitoring of contemporary processes and the study of palaeoenvironmental reconstructions using proxy indicators, continue to be important tasks for all of those disciplines involved in the study of environmental issues.

And as knowledge and understanding improves, so our perspective on certain issues can change. Reappraisal of the Sahelian fuelwood crisis, widely feared in the 1970s but now thought to be much less of a concern, is a case in point here. We can only base our approach to managing environmental issues on existing knowledge, while continuing to conduct research to improve our understanding.

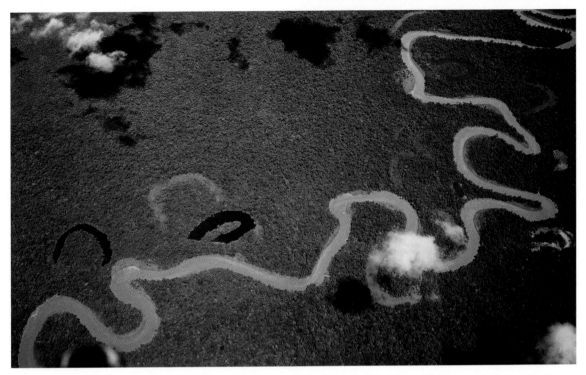

Figure 22.2 We remain remarkably ignorant of many aspects of the physical environment. This photograph is taken over tropical rain forest – a biome about which we know little – in New Guinea, a large island that remains relatively unexplored by scientists.

But in the meantime we must be aware of uncertainties, hence the emergence of important tenets such as the precautionary principle and 'no-regrets' approaches.

Some elements of human society emerge as common to several issues. Ownership, or a lack of ownership, is a pertinent issue in many atmospheric and marine environmental problems. Economic factors are also important. Poverty can drive people to degrade their resources, or force individuals to live in marginal and hazardous areas. Societies and governments may not tackle environmental problems because they lack the necessary economic resources even though workable solutions to their problems may be well known. This is not to say, however, that poor people necessarily cause environmental problems, nor that richer sectors of society do not cause them. Greater economic prosperity certainly tends to be equated with greater environmental impact: the ecological footprint of richer societies and countries is much larger than that of poorer groups (Fig. 22.3).

Political factors also play a key role. International political forces have worked together to develop many agreements and conventions designed to address environmental issues (see below). Political and economic power often go hand in hand. Many wars and other conflicts arise due to competition over resources, and inadequate enforcement of conservation measures may result from political priorities that lie elsewhere or through the weakening of civil authority, as several examples from the former Soviet Union indicate. Political corruption has featured prominently in the tropical deforestation process. Perceptions and priorities

Figure 22.3 The city of Los Angeles, USA, shrouded in smog caused by its own waste products. Urban areas, particularly those in rich countries of the North, represent a huge concentration of resources brought from all over the world. A key question that underlies many environmental issues is whether everyone on this planet can consume resources at the rates enjoyed by people who live in countries such as the USA.

are important too. The way we interact with the environment can change because our view of certain aspects of nature is subject to change. The motivation behind assessing the global area of forests, for example, has altered over the last 100 years or so. Initially driven by interest in timber resources, it is now more closely related to global environmental concerns such as biodiversity loss and climate change. This shift reflects a more general move in our view of the natural environment as a whole: from nature as resource to nature as life-sustaining global ecosystem that also harbours resources.

Perceptions of a particular landscape may vary with social and technological changes within a particular culture. Individuals within that culture may also see the same landscape in a different way, perhaps depending on socio-economic and political inequalities. Furthermore, different cultures may see different resources and/or challenges in the same places. The landscape of Greenland (Fig. 22.1) was viewed as very marginal in late medieval times by Norse settlers wanting to plough the land and herd animals, but their Inuit contemporaries considered the region to be exceptionally rich because they obtained their food resources by hunting.

Our approaches to explaining change in the environment are also subject to shifting perceptions and priorities, themselves in part reflected in shifts in intellectual fashion. A case in point is the intense current interest in the importance of climate as a driver of change in both the physical and human environment. The interest stems from concerns about anthropogenic impacts on global warming, which most agree is real enough, but one result has been an intellectual climate that is increasingly sympathetic to the idea of cultural catastrophes triggered by environmental change. Palaeoenvironmental researchers have produced numerous studies showing apparent correlations between climatic change and cultural collapse, while a few have used similar lines of evidence to argue that climatic change also appears to have played a significant role in the emergence of civilizations (see page 220). This fashion for climatic explanations of change marks the return to prominence of a form of environmental determinism.

However, there is a risk that we are putting too much emphasis on climate as a driver of change. There is the possibility that such associations may be purely coincidental. Indeed, we should also examine the numerous instances where cultures have survived rapid environmental change unperturbed or collapsed without any environmental forcing. A wider assessment of historical collapses of society has identified five groups of interacting factors – which may drive the change unilaterally or in combinations – as being especially important (Diamond, 2005): the damage that people have inflicted on their environment; climatic change; changes in friendly trading partners; the deleterious effects of enemies; and the society's political, economic and social responses to these shifts.

Examples in history, prehistory and indeed in the contemporary era will always be subject to new interpretations and fresh analyses. The supposedly textbook example cited in Chapter 3 of a culture that doomed itself by destroying its own habitat, that of Rapa Nui or Easter Island in the Pacific, has also been interpreted in several different ways (Table 22.1). One alternative explanation cites evidence for abrupt climatic and environmental change in the Pacific around AD 1300, ultimately driven by an increase in El Niño events. Another prefers a synergy of impacts, including the devastating ecological effects on the island's trees of rats inadvertently introduced by the original settlers, and the later impacts of European contact on demography.

Main driver of change	Causal chain	Reference
Ecocide	Deforestation leads to accelerated soil erosion, falling crop yields and food shortages resulting in intertribal warfare, social disintegration and population collapse	Bahn and Flenly (1992)
Environmental change	Climatic deterioration leads to resource depletion, increased competition and food shortages resulting in intertribal warfare, social disintegration and population collapse	Nunn (2000)
Biological invasion and genocide	Rats responsible for forest decline. European contact brings new diseases and slave-trading resulting in social disintegration and population collapse	Hunt (2007)

TABLE 22.1 Some suggested explanations for Rapa Nui's environmental catastrophe and population collapse

Another message from the preceding chapters of this book is that supposedly advanced societies can learn useful lessons about environmental management from indigenous cultures, which often remain 'closer to nature' than urban, industrialized groups. However, again, this is not necessarily to say that societies operating with rudimentary levels of technology are always better at avoiding environmental problems. Examples to the contrary have also been highlighted in this book: accelerated soil erosion rates in central Mexico were as great before the arrival of the plough brought by Spanish invaders, as after, and evidence suggests that at least half of Hawaiian bird species became extinct in the pre-European period.

These examples also serve to re-emphasize the fact that people have been leaving a significant mark on nature for a long time – in some cases a very long time. The first urban cultures began to develop around 5000 years ago (Chapter 10); we think the domestication of plants and animals began some 10 000 years BP (Chapter 13), and some believe overhunting by our Stone Age ancestors was responsible for the disappearance of large mammals such as the mammoth even before that (Chapter 15). The starting date for the so-called Anthropocene, the era when human action has emerged as a critical force in biophysical systems, is debatable. Such long histories of profound human influence may make the traditional division between the impact of nature on society on the one hand, and human impact on the environment on the other, inappropriate. The division will undoubtably continue because human actions represent the one set of driving forces for change that we can control in a predictable way. However, in some cases it may be that human activities and environmental change are better viewed together, as a co-evolutionary and adaptive process.

This book has also highlighted many areas where environmental issues have been tackled successfully. A general trend towards improving urban air quality has been documented with higher development levels, and there are many examples of waste disposal problems being ameliorated by viewing society's waste products as resources waiting to be used. Methods for rehabilitating and protecting the environment are constantly being developed, and the fact that many issues are interrelated means that efforts to tackle one issue often have beneficial effects for others. As Figure 22.4 shows, efforts to reduce air pollutants brings numerous benefits to many aspects of the physical and human environments.

Of course, the very rise in interest in sustainable development can be seen as an appropriate response by society to the scale and critical nature of many environmental issues. This book has been organized on an issue-by-issue basis, but the remainder of this chapter is devoted to a more regional approach, looking at the ways in which particular societies are reacting to the many environmental issues that affect them.

REGIONAL PERSPECTIVES

A distinction can be made between three global regions that should have different priorities in their contributions to global environmental sustainability (Goodland *et al.*, 1993a). The North must concentrate on reducing its long history of environmental damage due to overconsumption and affluence; the main priority in the South should be to stabilize population growth; and in the countries of the East, the former communist bloc, modernization of wasteful and polluting technology should be the central priority (Fig. 22.5). To promote these strategies, it is in the self-interest of the North to accelerate the transfer of technology to the East and South.

Measures of population density and relative affluence (which also has a major bearing on technological capacity) have been used to classify some major world regions, as shown in Figure 22.6. More detailed design and implementation of sustainable development strategies for these regions will vary according to their

on a number of general principles, which have continued to underpin subsequent development of policy. They are:

- *the polluter-pays principle* (polluters are liable for the costs of clean-up and the prevention of pollution)
- *stand-still principle* (polluted areas should not be polluted further and clean areas must remain clean)
- *principle of isolation and control* (pollution should be controlled at its source, not exported elsewhere through the air or water)
- *principle of priority for pollution abatement at source* (as opposed to end-of-pipe solutions)
- *the use of 'best technical means' technology* (to eliminate emissions when serious risks to public health are at stake regardless of economic costs, and the use of 'best practical means' technology when health effects are limited, so enabling industry to consider economic costs)
- *the principle of avoiding unnecessary pollution.*

This approach proved to be effective at dealing with the most obvious pollution problems. Air and water quality improved thanks to significant reductions in emissions of pollutants including heavy metals, SO_2 and phosphates from detergents. However, the excessive use of fertilizers and pesticides in agriculture, and emissions from the transport sector continued to cause serious pollution.

The second period, 1984 to 1989, saw a shift in emphasis from reacting to pollution problems to actively trying to prevent pollution before it becomes a problem. This shift was accompanied by a change in policy, away from the command-and-control approach of environmental laws, to a structure of economic incentives, social institutions and self-regulation to achieve sustainable development. Policies aimed to encourage pollution prevention by starting to involve all stakeholders, including business, government and local communities, in the design and implementation of programmes. This focus on preventing pollution at source spawned new instruments such as environmental care programmes for businesses and environmental impact assessments. This process enabled a shift in perception from seeing environmental standards as being in conflict with economic interests (because achieving the standards cost money) towards viewing a clean environment as a necessary precondition for a sound economy. The results from this period were also encouraging as chemical industries developed substitutes for phosphate detergents, agreements were reached to reduce packaging materials and the production of mercury batteries was stopped. Industry and energy suppliers made further drastic reductions in emissions of heavy metals and SO_2, and pollution from agriculture began to decline.

The third period in the evolution of Dutch environmental policy, from 1990 to 1999, saw the introduction of the National Environmental Policy Plans (NEPPs): NEPP1 in 1989, followed by NEPP2 in 1993 and NEPP3 in 1998. These NEPPs have continued the policy of emissions reductions, which aim to safeguard the quality of air, water and soil by setting targets for pollution prevention. The focus has been on eight themes: dispersal of toxic substances, waste disposal, disturbance by noise and external safety from hazards, eutrophication, acidification, climate change (global warming and ozone depletion), groundwater depletion, and squandering of resources. By this time a clear premise of the Dutch environmental management philosophy had emerged: that a high-quality environment cannot be achieved through conventional pollution control measures alone. A mixture of new, cleaner technologies and structural changes in patterns of production and consumption are also needed. The NEPPs have emphasized the need to improve eco-efficiency (the level of emissions and resources used per unit of production), and further encouraged the integration of ecological and economic concerns.

The style of policies to implement the NEPPs has also continued to develop away from environmental legislation and regulations towards more open decision-making with more flexibility and autonomy for local authorities and enterprises to define their own ways of achieving the targets set. When launching NEPP3, the Dutch government announced further significant achievements since NEPP1: energy efficiency in industry had increased by more than 10 per cent, the sale of CFCs ceased in 1995, the proportion of waste reused increased from 61 per cent to 72 per cent in the period 1990–96, and acidification had decreased by 50 per cent since 1985.

Contrasting recent performances for two sources of pollution are shown in Figure 22.7. The agricultural emissions of ammonia (largely from manure), a source of acidification in the Netherlands, rose through the early 1980s as the total agricultural manure production sharply increased, but has declined as low emission spreading techniques (injection into the subsoil) have increasingly been applied since 1990 (Fig. 22.7a). Having failed to hit the NEPP1 target for 2000, the NEPP4 target was set for 2030 in anticipation of a slowdown in the rate of emissions reduction. Progress towards the NEPP4 target for nitrogen oxides (NOx) emissions from motor traffic, set for 2010, is shown in Figure 22.7b. The emission of NOx has been declining since 1990, thanks to the use of three-way catalytic converters in passenger cars and delivery vans, and to the application of increasingly clean diesel engines.

Since the introduction of NEPP1 in 1989, the Netherlands has succeeded in achieving economic growth with a reduction in environmental pressure in many areas. Keijzers (2000) indicates that continued improvements in environmental performance have been seen in several sectors since NEPP1, including the construction and energy industries, waste disposal, sewage and water cleaning sectors. However, policies to curb energy use, to reduce emissions of CO_2 and NOx, and to minimize resource use were still well away from sustainable levels as described in NEPP1. Key areas for attention in NEPP4, launched in 2002,

Figure 22.7 Performance and targets under NEPPs in the Netherlands (from data at www.rivm.nl/environmentaldata/ accessed April 2002 and www.sharedspaces.nl/ accessed June 2007) for a) ammonia emissions by agriculture (from manure and fertilizers); b) NOx emissions from motor traffic.

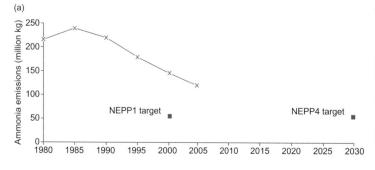

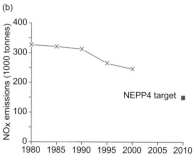

include managing CO_2 emissions, controlling future infrastructure development, minimizing resource use and reducing the burden on biodiversity.

Nonetheless, the Netherlands, like all countries, does not operate in a vacuum. The country is affected by pollutants that arrive from outside its borders, such as water pollution in the River Rhine and acid rain precursors from many parts of Europe. The low-lying country is also particularly vulnerable to any rise in sea level that may be consequent upon human-induced global warming. Dutch exports produced under a sustainable regime may be less competitively priced than equivalent products derived from unsustainable methods, and Dutch imports of resources from other countries may effectively contribute to environmentally damaging practices elsewhere. The scale of impact overseas is indicated in Figure 22.8, which shows the land used for the production of food and timber that was imported for consumption in the Netherlands. Indeed, this snapshot for the 1995 food and timber ecological footprint is one point in an upward trend in global land use by the Dutch for timber and agricultural products. The size of this footprint has increased by approximately 40 per cent over the 40-year period 1960–2000 (Rood *et al.*, 2004). While the NEPP is undoubtedly a very significant step in the right direction at the national level, its measures can only work effectively if paralleled by similar initiatives elsewhere. Hence, it is appropriate to look again at international efforts to promote sustainable development.

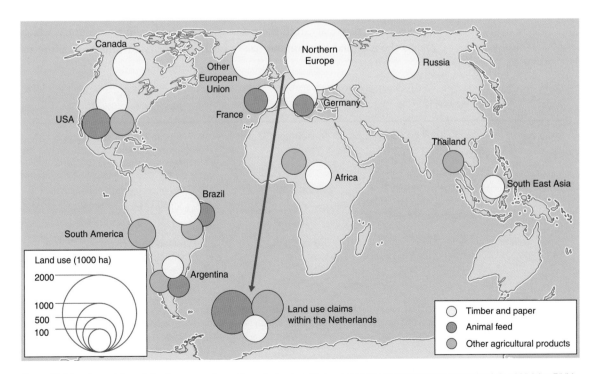

Figure 22.8 Land use claims relating to consumption patterns for food and timber production imported into the Netherlands in 1995 (after RIVM, 1999).

GLOBAL DIMENSIONS

International attempts to promote conservation and sustainable development have been mentioned already in this and other chapters. These include the establishment of the UN Environment Programme, the recommendations of organizations such as the World Commission on Environment and Development, and many global international agreements, such as the conventions on biological diversity and climate change negotiated at UNCED (the so-called Earth Summit held in Rio de Janeiro in 1992). There are also many other regional agreements and conventions.

Table 22.3 shows the major global conventions that address environmental issues. Such conventions typically arise as concern at the environmental effects of certain activities reaches a threshold at which global action is considered necessary. They reflect the fact that a sufficient number of countries recognize a common interest in trying to combat certain issues, including those rooted in both systemic and cumulative global environmental change. The international community can act quickly when issues are perceived to be particularly acute. The Chernobyl accident in April 1986 precipitated two conventions on nuclear accident notification and assistance in the same year.

The years indicated in the table are when the conventions were first agreed. A country becomes a signatory to a treaty when someone given authority by a national government signs it. Usually a signatory has no duty to perform the obligations under the treaty until the treaty comes into force in that country, which means the national government has to ratify the treaty, or otherwise adopt its

Topic	Convention	Agreed	Main aims
Antarctica	Antarctic Treaty and Convention	Washington DC, 1959	Ensure Antarctica is used for peaceful purposes, such as scientific research
Wetlands	Convention on Wetlands of International Importance Especially as Waterfowl Habitats	Ramsar, 1971	Stem progressive encroachment on and loss of wetlands
World heritage	Convention Concerning the Protection of the World Cultural and Natural Heritage	Paris, 1972	Establish a system of collective protection of cultural and natural heritage sites of outstanding universal value
Ocean dumping	Convention on the Prevention of Marine Pollution by Dumping of Wastes and Other Matter	London, Mexico City, Moscow and Washington DC, 1972	Control marine pollution by prohibiting the dumping of certain materials and regulating ocean disposal of others, encouragement of regional agreements and establishment of mechanisms to assess liability and settle disputes

TABLE 22.3 Major global environmental conventions

Topic	Convention	Agreed	Main aims
Biological and toxin weapons	Convention on the Prohibition of the Development, Production, and Stockpiling of Bacteriological (Biological) and Toxin Weapons, and on their Destruction	London, Moscow and Washington DC, 1972	Prohibit acquisition and retention of biological agents and toxins not justified for peaceful purposes, and the means of delivering them for hostile purposes
Endangered species	Convention on International Trade in Endangered Species of Wild Fauna and Flora	Washington DC, 1973	Protect endangered species from overexploitation by controlling trade in live or dead individuals and in their parts through a system of permits
Ship pollution	Protocol of 1978 Relating to the International Convention for the Prevention of Pollution from Ships, 1973	London, 1978	Modify the 1973 convention to eliminate international pollution by oil and other harmful substances and to minimize accidental discharge of such substances
Migratory species	Convention on the Conservation of Migratory Species of Wild Animals	Bonn, 1979	Promote international agreements to protect wild animals that migrate across international borders
Southern Ocean	Convention on the Conservation of Antarctic Marine Living Resources	Canberra, 1980	Safeguard the environment and protect marine ecosystems surrounding Antarctica
Law of the sea	UN Convention on the Law of the Sea	Montego Bay, 1982	Establish a comprehensive legal regime for the seas and oceans, including environmental standards and rules to control marine pollution
Ozone layer	Vienna Convention for the Protection of the Ozone Layer	Vienna, 1985	Protect human health and the environment by promoting research, monitoring of the ozone layer and control measures against activities that produce harmful effects
Nuclear accident notification	Convention on Early Notification of a Nuclear Accident	Vienna, 1986	Provide relevant information about nuclear accidents to minimize transboundary radiological consequences
Nuclear accident assistance	Convention on Assistance in the Case of a Nuclear Accident or Radiological Emergency	Vienna, 1986	Facilitate prompt provision of assistance following a nuclear accident or radiological emergency

TABLE 22.3 Continued

Topic	Convention	Agreed	Main aims
CFC control	Protocol on Substances that Deplete the Ozone Layer	Montreal, 1987	Require developed states to cut consumption of CFCs and halons with allowances for increases in consumption by developing countries
Hazardous waste movement	Basel Convention on the Control of Transboundary Movements of Hazardous Wastes and their Disposal	Basel, 1989	Establish obligations to reduce transboundary movements of wastes, minimize generation of hazardous wastes and ensure their environmentally sound management
Biodiversity	UN Convention on Biological Diversity	Nairobi, 1992	Protect biological resources, and regulate biotechnology firms' access to and ownership of genetic material, and compensation to developing countries for extraction of their genetic materials
Climate change	Convention on Climate Change	New York, 1993	Stabilize atmospheric concentrations of greenhouse gases
Desertification	UN Convention to Combat Desertification	Paris, 1994	Promote sustainable development of drylands
Persistent Organic Pollutants (POPs)	Convention on Persistent Organic Pollutants (POPs)	Stockholm, 2001	International control of 12 chemicals

TABLE 22.3 Continued

provisions in national law, and the treaty itself is ratified by a prescribed number of countries. This can take a long time. The UN Convention on the Law of the Sea, for example, was first signed in 1982, but did not come into force until 1994. Countries can still join conventions after the first signing session. The Convention on Wetlands of International Importance Especially as Waterfowl Habitats (the Ramsar Convention) was first signed by 18 countries in 1971, but by early 2008 the original 18 had been joined by 139 other contracting parties.

These conventions represent a significant step forward at the international level, but international agreements and conventions still have their weaknesses. Enforcement is a particular difficulty. While non-compliance with an agreement can lay a country open to criticism, compliance can rarely be enforced by law. Part of this problem is related to the difficulties of translating agreements in principle into national laws. Another weakness is structural. Any agreement requires compromise between the parties, and international agreements, often involving hundreds of nation states, can result in provisions that are imprecise and not very constraining.

Agenda 21 is not shown in Table 22.3 because it is not a binding treaty. It was, nonetheless, an important outcome of the Earth Summit, a sort of global action plan for achieving sustainable development during the twenty-first century. Agenda 21 is designed to reconcile conservation and development, and addresses general development issues, issues relating to specific resources, the roles of various groups, and means of implementation. Such implementation is the concern of individual countries and although it has no legal force, Agenda 21 has considerable political authority.

The integrated approach embodied in Agenda 21 emphasizes the fact that many of the subjects of the global environmental conventions shown in Table 22.3 are, of course, interlinked. For example, the links between three major global change issues discussed in detail at the Earth Summit – biodiversity, climate change and desertification/land degradation – are numerous. Land degradation can often result in a loss of biodiversity which can in turn have impacts on regional and global climate through changes in surface energy budgets and the carbon cycle. Changes in rainfall patterns and amounts, and the consequent production of biomass, will affect land degradation. Hence, any attempt to deal with one of these environmental issues will inevitably have impacts on others. So a scheme financed under the UN Convention to Combat Desertification to promote sustainable land use, for instance, may well also enhance biodiversity.

Many of these international conventions have also been associated with new global bodies established to assess the issues scientifically and to offer advice to policymakers. A good example is the Intergovernmental Panel on Climate Change (IPCC) which has made tremendous advances in our understanding of climate change since its establishment in 1988. A similar initiative took place between 2001 and 2005 in the form of the Millennium Ecosystem Assessment, which aimed to provide a scientific appraisal of the condition and trends in the world's ecosystems and the services they provide, as well as the scientific basis for action to conserve and use them sustainably.

These and other initiatives have all made a positive contribution, but they have done little to address one of the major underlying difficulties in achieving global sustainability: poverty and the unequal distribution of resources. Inequalities exist at all levels (see Chapter 2), but on the global scale an obvious imbalance is evident between North and South. Some minor, if significant, attempts have been made to address both debt problems and environmental problems in developing countries by converting part of the external debt of a country into a domestic obligation to support a specific programme. Some examples of existing 'debt-for-nature swaps' are detailed in Table 22.4. An international conservation group, or in some cases a national government, purchases part of a debtor country's foreign debt on the secondary market, at a fraction of the theoretical face value of the debt. The low cost of the original debt on the secondary market is a reflection of the fact that creditors have a low expectation of the debt itself being repaid. Once the debt has been acquired, the 'investing' conservation organization agrees a rate of exchange with the debtor country so that the debt is converted into local currency, which is then used to finance the intended aims.

Debtor	Date	Debt face value (US$ million)	Cost (US$ million)	Investor	Terms and aims
Bolivia	7/87	0.65	0.1	Conservation International	Full legal protection of Beni Biosphere Reserve, set-up of buffer zones and local management fund
Costa Rica	4/89	24.5	3.5	Government of Sweden	Expansion and protection of Guanacaste National Park
Madagascar	1/91	0.12	0.06	Conservation International	Interest from endowment fund for ecosystem management programmes, species inventories and environmental education
Poland	1/90	0.05	0.01	WWF-International and WWF-Sweden	Clean-up of River Vistula and development of Biebrza National Park
Sudan	12/88	0.8		Bank donation	Midland Bank donated US $0.8 million in loans to UNICEF to provide ten village water wells with hand pumps

Source: modified after WCMC (1992: Table 32.11).

TABLE 22.4 Examples of established debt-for-nature agreements

Supporters of debt-for-nature swaps point out that they are agreements in which all parties involved stand to gain. Conservation organizations increase the spending power of their money, through the difference between the secondary market cost and the face value of the debt purchased, and are able to exert influence on conservation policies in developing countries. The debtor gains by reducing its foreign debt, reducing the government's need to raise foreign currency to service its debts, and also wins finance to support conservation programmes, which the government has some control over. For some debtor countries, however, such agreements may be seen as an infringement upon national sovereignty, passing some control and influence over national resources to foreign interests.

Despite debt-for-nature swaps, part of the packages of development aid that flow from North to South, the problems of indebtedness and unequal trading relations remain essentially unchanged. Redistribution from rich to poor countries on any significant scale still appears to be politically impossible, yet it is the resolution or otherwise of this issue, perhaps more than any other, that will dictate the pace of global change towards sustainability.

Having drawn attention to these international dimensions to global environmental issues, it is appropriate also to highlight drawbacks that some identify with the underlying belief that these problems are solvable through globally co-ordinated action. Adger *et al.* (2001) continue the theme of synergies between issues in their analysis of the major discourses associated with four global envi-

Benstead, J.P., Stiassny, M.L.J., Loiselle, P.V., Riseng, K.J. and Raminosoa, N. 2000 River conservation in Madagascar. In Boon, P.J., Davies, B.R. and Petts, G.E. (eds), *Global perspectives on river conservation: science, policy and practice*. Chichester, Wiley: 205–31.

Bentley, N. 1998 An overview of the exploitation, trade and management of corals in Indonesia. *TRAFFIC Bulletin* 17: 67–78.

Bergström, M. 1990 The release in war of dangerous forces from hydrological facilities. In Westing, A.H. (ed.), *Environmental hazards of war*. London, Sage: 38–47.

Berkes, F. (ed.) 1989 *Common property resources: ecology and community-based sustainable development*. London, Belhaven.

Bertrand, F. 1993 *Contribution à l'étude de l'environnement et de la dynamique des mangroves de Guinée*. Paris, ORSTOM.

Berz, G.A. 1991 Global warming and the insurance industry. *Nature and Resources* 27(1): 19–28.

Betts, R.A., Cox, P.M., Lee, S.E. and Woodward, F.I. 1997 Contrasting physiological and structural vegetation feedbacks in climate change simulations. *Nature* 387: 796–9.

Bhatti, N., Streets, D.G. and Foell, W.K. 1992 Acid rain in Asia. *Environmental Management* 16: 541–62.

Bird, E.F.C. 1985 *Coastline changes: a global review*. Chichester, Wiley.

Biswas, A.K. 1990 Watershed management. In Thanh, N.C. and Biswas, A.K. (eds), *Environmentally-sound water management*. Delhi, Oxford University Press: 155–75.

Björk, S. and Digerfeldt, G. 1991 Development and degradation, redevelopment and preservation of Jamaican wetlands. *Ambio* 20: 276–84.

Black, M. 1994 *Mega-slums: the coming sanitary crisis*. London, Wateraid.

Black, R. 1994 Environmental change in refugee-affected areas of the Third World: the role of policy and research. *Disasters* 18: 107–16.

Blaikie, P. 1985 *The political economy of soil erosion*. London, Longman.

Blaikie, P. 1989 Explanation and policy in land degradation and rehabilitation for developing countries. *Land Degradation and Rehabilitation* 1: 23–37.

Blaikie, P., Cannon, T., Davis, I. and Wisner, B. 1994 *At risk: natural hazards, people's vulnerability and disasters*. London, Routledge.

Blum, E. 1993 Making biodiversity conservation profitable: a case study of the Merck/INBio agreement. *Environment* 35(4): 16–45.

Blunden, J. 1985 *Mineral resources and their management*. London, Longman.

Boardman, J. 1990 *Soil erosion in Britain: costs, attitudes and policies*. Social Audit Paper 1. University of Sussex, Brighton, Education Network for Environment and Development.

Bond, A.R. and Piepenburg, K. 1990 Land reclamation after surface mining in the USSR: economic, political, and legal issues. *Soviet Geography* 31: 332–65.

Bormann, F.H. and Likens, G.E. 1979 *Pattern and process in a forested ecosystem*. New York, Springer Verlag.

Boroffka, N., Oberhänsli, H., Sorrel, P., Demory, F., Reinhardt, C., Wünnemann, B., Alimov, K., Baratov, S., Rakhimov, K., Saparov, N., Shirinov, T., Krivonogov, S.K. and Röhl, U. 2006 Archaeology and climate: settlement and lake-level changes at the Aral Sea. *Geoarchaeology* 21: 721–34.

Borysova, O., Kondakov, A., Paleari, S., Rautalahti-Miettinen, E., Stolberg, F. and Daler, D. 2005 *Eutrophication in the Black Sea region: impact assessment and causal chain analysis*. Kalmar, Sweden, University of Kalmar.

Boserüp, E. 1965 *The conditions of agricultural growth: the economics of agrarian change under population pressure*. London, Allen & Unwin.

Bosson, R. and Varon, B. 1977 *The mining industry and the developing countries*. New York, Oxford University Press.

Boutron, C.F., Görlach, U., Candelone, J.-P., Bolshov, M.A. and Delmas, R.J. 1991 Decrease in anthropogenic lead, cadmium and zinc in Greenland snows since the late 1960s. *Nature* 353: 153–6.

Bowonder, B., Prasad, S.S.R. and Unni, N.V.M. 1988 Dynamics of fuelwood prices in India. *World Development* 16: 1213–29.

Boyce, J.K. 1990 Birth of a megaproject: political economy of flood control in Bangladesh. *Environmental Management* 14: 419–28.

Bozheyeva, G., Kunakbayev, Y. and Yeleukenov, D. 1999 *Former Soviet biological weapons facilities in Kazakhstan: past, present, and future*. Monterey Institute of International Studies, Center for Nonproliferation Studies Occasional Papers 1.

Bradshaw, A.D. and Chadwick, M.J. 1980 *The restoration of land*. Oxford, Blackwell Scientific.

Bradshaw, C.J.A., Sodhi, N.S., Peh, K.S.-H. and Brook, B.W. 2007 Global evidence that deforestation amplifies flood risk and severity in the developing world. *Global Change Biology* 13: 2379–95.

Brandon, C. and Ramankutty, R. 1993 *Toward an environmental strategy for Asia*. World Bank Discussion Paper 224.

Braun, S. and Fluckiger, W. 1984 Increased population of the aphis *Aphis pomi* at a motorway. Part 2 the effect of drought and deicing salt. *Environmental Pollution (series A)* 36: 261–70.

Bravo, A.H., Soto, A.R., Sosa, E.R., Sanchez, A.P., Alarcón, J.A.L., Kahl, J. and Ruíz, B.J. 2006 Effect of acid rain on building material of the El Tajin archaeological zone in Veracruz, Mexico. *Environmental Pollution* 144: 655–60.

Briscoe, J. 1987 A role for water supply and sanitation in the child survival revolution. *Bulletin of the Pan American Health Organization* 21: 92–105.

British Geological Survey 2007 *World mineral production 2001–05.* Keyworth, Nottingham, British Geological Survey.

Broad, R. 1994 The poor and the environment: friends or foe? *World Development* 22: 811–22.

Brook, B.W., Sodhi, N.S. and Ng, P.K.L. 2003 Catastrophic extinctions follow deforestation in Singapore. *Nature* 424: 420–3.

Brookes, A. 1985 River channelization: traditional engineering methods, physical consequences, and alternative practices. *Progress in Physical Geography* 9: 44–73.

Brooks, N. 2006 Cultural responses to aridity in the Middle Holocene and increased social complexity. *Quaternary International* 151: 29–49.

Brown, S. and Lugo, A.E. 1990 Tropical secondary forests. *Journal of Tropical Ecology* 6: 1–32.

Bruinsma, J. 2003 *World agriculture: towards 2015/2030: an FAO perspective.* London, Earthscan.

Bryant, D., Burke, L., McManus, J. and Spalding, M. 1998 *A map-based indicator of threats to the world's coral reefs.* Washington DC, World Resources Institute.

Bryson, R.A. and Barreis, D.A. 1967 Possibility of major climatic modifications and their implications: northwest India, a case for study. *Bulletin of the American Meteorological Society* 48: 136–42.

Bucher, E.H. 1992 The causes of extinction of the passenger pigeon. *Current Ornithology* 9: 1–36.

Burke, L., Kura, Y., Kassem, K., Revenga, C., Spalding, M. and McAllister, D. 2000 *Pilot analysis of global ecosystems (PAGE): Coastal ecosystems.* Washington DC, World Resources Institute.

Burt, T. 1993 From Westminster to Windrush: public policy in the drainage basin. *Geography* 78: 388–400.

Burt, T. 1994 Long-term study of the natural environment – perceptive science or mindless monitoring. *Progress in Physical Geography* 18: 475–96.

Burt, T., Heathwaite, A.L. and Trudgill, S.T. 1993 *Nitrate: processes, patterns and management.* Chichester, Wiley.

Burton, I., Kates, R.W. and White, G.F. 1978 *The environment as hazard.* New York, Oxford University Press.

Buschiazzo, D.E., Aimar, S.B. and Garcia Queijeiro, J.M. 1999 Long-term maize, sorghum and millet monoculture effects on an Argentina typic ustipsamment. *Arid Soil Research and Rehabilitation* 13: 1–15.

Caddy, J.F. and Gulland, J.A. 1983 Historical patterns of fish stocks. *Marine Pollution* 7: 267–78.

Capra, F. 1982 *The turning point: science, society and the rising culture.* New York, Simon & Schuster.

Carapico, S. 1985 Yemeni agriculture in transition. In Beaumont, P. and McLachlan, K. (eds), *Agricultural development in the Middle East.* Chichester, Wiley: 241–54.

Carreira, J.A. and Neill, F.X. 1995 Mobilization of nutrients by fire in a semiarid gorse-scrubland ecosystem of southern Spain. *Arid Soil Research and Rehabilitation* 9: 73–89.

Carson, R. 1962 *Silent spring.* Boston, Houghton Mifflin.

Carter, F.W. 1993a Czechoslovakia. In Carter, F.W. and Turnock, D. (eds), *Environmental problems in Eastern Europe.* London, Routledge: 63–88.

Carter, F.W. 1993b Poland. In Carter, F.W. and Turnock, D. (eds), *Environmental problems in Eastern Europe.* London, Routledge: 107–34.

Caughley, G. 1979 What is this thing called carrying capacity? In Boyce, M.S. and Hayden-Wing, L.D. (eds), *North American elk: ecology, behaviour and management.* Laramie, University of Wyoming Press: 2–8.

Cavanagh, J.E., Clarke, J.H. and Price, R. 1993 Ocean energy systems. In Johansson, T.B., Kelly, H., Reddy, A.K.N. and Williams, R.H. (eds), *Renewable energy: sources for fuels and electricity.* New York, Island Press: 513–47.

Caviedes, C.N. and Fik, T.J. 1992 The Peru–Chile eastern Pacific fisheries and climatic oscillation. In Glantz, M.H. (ed.), *Climatic variability, climate change and fisheries.* Cambridge, Cambridge University Press: 355–75.

Cederholm, C.J., Kunze, M.D., Murota, T. and Sibatani, A. 1999 Pacific salmon carcasses: essential contributions of nutrients and energy for aquatic and terrestrial ecosystems. *Fisheries* 24(10): 6–15.

Chakela, Q. and Stocking, M. 1988 An improved methodology for erosion hazard mapping. Part II, Application to Lesotho. *Geografiska Annaler* 70(A): 181–9.

Chandler, A.M. 1997 Engineering design lessons from Kobe. *Nature* 387: 227–9.

Chao, B.F. 1995 Anthropological impact on global geodynamics due to water impoundment in major reservoirs. *Geophysical Research Letters* 22: 3533–6.

Chape, S., Blyth, S., Fish, L., Fox, P. and Spalding, M. 2003 *2003 United Nations list of protected areas.* Gland, Switzerland, IUCN and Cambridge, UK, UNEP–WCMC.

Chapman, D. (ed.) 1996 *Water quality assessments*, 2nd edn. London, E & FN Spon.

Charlson, R.J. and Wigley, T.M.L. 1994 Sulfate aerosol and climatic change. *Scientific American* 270(2): 28–35.

Charney, J., Stone, P.H. and Quirk, W.J. 1975 Drought in the Sahara: a bio-geophysical feedback mechanism. *Science* 187: 434–5.

Chen, R.Z., Peng, G.Y. and Hunag, F.X. 1990 Effect of simulated acid rain on the growth and yield of soybean and peanut. *Journal of Ecology (China)* 9: 58–60.

Chernobyl Forum 2005 *Chernobyl's legacy: health, environmental and socio-economic impacts*. Vienna, International Atomic Energy Agency.

Chester, D. 1993 *Volcanoes and society*. London, Edward Arnold.

Chester, D.K., Degg, M., Duncan, A.M. and Guest, J.E. 2001 The increasing exposure of cities to the effects of volcanic eruptions: a global survey. *Environmental Hazards* 2: 89–103.

Chien, N. 1985 Changes in river regime after the construction of upstream reservoirs. *Earth Surface Processes and Landforms* 10: 143–59.

Chorus, I. and Bartram, J. 1999 *Toxic cyanobacteria in water: a guide to their public health consequences, monitoring and management*. World Health Organization, E & FN Spon.

Choun, H.F. 1936 Dust storms in southwestern plains area. *Monthly Weather Review* 64: 195–9.

Christensen, B. 1983 Mangroves – what are they worth? *Unasylva* 35: 2–15.

Church, J.A. and White, N.J. 2006 A 20th century acceleration in global sea-level rise. *Geophysical Research Letters* 33: L01602.

CIDA (Canadian International Development Agency) 2000 *Canada Climate Change Development Fund: management framework and business plan*. Ottawa, CIDA, 13 July.

Cincotta, R.P., Wisnewski, J. and Engelman, R. 2000 Human population in the biodiversity hotspots. *Nature* 404: 990–2.

CIPRCP (Commission Internationale pour la Protection du Rhin Contre la Pollution) 1984 *Rapport Annual 1984*. Koblenz, CIPRCP.

CIRIA (Construction Industry Research and Information Association) 1989 *The engineering implications of rising ground water levels in the deep aquifer beneath London*. London, CIRIA.

Ciudad de México 2007 *La calidad del aire en la ZMVM 1986–2006*. México DF, Ciudad de México.

Clark, R.B. 1992 *Marine pollution*, 3rd edn. Oxford, Clarendon Press.

Clark, W.C. 1989 Managing planet Earth. *Scientific American* 261(3): 19–26.

Clarke, R. and King, J. 2004 *The water atlas*. New York, New Press.

Clayton, K. 1991 Scaling environmental problems. *Geography* 76: 2–15.

Clements, F.E. 1916 *Plant succession: an analysis of the development of vegetation*. Publication 242. Washington DC, Carnegie Institute.

Coates, L. 1999 Flood fatalities in Australia, 1788–1996. *Australian Geographer* 30: 391–408.

Cobb, C.W. and Cobb, J.B. 1994 The green national product: a proposed index of sustainable economic welfare. Lanham MD, University Press of America.

Cohen, M.N. 1977 *The food crisis in prehistory: overpopulation and the origins of agriculture*. New Haven, Yale University Press.

Cohn, J.P. 1990 Elephants: remarkable and endangered. *BioScience* 40: 10–14.

Colby, M.E. 1989 *The evolution of paradigms of environmental management in development*. World Bank Strategic Planning and Review Discussion Paper. Washington DC, World Bank.

Colinvaux, P. 1993 *Ecology 2*. New York, Wiley.

Collar, N.J., Crosby, M.J. and Stattersfield, A.J. 1994 *Birds to watch 2. The world list of threatened birds*. Cambridge, BirdLife International.

Collier, P. and Hoeffler, A. 2000 Greed and grievance in civil war. World Bank, Policy Research Working Paper 2355.

Collins, C.O. and Scott, S.L. 1993 Air pollution in the Valley of Mexico. *Geographical Review* 83: 119–33.

Collins, N.M., Sayer, J.A. and Whitmore, T.C. (eds) 1991 *The conservation atlas of tropical forests: Asia and the Pacific*. London, Macmillan/IUCN.

Confalonieri, U. 1998 Malaria in the Brazilian Amazon. In WRI, *World resources 1998–99*. New York, Oxford University Press: 48–9.

Connell, J.H. 1978 Diversity in tropical rain forests and coral reefs. *Science* 199: 1302–10.

Connelly, N.A., O'Neill, C.R., Knuth, B.A. and Brown, T.L. 2007 Economic impacts of zebra mussels on drinking water treatment and electric power generation facilities. *Environmental Management* 40: 105–12.

Conway, G.R. and Pretty, J.N. 1991 *Unwelcome harvest: agriculture and pollution*. London, Earthscan.

Cooke, R.U. 1984 *Geomorphological hazards in Los Angeles*. London, Allen & Unwin.

Cooke, R.U. 1989 Geomorphological contributions to acid rain research: studies of stone weathering. *Geographical Journal* 155: 361–6.

Cooke, R.U. and Doornkamp, J.C. 1990 *Geomorphology in environmental management*, 2nd edn. Oxford, Clarendon Press.

Corlett, R.T. 1992 The ecological transformation of Singapore, 1819–1900. *Journal of Biogeography* 19: 411–20.

Corte-Real, J., Sorani, R. and Conte, M. 1998 Climate change. In Mairota, P., Thornes, J.B. and Geeson, N. (eds), *Atlas of Mediterranean environments in Europe: the desertification context*. Chichester, Wiley: 34–6.

Coull, J.R. 1993 Will a blue revolution follow the green revolution? The modern upsurge of aquaculture. *Area* 25: 350–7.

Crocker, R.L. and Major, J. 1955 Soil development in relation to vegetation and surface age at Glacier Bay, Alaska. *Journal of Ecology* 43: 427–48.

Crowder, B.M. 1987 Economic costs of reservoir sedimentation: a regional approach to estimating cropland erosion damages. *Journal of Soil and Water Conservation* 42: 194–7.

Crowson, P. 1992 *Mineral resources: the infinitely finite*. Ottawa, The International Council on Metals and the Environment.

Crutzen, P.J. and Stoermer, E.F. 2000 The 'anthropocene'. IGBP Newsletter 41: 17–18.

Csirke, J. 1988 Small shoaling pelagic fish stocks. In Gulland, J.A. (ed.), *Fish population dynamics*, 2nd edn. Chichester, Wiley: 277–84.

Curtis, D., Hubbard, M. and Shepherd, A. (eds) 1988 *Preventing famine: policies and prospects for Africa*. London, Routledge.

D'Yakanov, K.N. and Reteyum, A.Y. 1965 The local climate of the Rybinsk reservoir. *Soviet Geography* 6: 40–53.

Daly, H.E. 1987 The economic growth debate: what some economists have learned but many others have not. *Journal of Environmental Economics and Management* 14: 323–36.

Daly, H.E. 1993 The perils of free trade. *Scientific American* 269(5): 24–9.

Davies, B.R., Boon, P.J. and Petts, G.E. 2000 River conservation: a global imperative. In Boon, P.J., Davies, B.R. and Petts, G.E. (eds), *Global perspectives on river conservation: science, policy and practice*. Chichester, Wiley: xi–xvi.

Davis, M.B. 1976 Erosion rates and land use history in southern Michigan. *Environmental Conservation* 3: 139–48.

Davis, T.J. (ed.) 1993 *Towards the wise use of wetlands*. Gland, Wise Use Project, Ramsar Convention Bureau.

de Jong, J. and Wiggens, A.J. 1983 Polders and their environment in the Netherlands. In *Polders of the world, an international symposium: final report*. Wageningen, International Institute for Land Reclamation and Improvement: 221–41.

de Mora, S.J. and Turner, T. 2004 The Caspian Sea: a microcosm for environmental science and international cooperation. *Marine Pollution Bulletin* 48: 26–9.

De Noni, G., Trujillo, G. and Viennot, M. 1986 L'érosion et la conservation des sols en Equateur. *Cahiers ORSTOM Série Pédologie* 22: 235–45.

de Vries, H.J.M. 1989 *Sustainable development*. Groningen, Netherlands, ISRIC.

DEA (Danish Energy Authority) 2005 *Offshore wind power – Danish experiences and solutions*. Copenhagen, DEA.

Dearing, J.A. 2006 Climate-human-environment interactions: resolving our past. *Climate of the Past* 2: 187–203.

DECADE (Domestic Equipment and Carbon Dioxide Emissions) 1995 *Second year report*. Oxford, University of Oxford Environmental Change Unit, Energy and Environment Programme.

Décamps, H. and Fortuné, M. 1991 Long-term ecological research and fluvial landscapes. In Risser, P.G. (ed.), *Long-term ecological research*. SCOPE Report 47. Chichester, Wiley: 135–51.

Deegan, J. 1987 Looking back at Love Canal. *Environmental Science and Technology* 21: 328–31.

Deichmann, U. and Eklundh, L. 1991 *Global digital datasets for land degradation studies: a GIS approach*. UNEP/GEMS GRID Case Study Series 4. Nairobi, UNEP.

Dejene, A. and Olivares, J. 1991 *Integrating environmental issues into a strategy for sustainable agricultural development: the case of Mozambique*. World Bank Technical Paper 146.

deMenocal, P.B. 2001 Cultural responses to climate change during the late Holocene. *Science* 292: 667–3.

Desbiens, C. 2004 Producing North and South: a political geography of hydro development in Québec. *The Canadian Geographer* 48: 101–18.

Dhakal, S. 2004 *Urban energy use and greenhouse gas emissions in Asian mega-cities: policies for a sustainable future*. Kitakyushu, Japan, Institute for Global Environmental Strategies.

Diamond, J. 2005 *Collapse: how societies choose to fail or survive*. New York, Viking Penguin.

Diamond, J.M. 1984 Historic extinctions: a Rosetta Stone for understanding prehistoric extinctions. In Martin, P.S. and Klein, R.G. (eds), *Quaternary extinctions: a prehistoric revolution*. Tucson, University of Arizona Press: 824–62.

Diarra, D.C. and Akuffo, F.O. 2002 Solar photovoltaic in Mali: potential and constraints. *Energy Conversion and Management* 43: 151–63.

Dickinson, G., Murphy, K. and Springuel, I. 1994 The implications of the altered water regime for the ecology and sustainable development of Wadi Allaqi, Egypt. In Millington, A.C. and Pye, K. (eds), *Environmental change in drylands: biogeographical and geomorphological perspectives*. Chichester, Wiley: 379–91.

Dierber, F.E. and Kiattisimkul, W. 1996 Issues, impacts, and implications of shrimp aquaculture in Thailand. *Environmental Management* 20: 649–66.

Dijkema, G.P.J., Reuter, M.A. and Verhoef, E.V. 2000 A new paradigm for waste management. *Waste Management* 20: 633–8.

Dikou, A. and van Woesik, R. 2006 Survival under chronic stress from sediment load: Spatial patterns of hard coral communities in the southern islands of Singapore. *Marine Pollution Bulletin* 52: 7–21.

Dinerstein, E., Loucks, C., Wikramanayake, E., Ginsberg, J., Sanderson, E., Seidensticker, J., Forrest, J., Bryja, G., Heydlauff, A., Klenzendorf, S., Leimgruber, P.,

Greenwood, B. and Mutabingwa, T. 2002 Malaria in 2002. *Nature* 415: 670–2.

Grenon, M. and Batisse, M. (eds) 1989 *Futures for the Mediterranean basin: the Blue Plan*. New York, Oxford University Press.

Grigg, D.B. 1992 *The transformation of agriculture in the West*. Oxford, Blackwell.

Grigg, D.B. 1993 The role of livestock products in world food consumption. *Scottish Geographical Magazine* 109: 66–74.

Groombridge, B. and Jenkins, M.D. 2000 *Global Biodiversity: Earth's living resources in the 21st century*. Cambridge, WCMC.

Grossman, L.S. 1992 Pesticides, caution, and experimentation in Saint Vincent, Eastern Caribbean. *Human Ecology* 20: 315–36.

Grove, R. 1990 The origins of environmentalism. *Nature* 345: 11–14.

Grubb, M.J. and Meyer, N.I. 1993 Wind energy: resources, systems and regional strategies. In Johansson, T.B., Kelly, H., Reddy, A.K.N. and Williams, R.H. (eds), *Renewable energy: sources for fuels and electricity*. New York, Island Press: 157–212.

Gunn, J.M. and Keller, W. 1990 Biological recovery of an acid lake after reductions in industrial emissions of sulphur. *Nature* 345: 431–3.

Gupta, H.K. 2002 A review of recent studies of triggered earthquakes by artificial water reservoirs with special emphasis on earthquakes in Koyna, India. *Earth-Science Reviews* 58: 279–310.

Hägerstrand, T. and Lohm, U. 1990 Sweden. In Turner II, B.L., Clark, W.C., Kates, R.W., Richards, J.F., Mathews, J.T. and Meyer, W.B. (eds), *The Earth as transformed by human action*. Cambridge, Cambridge University Press: 605–22.

Hall, D.O. and Rosillo-Calle, F. 1991 *Biomass in developing countries*. Report to the Office of Technology Assessment, Washington DC.

Hall, D.O., Rosillo-Calle, F., Williams, R.H. and Woods, J. 1993 Biomass for energy: supply prospects. In Johansson, T.B., Kelly, H., Reddy, A.K.N. and Williams, R.H. (eds), *Renewable energy: sources for fuels and electricity*. New York, Island Press: 595–651.

Hall, D.R. 1993 Albania. In Carter, F.W. and Turnock, D. (eds), *Environmental problems in Eastern Europe*. London, Routledge: 7–37.

Halls, A.J. (ed.) 1997 *Wetlands, biodiversity and the Ramsar Convention: the role of the Convention on Wetlands in the conservation and wise use of biodiversity*. Gland, Ramsar Convention Bureau.

Hanan, N.P., Prevost, Y., Diouf, A. and Diallo, O. 1991 Assessment of desertification around deep wells in the Sahel using satellite imagery. *Journal of Applied Ecology* 28: 173–86.

Hansen, J.R., Hansson, R. and Norris, S. 1996 *The State of the European Arctic environment*. EEA Environmental Monograph 3.

Hardin, G. 1968 The tragedy of the commons. *Science* 162: 1243–8.

Hardoy, J.E., Mitlin, D. and Satterthwaite, D. 1992 *Environmental problems in third world cities*. London, Earthscan.

Hardoy, J.E., Mitlin, D. and Satterthwaite, D. 2001 *Environmental problems in an urbanizing world*. London, Earthscan.

Harper, P.P. 1992 La Grande Rivière: a subarctic river and hydroelectric megaproject. In Calow, P. and Petts, G.E. (eds), *The rivers handbook*, vol. 1. Oxford, Blackwell Scientific: 411–25.

Hartig, J.H. and Vallentyne, J.R. 1989 Use of an ecosystem approach to restore degraded areas of the Great Lakes. *Ambio* 18: 423–8.

Hassan, F.A. 1980 Prehistoric settlement along the Main Nile. In Williams, M.A.J. and Faure, H. (eds), *The Sahara and the Nile*. Rotterdam, Balkema: 421–50.

Hawksworth, D.L. 1990 The long-term effects of air pollutants on lichen communities in Europe and North America. In Woodwell, G.M. (ed.), *The Earth in transition: patterns and processes of biotic impoverishment*. Cambridge, Cambridge University Press: 45–64.

Hay, S.I., Cox, J., Rogers, D.J., Randolph, S.E., Stern, D.I., Shanks, G.D., Myers, M.F. and Snow, R.W. 2002 Climate change and the resurgence of malaria in the East African highlands. *Nature* 415: 905–9.

Hay, S.I., Guerra, C.A., Tatem, A.J., Noor, A.M. and Snow, R.W. 2004 The global distribution and population at risk of malaria: past, present, and future. *The Lancet Infectious Diseases* 4: 327–36.

Haynes, R.J. and Williams, P.H. 1993 Nutrient cycling and soil fertility in the grazed pasture ecosystem. *Advances in Agronomy* 49: 119–99.

Hays, J.D., Imbrie, J. and Shackleton, N.J. 1976 Variations in the earth's orbit: pacemaker of the ice ages. *Science* 235: 1156–67.

Heath, J., Pollard, E. and Thomas, J.A. 1984 *Atlas of butterflies in Britain and Ireland*. Harmondsworth, Viking.

Heliotis, F.D., Karandinos, M.G. and Whiton, J.C. 1988 Air pollution and the decline of the fir forest in Parnis National Park, near Athens, Greece. *Environmental Pollution* 54: 29–40.

Hellawell, J.M. 1988 River regulation and nature conservation. *Regulated Rivers: Research and Management* 2: 425–43.

Hellden, U. 1988 Desertification monitoring: is the desert encroaching? *Desertification Control Bulletin* 17: 8–12.

Hellden, U. 1991 Desertification – time for an assessment? *Ambio* 20: 372–83.

Henderson, S., Dawson, T.P. and Whittaker, R.J. 2006 Progress in invasive plants research. *Progress in Physical Geography* 30: 25–46.

Henderson-Sellers, A. 1994 Numerical modelling of global climates. In Roberts, N. (ed.), *The changing global environment.* Oxford, Blackwell: 99–124.

Hengeveld, R. 1989 *Dynamics of biological invasions.* London, Chapman & Hall.

Hernández Tejeda, T. and de Bauer, L.I. 1986 Photochemical oxidant damage on *Pinus hartwegii* at the Desierto de los Leones, Mexico DF. *Phytopathology* 76: 377.

Hewitt, K. and Burton, I. 1971 *The hazardousness of a place: a regional ecology of damaging events.* Toronto, University of Toronto Geography Department.

Hilz, C. and Radka, M. 1991 Environmental negotiation and policy: the Basel Convention on transboundary movement of hazardous wastes and their disposal. *International Journal of Environment and Pollution* 1: 55–72.

Hinrichsen, D. and Láng, I. 1993 Hungary. In Carter, F.W. and Turnock, D. (eds), *Environmental problems in Eastern Europe.* London, Routledge: 89–106.

Hinzman, L.D. and 34 others 2005 Evidence and implications of recent climate change in northern Alaska and other Arctic regions. *Climatic Change* 72: 251–98.

Hira, P.R. 1969 Transmission of schistosomiasis in Lake Kariba, Zambia. *Nature* 2124: 670–2.

Hirst, R.A., Pywell, R.F. and Putwain, P.D. 2000 Assessing habitat disturbance using an historical perspective: The case of Salisbury Plain military training area. *Journal of Environmental Management* 60: 181–93.

Hobbelink, H. 1991 *Biotechnology and the future of world agriculture.* London, Zed Books.

Hodgson, D.A. and Johnston, N.M. 1997 Inferring seal populations from lake sediments. *Nature* 387: 30–1.

Holdgate, M.W. 1991 Conservation in a world context. In Spellerberg, I.F., Goldsmith, F.B. and Morris, M.G. (eds), *The scientific management of temperate communities for conservation.* Oxford, Blackwell Scientific: 1–26.

Hole, D.G., Perkins, A.J., Wilson, J.D., Alexander, I.H., Grice, P.V. and Evans, A.D. 2005 Does organic farming benefit biodiversity? *Biological Conservation* 122: 113–30.

Holland, G.J. and Webster, P.J. 2007 Heightened tropical cyclone activity in the North Atlantic: natural variability or climate trend? *Philosophical Transactions of the Royal Society A* doi:10.1098/rsta.2007.2083.

Holling, C.S. 1995 What barriers? What bridges? In Gunderson, L.H., Holling, C.S. and Light, S.S. (eds), *Barriers and bridges to the renewal of ecosystems and institutions.* New York, Columbia University Press: 10–20.

Holmberg, J. 1991 *Poverty, environment and development: proposals for action.* Stockholm, Swedish International Development Agency.

Homer-Dixon, T.F. 1999 Environment, scarcity and violence. Princeton, Princeton University Press.

Homer-Dixon, T.F., Boutwell, J.H. and Rathjens, G.W. 1993 Environmental change and violent conflict. *Scientific American* 268(2): 16–23.

Houghton, J.T., Ding, Y., Griggs, D.J., Noguer, M., van der Linden, P.J. and Xiaosu, D. (eds) 2001 *Climate change 2001: the scientific basis.* Cambridge, Cambridge University Press.

Houghton, J.T., Jenkins, G.J. and Ephraums, J.J. (eds) 1990 *Climate change: the IPCC scientific assessment.* Cambridge, Cambridge University Press.

Howard, K.W.F. and Haynes, J. 1993 Groundwater contamination due to road de-icing chemicals. *Geoscience Canada* 20: 1–8.

Howells, G. 1990 *Acid rain and acid waters.* London, Ellis Horwood.

Hoyt, E. 2000 *Whale watching 2000: worldwide tourism numbers, expenditures, and expanding socioeconomic benefits.* Cape Cod, International Fund for Animal Welfare.

Hudson, N.W. 1991 A study of the reasons for success or failure of soil conservation projects. *FAO Soils Bulletin* 64.

Hughes, T.P. 1994 Catastrophes, phase shifts, and large-scale degradation of a Caribbean coral reef. *Science* 265: 1547–51.

Hulme, M. 2001 Climatic perspectives on Sahelian desiccation: 1973–1998. *Global Environmental Change* 11: 19–29.

Humborg, C., Ittekkot, V., Cociasu, A. and Bodungen, B.V. 1997 Effect of Danube River dam on Black Sea biogeochemistry and ecosystem structure. *Nature* 386: 385–8.

Humphreys, D. 1993 *The phantom of full cost pricing.* London, Rio Tinto Zinc.

Hunt, T.L. 2007 Rethinking Easter Island's ecological catastrophe. *Journal of Archaeological Science* 34: 485–502.

Hunt, T.L. and Lipo, C.P. 2006 Late colonization of Easter Island. *Science* 311: 1603–6.

Huntingdon, E. 1907 *The pulse of Asia: a journey in Central Asia illustrating the geographic basis of history.* Boston, Houghton Mifflin.

Hurni, H. 1993 Land degradation, famine, and land resource scenarios in Ethiopia. In Pimental, D. (ed.), *World soil erosion and conservation.* Cambridge, Cambridge University Press: 27–61.

Hurst, P. 1992 Pesticide reduction programs in Denmark, the Netherlands, and Sweden. *International Environmental Affairs* 4: 234–53.

IAEA (International Atomic Energy Agency) 1991 *The International Chernobyl Project: summary brochure, assessment of radiological consequences and evaluation of protective measures.* Report by International Advisory Committee, IAEA, Vienna.

IAEA 2006 *Energy, electricity and nuclear power estimates for the period up to 2030.* Vienna, International Atomic Energy Agency.

IEA (International Energy Agency) 2006 Key world energy statistics. Paris, IEA.

IFC (International Finance Corporation) 2002 *Treasure or trouble? Mining in developing countries.* Washington DC, IFC.

IGES (Institute for Global Environmental Strategies) 2006 *Sustainable groundwater management in Asian cities.* Kanagawa, Japan, IGES.

IGN 1992 Mali: transect methodology to assess ecosystem change. In *UNEP World Atlas of Desertification.* London, Edward Arnold: 62–5.

Innes, J.L. 1992 Forest decline. *Progress in Physical Geography* 16: 1–64.

Intergovernmental Panel on Climate Change (IPCC) 1992 *Climate change 1992: the supplementary report to the IPCC scientific assessment.* Report by working group I. Cambridge, Cambridge University Press.

International Energy Outlook 1998. Washington DC, US Department of Energy.

IPS (International Peat Society) 2001 *Peat production by country in 1999.* Jyväskylä, IPS.

Irish Peatland Conservation Council (IPCC) 1998 *Towards a conservation strategy for the bogs of Ireland.* Dublin, IPCC.

IUCN (International Union for Conservation of Nature and Natural Resources) 1988 *Coral reefs of the world.* Volume 3: *Central and Western Pacific.* Cambridge, IUCN.

IUCN 1992 *Angola: environmental status quo assessment.* Harare, IUCN Regional Office Southern Africa.

IUCN 2004 *The 2004 Red List of threatened species.* Gland, IUCN.

IUCN/UNEP 1986a *Review of the protected areas system in the Indo-Malayan realm.* Gland, IUCN.

IUCN/UNEP 1986b *Review of the protected areas system in the Afrotropical realm.* Gland, IUCN.

IUCN/UNEP/WWF 1980 *World conservation strategy: living resource conservation for sustainable development.* Gland, IUCN.

IUCN/UNEP/WWF 1991 *Caring for the Earth: a strategy for sustainable living.* Gland, IUCN.

Ives, J.D. and Messerli, B. 1989 *The Himalayan dilemma: reconciling development and conservation.* London, Routledge.

Iwama, G.K. 1991 Interactions between aquaculture and the environment. *Critical Reviews in Environmental Control* 21: 177–216.

Jablonski, D. 2004 Extinction: past and present. *Nature* 427: 589.

Jackson, J., Kirby, M., Berger, W., Bjorndal, K., Dotsford, L., Bourque, B., Brabury, R., Cooke, R., Erlandson, J.,

Estes, J., Hughes, T., Kidwell, S., Lange, C., Lenihan, H., Pandolfi, J., Peterson, C., Steneck, R., Tigner, M. and Warner, R. 2001 Historical overfishing and the recent collapse of coastal ecosystems. *Science* 293: 629–38.

Jagtap, T.G., Chavan, V.S. and Untaawale, A.G. 1993 Mangrove ecosystems of India: a need for protection. *Ambio* 22: 252–4.

Janzen, J. 1994 Somalia. In Glantz, M.H. (ed.), *Drought follows the plow.* Cambridge, Cambridge University Press: 45–57.

Jasani, B. 1975 Environmental modification – new weapons of war? *Ambio* 4: 191–8.

Jenkins, R. 1987 *Transnationals and uneven development.* London, Croom Helm.

Jepson, P., Harvie, J.K., Mackinnon, K. and Monk, K.A. 2001 The end for Indonesia's lowland forests? *Science* 292: 859–61.

Jeyaratnam, J. 1990 Acute pesticide poisoning: a major global health problem. *World Health Statistics Quarterly* 43: 139–44.

Jickells, T.D., Carpenter, R. and Liss, P.S. 1990 Marine environment. In Turner II, B.L., Clark, W.C., Kates, R.W., Richards, J.F., Mathews, J.T. and Meyer, W.B. (eds), *The Earth as transformed by human action.* Cambridge, Cambridge University Press: 313–34.

Jimenez, R.D. and Velasquez, A. 1989 Metropolitan Manila: a framework for its sustained development. *Environment and Urbanization* 1: 51–8.

Jodha, N.S. 1992 *Common property resources.* World Bank Discussion Paper, August 1992, Washington DC.

Johansson, T.B., Kelly, H., Reddy, A.K.N. and Williams, R.H. 1993 Renewable fuels and electricity for a growing world economy: defining and achieving the potential. In Johansson, T.B., Kelly, H., Reddy, A.K.N. and Williams, R.H. (eds), *Renewable energy: sources for fuels and electricity.* New York, Island Press: 1–71.

Johns, A.D. 1992 Species conservation in managed tropical forests. In Whitmore, T.C. and Sayer, J.A. (eds), *Tropical deforestation and species extinction.* London, Chapman & Hall: 15–53.

Johns, A.G. and Johns, B.G. 1995 Tropical forests and primates: long-term co-existence? *Oryx* 29: 205–11.

Johnson, D.B. and Hallberg, K.B. 2005 Acid mine drainage remediation options: a review. *Science of the Total Environment* 338: 3–14.

Johnston, G.H. 1981 *Permafrost engineering, design and construction.* Toronto, Wiley.

Jokiel, P.L. and Brown, E.K. 2004 Global warming, regional trends and inshore environmental conditions influence coral bleaching in Hawaii. *Global Change Biology* 10: 1627–41.

Jones, D.K.C., Cooke, R.U. and Warren, A. 1986 Geomorphological investigation, for engineering purposes, of blowing sand and dust hazard. *Quarterly Journal of Engineering Geology* 19: 251–70.

Jones, P.D., Briffa, K.R., Barnett, T.P. and Tett, S.F.B. 1998 High-resolution palaeoclimatic records for the last millennium: interpretation, integration and comparison with General Circulation Model control-run temperatures. *The Holocene* 8: 455–71.

Jutila, E. 1992 Restoration of salmonid rivers in Finland. In Boon, P.J., Calow, P. and Petts, G.E. (eds), *River conservation and management*. Chichester, Wiley: 353–62.

Kaiser, J. 1996 Acid rain's dirty business: stealing minerals from soil. *Science* 272: 198.

Kajak, Z. 1992 The River Vistula and its floodplain valley (Poland): its ecology and importance for conservation. In Boon, P.J., Calow, P. and Petts, G.E. (eds), *River conservation and management*. Chichester, Wiley: 35–49.

Kallend, A.S., Marsh, A.R.W., Pickles, J.H. and Proctor, M.V. 1983 Acidity of rain in Europe. *Atmospheric Environment* 17: 127–37.

Kashulina, G., Reimann, C., Finne, T.E., Halleraker, J.H., Äyräs, M. and Chekushin, V.A. 1997 The state of the ecosystems in the central Barents Region: scale, factors and mechanism of disturbance. *Science of the Total Environment* 206: 203–25.

Kates, R.W., Turner II, B.L. and Clark, W.C. 1990 The great transformation. In Turner II, B.L., Clark, W.C., Kates, R.W., Richards, J.F., Mathews, J.T. and Meyer, W.B. (eds), *The Earth as transformed by human action*. Cambridge, Cambridge University Press: 1–17.

Kawasaki, T. 1983 Why do some pelagic fishes have wide fluctuations in their numbers? Biological basis of fluctuation from the viewpoint of evolutionary ecology. In Sharp, G.D. and Csirke, J. (eds), Reports of the expert consultation to examine changes in abundance and species composition of neritic fish resources. *FAO Fisheries Report* 291: 1065–80.

Keijzers, G. 2000 The evolution of Dutch environmental policy: the changing ecological arena from 1970 to 2000 and beyond. *Journal of Cleaner Production* 8: 179–200.

Kerpelman, C. 1990 *Preliminary study on the identification of disaster-prone countries based on economic impact*. Geneva, Office of the United Nations Disaster Relief Organization.

Khakimov, F.I. 1989 *Soil reclamation conditions of delta desertification: tendencies of transformation and spatial differentiation*. Pushchino, Nauchnyi Tsentr Biologicheskikh Issledovaniy AN SSR (in Russian).

Khalaf, F.I. 1989 Desertification and aeolian processes in Kuwait. *Journal of Arid Environments* 12: 125–45.

Khalil, G.M. 1992 Cyclones and storm surges in Bangladesh: some mitigative measures. *Natural Hazards* 6: 11–24.

Khan, A.U. 1994 History of decline and present status of natural tropical thorn forest in Punjab. *Biological Conservation* 67: 205–10.

Khordagui, H.K. 1992 A conceptual approach to selection of a control measure for residual chlorine discharge in Kuwait Bay. *Environmental Management* 16: 309–16.

Kiersch, G.A. 1965 The Vaiont reservoir disaster. *Mineral Information Service* 18: 129–38.

Kim, K.C. 1997 Preserving biodiversity in Korea's demilitarized zone. *Science* 278: 242.

Kim, S.S. 1984 *The quest for a just world*. Boulder, Westview Press.

Kinlen, L.J. 1988 Evidence for an infective cause of childhood leukaemia: comparison of a Scottish new town with nuclear reprocessing sites in Britain. *Lancet* 10 December: 1323–7.

Kirkitsos, P. and Sikiotis, D. 1996 Deterioration of Pentelic marble, Portland limestone and Baumberger sandstone in laboratory exposures to NO_2: a comparison with exposures to gaseous HNO_3. *Atmospheric Environment* 30: 941–50.

Kiss, A. 1985 The protection of the Rhine against pollution. *Natural Resources Journal* 25: 613–32.

Kivinen, E. and Pakarinen, P. 1981 Geographical distribution of peat resources and major peatland complex types in the world. *Annals, Academy Sciencia Fennicae* A132: 1–28.

Klein, B.C. 1989 Effects of forest fragmentation on dung and carrion beetle communities in central Amazonia. *Ecology* 70: 1715–25.

Klein, D.R. 1971 Reaction of reindeer to obstructions and disturbances. *Science* 173: 393–8.

Klinger, L.F. and Erickson III, D.J. 1997 Geophysical coupling of marine and terrestrial ecosystems. *Journal of Geophysical Research* 102(D21): 25359–70.

Knox, J.C. 1993 Large increases in flood magnitude in response to modest changes in climate. *Nature* 361: 430–2.

Knox, P. and Agnew, J. 1994 *The geography of the world economy*, 2nd edn. London, Edward Arnold.

Kobayashi, Y. 1981 Causes of fatalities in recent earthquakes in Japan. *Journal of Disaster Science* 3: 15–22.

Koca, M.Y. and Kincal, C. (2004) Abandoned stone quarries in and around the Izmir city centre and their geo-environmental impacts. *Engineering Geology* 75: 49–67.

Koike, K. 1985 Japan. In Bird, E.C.F. and Schwartz, M.L. (eds), *The world's coastline*. Stroudsburg, Van Nostrand Reinhold: 843–55.

Kreimer, A., Lobo, T., Menezes, B., Munasinghe, M. and Parker, R. 1993 *Towards a sustainable urban environment: the Rio de Janeiro study*. World Bank Discussion Paper 195.

KREM (Korean Republic Environment Ministry) *Green Korea 2006*. Gwacheon, KREM.

Krimgold, F. 1992 Modern urban infrastructure: the Armenian case. In Kreimer, A. and Munasinghe, M. (eds), *Environmental management and urban vulnerability*. World Bank Discussion Paper 168: 263–5.

Kroonenberg, S.B., Badyukovab, E.N., Stormsa, J.E.A., Ignatovb, E.I. and Kasimov, N.S. 2000 A full sea-level cycle in 65 years: barrier dynamics along Caspian shores. *Sedimentary Geology* 134: 257–74.

Kummer, D.M. 1991 *Deforestation in the postwar Philippines*. Chicago, University of Chicago Press.

Lacerda, L.D. 1997 Global mercury emissions from gold and silver mining. *Water, Air and Soil Pollution* 97: 209–21.

Lahlou, A. 1996 Environmental and socio-economic impacts of erosion and sedimentation in North Africa. In Walling, D.E. and Webb, B.W. (eds), *Erosion and sediment yield: global and regional perspectives*. Wallingford, International Association of Hydrological Sciences Publication 236: 491–500.

Lajewski, C.K., Mullins, H.T., Patterson, W.P. and Callinan, C.W. 2003 Historic calcite record from the Finger Lakes, New York: impact of acid rain on a buffered terrain. *Geological Society of America Bulletin* 115: 373–84.

Lal, R. 1993 Soil erosion and conservation in West Africa. In Pimental, D. (ed.), *World soil erosion and conservation*. Cambridge, Cambridge University Press: 7–25.

Lal, R. and Stewart, B.A. 1990 Need for action: research and development priorities. *Advances in Soil Science* 11: 331–6.

Lambert, J.H., Jennings, J.N., Smith, C.T., Green, C. and Hutchinson, J.N. 1970 *The making of the Broads: a reconsideration of their origin in the light of new evidence*. Royal Geographical Society Research Series 3. London, Royal Geographical Society.

Lamprey, H.F. 1975 *Report on the desert encroachment reconnaissance in northern Sudan, October 21–November 10, 1975*. Khartoum, National Council for Research, Ministry of Agriculture, Food and Resources.

Landsberg, H.E. 1981 *The urban climate*. New York, Academic Press.

Langdale, G.W., Mills, W.C. and Thomas, A.W. 1992 Conservation tillage development for soil erosion control in the southern Piedmont. In Hurni, H. and Kebede, T. (eds), *Erosion, conservation and small-scale farming*. Bern, Geographia Bernensia: 453–8.

Langford, T.E.L. 1990 *Ecological effects of thermal discharges*. London, Elsevier Applied Science.

Larson, W.E., Pierce, F.J. and Dowdy, R.H. 1983 The threat of soil erosion to long-term crop production. *Science* 219: 458–65.

Larssen, T., Lydersen, E., Tang, D., He, Y., Gao, J., Liu, H., Duan, L., Seip, H.M., Vogt, R.D., Mulder, J., Shao, M., Wang, Y., Shang, H., Zhang, X., Solberg, S., Aas, W., Okland, T., Eilertsen, O., Angell, V., Li, Q., Zhao, D., Xiang, R., Xiao, J. and Luo, J. 2006 Acid rain in China. *Environmental Science & Technology* 40: 418–25.

Laurance, W.F., Delamônica, P., Laurance, S.G., Vasconcelos, H.L. and Lovejoy, T.E. 2000 Rainforest fragmentation kills big trees. *Nature* 404: 836.

Lawrence, G.B. 2002 Persistent episodic acidification of streams linked to acid rain effects on soil. *Atmospheric Environment* 36: 1589–98.

Lay, T., Kanamori, H., Ammon, C.J., Nettles, M., Ward, S.N., Aster, R., Beck, S.L., Bilek, S.L., Brudzinski, M.R., Butler, R., DeShon, H.R., Ekstrom, G., Satake, K. and Sipkin, S. 2005 The great Sumatra-Andaman earthquake of 26 December 2004. *Science* 308: 1127–32.

Layrisse, M. 1992 The 'holocaust' of the Amerindians. *Interciencia* 17: 274.

Le Ble, S. and Cuignon, R. 1988 Mise en évidence de l'influence du canal du Dique sur l'archipel du Rosaire (Colombie): circulation des eaux et dispersion des rejets en suspension. *Bulletin Institut de Géologie du Bassin d'Aquitaine* 44: 5–13.

Leach, G. and Mearns, R. 1988 *Beyond the fuelwood crisis: people, land and trees in Africa*. London, Earthscan.

Ledec, G., Quintero, J.D. and Mejia, M.C. 1997 *Good dams and bad dams: environmental and social criteria for choosing hydroelectric project sites*. Washington DC, World Bank Sustainable Dissemination Note 1.

Lee, K.N. 1989 The Columbia River basin: experimenting with sustainability. *Environment* 31: 6–11, 30–3.

Lelek, A. 1989 The Rhine river and some of its tributaries under human impact in the last two centuries. *Canadian Special Publication of Fisheries and Aquatic Science* 106: 469–87.

Lepers, E. 2003 Synthesis of the main areas of land-cover and land-use change. Millennium Ecosystem Assessment, Final Report. New York, Island Press.

Leprun, J.-C., da Silveira, C.O. and Sobral Filho, R.M. 1986 Efficacité des pratiques culturales antiérosives testées sous différents climats brésiliens. *Cahiers ORSTOM Série Pédologie* 22: 223–33.

Lerner, D.N. and Tellam, J.H. 1993 The protection of urban groundwater from pollution. In Currie, J.C. and Pepper, A.T. (eds), *Water and the environment*. Chichester, Ellis Horwood: 322–35.

Levins, R., Awerbuch, T., Brinkman, U., Eckardt, I., Epstein, P., Makhoul, N., Albuquerque de Possas, C., Puccia, C., Spielman, A. and Wilson, M.E. 1994 The emergence of new diseases. *American Scientist* 82: 52–60.

Lewis, L.A. and Berry, L. 1988 *African environments and resources*. London, Allen & Unwin.

Lin, J.C. 1996 Coastal modification due to human influence in south-western Taiwan. *Quaternary Science Reviews* 15: 895–900.

Lisk, D.J. 1991 Environmental effects of landfills. *Science of the Total Environment* 100: 415–68.

Liu, C.W., Lin, K.H. and Kuo, Y.M. 2003 Application of factor analysis in the assessment of groundwater quality in a blackfoot disease area in Taiwan. *Science of the Total Environment* 313: 77–89.

Liu, J., Linderman, M., Ouyang, Z., An, L., Yang, J. and Zhang, H. 2001 Ecological degradation in protected areas: the case of Wolong Nature Reserve for giant pandas. *Science* 292: 98–101.

Lloyd, G.O. and Butlin, R.N. 1992 Corrosion. In Radojevic, M. and Harrison, R.M. (eds), *Atmospheric acidity: sources, consequences and abatement*. London, Elsevier Applied Science: 405–34.

Lockeretz, W. 1978 The lessons of the dust bowl. *American Scientist* 66: 560–9.

Lockeretz, W. 1988 Open questions in sustainable agriculture. *American Journal of Alternative Agriculture* 3: 174–81.

Loeb, V., Siegel, V., Holm-Hansen, O., Hewitt, R., Fraser, W., Trivelpiece, W. and Trivelpiece, S. 1997 Effects of sea-ice extent and krill or salp dominance on the Antarctic food web. *Nature* 387: 897–900.

Loevinsohn, M.E. 1994 Climatic warming and increased malaria incidence in Rwanda. *Lancet* 343: 714–17.

Löffler, E. and Kubinok, J. 1988 Soil salinization in north-east Thailand. *Erdkunde* 42: 89–100.

Löfstedt, R. 1998 Sweden's biomass controversy: a case study of communicating policy issues. *Environment* 40(4): 16–20, 42–5.

Lonergan, S.C. 1993 Impoverishment, population, and environmental degradation: the case for equity. *Environmental Conservation* 20: 328–34.

Lorius, C., Jouzel, J., Raynaud, D., Hansen, J. and Le Treut, H. 1990 The ice-core record: climate sensitivity and future greenhouse warming. *Nature* 347: 139–45.

Lottermoser, B.G. and Morteani, G. 1993 Sewage sludge: toxic substances, fertilizers, or secondary metal resources? *Episodes* 16: 329–33.

Lovei, M. 1998 *Phasing out lead from gasoline: worldwide experience and policy implications*. World Bank Technical Paper No. 397, Pollution Management Series.

Lovelock, J.E. 1989 *The ages of Gaia*. Oxford, Oxford University Press.

Lovelock, J. 2006 *The revenge of Gaia: why the earth is fighting back - and how we can still save humanity*. London, Allen Lane.

Lowe, M.D. 1991 *Shaping cities: the environmental and human dimensions*. Worldwatch Paper 105. Washington DC, Worldwatch Institute.

Lowe, M.D. 1994 Reinventing transport. In Brown, L.R. (ed.), *State of the world 1994*. New York, W.W. Norton: 81–98.

Lugo, A.E. 1988 Estimating reductions in the diversity of tropical forest species. In Wilson, E.O. and Peter, F.M. (eds), *Biodiversity*. Washington DC, National Academy Press: 58–70.

Lundgren, L.W. 1999 *Environmental geology*, 2nd edn. Upper Saddle River, Prentice Hall.

Lupinacci, J. 2000 Creating corporate value and environmental benefit with improved energy performance. *Environmental Quality Management* 10(2): 11–17.

MacArthur, R.H. and Wilson, E.O. 1967 *The theory of island biogeography*. Princeton, Princeton University Press.

McCabe, J.T. 1990 Turkana pastoralism: a case against the tragedy of the commons. *Human Ecology* 18: 81–103.

McCall, G.J.H. 1998 Geohazards and the urban environment. In Maund, J.G. and Eddlestone, M. *Geohazards in engineering geology*. London, Geological Society: 309–18.

McCauley, J.F., Breed, C.S., Grolier, M.J. and Mackinnon, D.J. 1981 The US dust storm of February 1977. In Péwé, T.L. (ed.), *Desert dust: origins, characteristics and effects on man*. Geological Society of America Special Paper 186: 123–47.

McCully, P. 1996 *Silenced rivers: the ecology and politics of large dams*. London, Zed Books.

McFarland, M. 1989 Chlorofluorocarbons and ozone. *Environmental Science and Technology* 23: 1203–8.

McGinley, P.C. 1992 Regulation of the environmental impacts of coal mining in the USA: market economics, cost–benefit analysis and mistakes of the past. *Natural Resources Forum* 16: 261–70.

McGuffie, K., Henderson-Sellers, A. and Zhang, H. 1998 Modelling climatic impacts of future rainforest destruction. In Maloney, B.K. (ed.), *Human activities and the tropical rainforest*. Dordrecht, Kluwer: 169–93.

Macklin, M.G., Hudson-Edwards, K.A. and Dawson, E.J. 1997 The significance of pollution from historic metal mining in the Pennine orefields on river sediment contaminant fluxes to the North Sea. *Science of the Total Environment* 194–5: 391–7.

McNeely, J. 1988 *Economics and biological diversity*. Gland, IUCN.

McNeely, J. 1994 Lessons from the past: forests and biodiversity. *Biodiversity and Conservation* 3: 3–20.

McTainsh, G. and Strong, C. 2007 The role of aeolian dust in ecosystems. *Geomorphology* 89: 39–54.

Maddox, J. 1990 Clouds and global warming. *Nature* 247: 329.

Magrath, W. and Arens, P. 1989 *The costs of soil erosion in Java: a natural resource accounting approach*. World Bank Environment Department Working Paper 18.

Magrin, G.O., Travasso, M.I. and Rodríguez, G.R. 2005 Changes in climate and crop production during the 20th century in Argentina. *Climatic Change* 72: 229–49.

Mahmood, R., Foster, S.A., Keeling, T., Hubbard, K.G., Carlson, C. and Leepe, R. 2006 Impacts of irrigation on 20th century temperature in the northern Great Plains. *Global and Planetary Change* 54: 1–18.

Maitland, P.S. 1991 Conservation of fish species. In Spellerberg, I.F., Goldsmith, F.B. and Morris, M.G. (eds), *The scientific management of temperate communities for conservation*. Oxford, Blackwell Scientific: 129–48.

Maki, A.W. 1991 The Exxon oil spill: initial environmental impact assessment. *Environmental Science and Technology* 25: 24–29.

Malm, O., Pfeiffer, W.C., Souza, C.M.M. and Reuther, R. 1990 Mercury pollution due to gold mining in the Madeira River basin, Brazil. *Ambio* 19: 11–15.

Malthus, T.R. 1798 *An essay on the principle of population*. London, Johnson.

Mani, M. and Wheeler, D. 1998 In search of pollution havens? Dirty industry in the world economy, 1960 to 1995. *The Journal of Environment and Development* 7: 215–47.

Mann, R.H.K. 1988 Fish and fisheries of regulated rivers in the UK. *Regulated Rivers: Research and Management* 2: 411–24.

Maragos, J.E. 1993 Impact of coastal construction on coral reefs in the US-affiliated Pacific Islands. *Coastal Management* 21: 235–69.

Margarita, M. and Loyarte, G. 1996 Climatic fluctuations as a source of desertification in a semi-arid region of Argentina. *Desertification Control Bulletin* 28: 8–14.

Marples, D.R. 1992 Post-Soviet Belarus and the impact of Chernobyl. *Post-Soviet Geography* 33: 419–31.

Marsh, G.P. 1874 *The Earth as modified by human actions*. New York, Sampson Low.

Marshall, B.E. and Junor, F.J.R. 1981 The decline of *Salvinia molesta* on Lake Kariba. *Hydrobiologia* 83: 477–84.

Martin, P.S. and Klein, R.G. 1984 *Pleistocene extinctions*. Tucson, University of Arizona Press.

Maslin, M., Malhi, Y., Phillips, O. and Cowling, S. 2005 New views on an old forest: assessing the longevity, resilience and future of the Amazon rainforest. *Transactions of the Institute of British Geographers* 30: 477–99.

Mather, A.S. 1990 *Global forest resources*. London, Belhaven.

Mather, A.S. 2005 Assessing the world's forests. Global Environmental Change Part A, 15: 267–80.

May, R.M. 1978 Human reproduction reconsidered. *Nature* 272: 491–5.

Maynard, R. 2004 Key airborne pollutants – the impact on health. *Science of the Total Environment* 334: 9–13.

MEA (Millennium Ecosystem Assessment) 2005 *Ecosystems and human well-being: synthesis*. Washington DC, Island Press.

Meadows, D.H., Meadows, D.L., Randers, J. and Behrens III, W.W. 1972 *The limits to growth: a report to the Club of Rome's project on the predicament of mankind*. New York, Potomac Associates.

Meadows, D.H., Randers, J. and Meadows, D.L. 2004 *The Limits to Growth: the 30-year update*. London, Earthscan.

Meadows, P.S. and Campbell, J.I. 1988 *An introduction to marine science*. London, Blackie & Son.

Mee, L.D. 1992 The Black Sea crisis: a need for concerted international action. *Ambio* 21: 278–86.

Meech, J.A., Veiga, M.M. and Tromans, D. 1998 Reactivity of mercury from gold mining activities in darkwater ecosystems. *Ambio* 27: 92–8.

Meierding, T.C. 1993 Marble tombstone weathering and air pollution in North America. *Annals of the Association of American Geographers* 83: 568–88.

Mellquist, P. 1992 River management – objectives and applications. In Boon, P.J., Calow, P. and Petts, G.E. (eds), *River conservation and management*. Chichester, Wiley: 1–8.

Menzel, A. and Fabian, P. 1999 Growing season extended in Europe. *Nature* 397: 659.

Metcalfe, S. and Derwent, R.G. 2005 *Atmospheric Pollution and Environmental Change*. London, Hodder Arnold.

Meybeck, M. 1982 Carbon, nitrogen and phosphorus transport by world rivers. *Science* 282: 401–50.

Meybeck, M., Chapman, D. and Helmer, R. 1989 *Global freshwater quality: a first assessment*. Oxford, Blackwell.

Meynell, P.-J. 1993 Developing collaboration to protect Saudi Arabia's wetlands. *IUCN Wetlands Programme Newsletter* 7: 11–12.

Micklin, P. 2007 The Aral Sea disaster. *Annual Review of Earth and Planetary Sciences* 35: 47–72.

Middleton, N.J. 1985 Effect of drought on dust production in the Sahel. *Nature* 316: 431–4.

Middleton, N.J. 1991 *Desertification*. Oxford, Oxford University Press.

Middleton, N.J. 2002 The Aral Sea. In Shahgedanova, M. (ed.), *The physical geography of Northern Eurasia*, Oxford, Oxford University Press: 497–510.

Middleton, N.J. and Thomas, D.S.G. 1997 *World atlas of desertification*, 2nd edn. London, Arnold.

Middleton, N.J. and van Lynden, G.W.J. 2000 Secondary salinization in South and Southeast Asia. *Progress in Environmental Science* 2: 1–19.

Miller, G., Mangan, J., Pollard, D., Thompson, S., Felzer, B. and Magee, J. 2005 Sensitivity of the Australian Monsoon to insolation and vegetation: implications for human impact on continental moisture balance. *Geology* 33: 65–8.

Milliman, J.D. 1990 Fluvial sedimentation in coastal seas: flux and fate. *Nature and Resources* 26(4): 12–22.

Milly, P.C.D., Wetherald, R.T., Dunne, K.A. and Delworth, T.L. 2002 Increasing risk of great floods in a changing climate. *Nature* 415: 514–17.

Mistry, J.F. 1989 Salinity ingress in the coastal area of Saurashtra-Gujarat State (India). *ICID Bulletin* 32: 52–60.

Mittermeir, R., Konstant, B., Nicoll, M. and Langrand, O. 1992 *Lemurs of Madagascar: an action plan for their conservation 1993–1999*. Gland, IUCN.

Moffatt, I. 1999 Edinburgh: a sustainable city? *International Journal of Sustainable Development and World Ecology* 6: 135–48.

Moleele, N.M., Ringrose, S., Matheson, W. and Vanderpost, C. 2002 More woody plants? the status of bush encroachment in Botswana's grazing areas. *Journal of Environmental Management* 64: 3–11.

Molina, M.J. and Molina, L.T. 2004 Megacities and atmospheric pollution. *Journal of the Air and Waste Management Association* 54: 644–80.

Molina, M.J. and Rowland, F.S. 1974 Stratospheric sink chlorofluoromethanes: chlorine atom catalyzed destruction of ozone. *Nature* 249: 810–14.

Monteiro, C.A. de F. 1989 Environmental quality in the great national metropolis and its industrial portuary appendix. In Gerasimov, I.P. (ed.), *Environmental problems in cities of developing countries*. Moscow, UNEP: 26–39.

Moore, D. and Driver, A. 1989 The conservation role of water supply reservoirs. *Regulated Rivers: Research and Management* 4: 203–12.

Moore, N.W., Hooper, M.D. and Davis, B.N.K. 1967 Hedges, I. Introduction and reconnaissance studies. *Journal of Applied Ecology* 4: 201–20.

Moran, E.F. 1981 *Developing the Amazon*. Bloomington, Indiana University Press.

Moreira, J.R. and Poole, A.D. 1993 Hydropower and its constraints. In Johansson, T.B., Kelly, H., Reddy, A.K.N. and Williams, R.H. (eds), *Renewable energy: sources for fuels and electricity*. New York, Island Press: 73–119.

Mortimore, M. 1987 Shifting sands and human sorrow: social response to drought and desertification. *Desertification Control Bulletin* 14: 1–14.

Mortimore, M. and Turner, B. 2005 Does the Sahelian smallholder's management of woodland, farm trees, rangeland support the hypothesis of human-induced desertification? *Journal of Arid Environments* 63: 567–95.

Motz, H. and Geiseler, J. 2001 Products of steel slags an opportunity to save natural resources. *Waste Management* 21: 285–93.

Mukherjee, M.D. 1996 Pisciculture and the environment: an economic evaluation of sewage-fed fisheries in east Calcutta. *Science, Technology and Development* 14: 73–99.

Murray, I. 1994 Time and tide rip into the frontier of old England. *Times* 23 March: 7.

Murray, J.E., Johnson, M.S. and Clarke, B. 1988 The extinction of Partula on Moorea. *Pacific Science* 42: 150–3.

Musannif, B. 1992 Integrated approach to energy efficient housing refurbishment. *Energy Management* July/August: 22–3.

Myers, N. 1979 *The sinking ark: a new look at the problem of disappearing species*. Oxford, Pergamon.

Myers, N., Mittermeier, R.A., Mittermeier, C.G., Da Fonseca, G.A.B. and Kent, J. 2000 Biodiversity hotspots for conservation priorities. *Nature* 403: 853–8.

Mylona, S. 1993 *Trends of sulphur dioxide emissions, air concentrations and depositions of sulphur in Europe since 1880*. EMEP/MSC-W Report 2/93. Oslo, EMEP.

Nandeesha, M.C. 2002 Sewage fed aquaculture systems of Kolkata: a century-old innovation of farmers. *Aquaculture Asia* 7: 28–32.

Naylor, R. 1996 Invasions in agriculture: assessing the cost of the golden apple snail in Asia. *Ambio* 25: 443.

Naylor, R.L., Goldburg, R.J., Primavera, J.H., Kautsky, N., Beveridge, M.C.M., Clay, J., Folke, C., Lubchenco, J., Mooney, H. and Troell, M. 2000 Effect of aquaculture on world fish supplies. *Nature* 405: 1017–24.

Nelson, F.E., Anisimov, O.A. and Shiklomanov, N.I. 2002 Climate change and hazard zonation in the circum-Arctic permafrost regions. *Natural Hazards* 26: 203–25.

Nelson, P.M. (ed.) 1987 *Transportation noise reference handbook*. London, Butterworth.

NEPA (National Environmental Protection Agency) 1997 *1996 report on the state of the environment*. Beijing, NEPA.

Nepstad, D., Schwartzman, S., Bamberger, B., Santilli, M., Ray, D., Schlesinger, P., Lefebvre, P., Alencar, A., Prinz, E., Fiske, G. and Rolla, A. 2006 Inhibition of Amazon deforestation and fire by parks and indigenous lands. *Conservation Biology* 20: 65–73.

Neumann, A.C. and Macintyre, I. 1985 Reef response to sea level rise: keep-up, catch-up or give-up. *Proceedings of the 5th International Coral Reef Congress, Tahiti* 3: 105–10.

Newcombe, K. 1984 *An economic justification for rural afforestation: the case of Ethiopia*. World Bank Energy Department Paper 16.

Nichol, J.E. 1989 Ecology of fuelwood production in Kano region, northern Nigeria. *Journal of Arid Environments* 16: 347–60.

Nicholls, N. 1997 Increased Australian wheat yield due to recent climate trends. *Nature* 387: 484–5.

Nicol, S. 2006 Krill, currents, and sea ice: Euphausia superba and its changing environment. *BioScience*, 56: 111–20.

Nicol, S. and de la Mare, W. 1993 Ecosystem management and the Antarctic krill. *American Scientist* 81: 36–47.

Nilsson, C., Reidy, C.A., Dynesius, M. and Revenga, C. 2005 Fragmentation and flow regulation of the world's large river systems. *Science* 308: 405–8.

Nilsson, K. 1991 Emission standards for waste incineration. *Waste Management and Research* 9: 224–7.